# INTERNATIONAL
# AIR TRANSPORT
# IN A CHANGING WORLD

## UTRECHT STUDIES IN AIR AND SPACE LAW

1. Marie Helen PICHLER, *Copyright Problems of Satellite and Cable Television in Europe*, ISBN 0-86010-952-6.

2. Andrew J. YOUNG, *Law and Policy in the Space Stations' Era*, ISBN 90-247-3722-2.

# International
# air transport
# in a changing world

*Jacques Naveau*

*Attorney at Law*
*Professor of Air Law*
*Brussels University*

BRUYLANT
BRUSSELS

MARTINUS NIJHOFF
LONDON/DORDRECHT/BOSTON

1 9 8 9

Naveau, Jacques, 1930-
  International air transport in a changing world.
  (Utrecht studies in air and space law)
Enl. updated English version of the 1st French ed. published in 1980 under title :
Droit du transport aérien international.
1. Aeronautics, Commercial — Law and legislation.
I. Title. II. Series.
K4095.4.N3913 1988      343.097      88-25345
ISBN 90-247-3727-3 (Nijhoff) 342.397

ISBN 2-8027-0424-9 Bruylant - D/1989/0023/10
ISBN 90-247-3727-3 Martinus Nijhoff Publishers

© 1989 Etablissements Emile Bruylant
Rue de la Régence 67, 1000 Brussels, Belgium

Martinus Nijhoff Publishers
P.O. Box 163, 3300 AD Dordrecht, The Netherlands

PRINTED IN BELGIUM

# ABSTRACTS

"The idea that national interests are not always best advanced in the context of traditional 'national sovereignty' is a relatively new and unfamiliar one." (Lord CLOCKFIELD).

"Economic interdependence is a fact. We must resolve the paradox of growing mutual dependence and burgeoning national and regional identities." (Henry KISSINGER).

"It is a European way of thinking that submits peoples to States and the world to super-powers. " (André GLUCKSMANN).

"I will not speak to you about yesterday because I was not the same person." (Lewis CARROLL, *Alice in Wonderland*).

"Indeed, we must change because the future is no longer what it used to be. The difference lies in the fact that its relation to the present is essentially new." (Aurelio PECCEI).

"Yet, the future is filled with promises. Challenges are often fortifying and the unknown replete with pleasant surprises provided we keep our heads cool." (Gilbert PÉRIER).

# TABLE OF CONTENTS

# PART III

## THE ACQUISITION
## OF COMMERCIAL RIGHTS

# PART IV

## THE EVOLUTION
## OF THE REGULATORY SYSTEM

# PART V

## THE DEVELOPING WORLD

## PART VI

### THE STATE OF EUROPE

## PART VII

### PERSPECTIVES

# PART VIII

## CONCLUSIONS

# PREFACE

*The present study constitutes the third volume of the Utrecht Studies in Air and Space Law, a series of books published as part of the Project on Air and Space Law under the auspices of the Netherlands Institute of Social and Economic Law Research (NISER).*

*The project is aimed at the furtherance of research in the field of air and space law by conducting such research itself, by promoting research by others in the field and by facilitating the publication of the results of that research. The project is guided in its activities by an Advisory Board consisting of Dr. Marietta Benkö, Institute of Air and Space Law, Cologne University, Cologne, FRG; Professor Pieter van Dijk, Faculty of Law, Utrecht University, Utrecht, the Netherlands; Professor He Qizhi, Beijing College of Foreign Affairs, Beijing, China, and Professor Caesar Voûte, formerly of the International Institute for Aerospace Survey and Earth Sciences ITC, Enschede, the Netherlands.*

*The present volume deals with the regulation of air transport against the background of political, economic and social developments in the world. The 1944 Chicago Convention still constitutes the main basis of the legal framework of air transport. However, particularly during the last twenty years, the regulatory system of the Chicago Convention has been challenged by far-reaching societal changes. These changes, which are mainly fueled by the unprecedented developments in technology, have,* inter alia, *resulted in the widening of gaps between various nations in the political, economic, social and also the legal field.*

*This book argues that in order to keep up with these societal changes the consideration and adaptation of existing air transport are called for. Furthermore, it is proposed that a regional approach is taken in this effort.*

*Dr. Naveau is a recognized expert in matters of air transport, not only from an academic point of view, but also on account of his practical activities in the legal field for the Belgian Airline Company SABENA.*

*The present book, which is an enlarged, updated, English version of the*

*1980 French first edtion entitled „ Droit du Transport Aérien Internatio-
nal" may serve both academic law research and practitioners of air policy
and air law.*

*Utrecht, February 1988.*

Dr. G. C. M. REIJNEN,                    Professor Dr. G. J. H. VAN HOOF,
Co-ordinator, Project on                              Director, NISER
Air and Space Law

# FOREWORD

International air transport is a complex activity. Anyone called upon to make decisions, give advice or opinions in this field is often painfully aware of the dilemma of integrating the known and the unknown, the facts of life and the facts of law, *politics and economics.*

The man in the street, who is the user or potential user of the air transport systems, wishes to benefit from *safe* and *reliable services* maintained at very high standards.

He also wants those services to be adequately *competitive,* and *air fares* to be *lower* and more *transparent* than they currently often are. However, he may well suspect that there is more at stake in this industry than merely pricing policies in the market-place. Air transport may not be as unique an activity as some would like to make us believe in order to maintain over-protection by national governments, but *it cannot be easily compared with any other commercial activity.*

Legislators, ministers, diplomats, analysts and many others would appreciate easy access to this unique activity of our time, one which has changed, and continues to change, the world in which we live.

But the way in which the service is perceived differs according to the particular social and economic environment in which it is operated. Indeed, the confrontation between theories and interests in different parts of the world is extremely confusing.

In many instances, ignorance and misconceptions are at the root of wrong attitudes or of ineffective policy decisions.

Legal experts in industry find it difficult to catch up with developments, as previously integrated systems disintegrate and neighbouring fields of law affect civil aviation. Meanwhile, academics ignore the hectic adventures of the market-place : their teaching runs the risk of being as remote from present-day realities and tomorrow's requirements as pre-war chemistry or pre-Keynes economy.

Political assessments are made difficult by the swift pace of simultaneous developments in different fields, which are rarely interconnected. (After all, air transport may not be the constant major concern of politicians, and they can be forgiven for not devoting much of their time to research in this field.)

There have been notorious instances in which many countries, and not only the smallest, have committed errors of consequence. The policy of the United States under the Carter administration is one such example. Though the government wanted to promote the "open sky" policy and launched negotiations to that effect with foreign governments, the campaign soon collapsed and raised a worldwide uproar because relevant factors in all parts of the world had not been taken into account, and the reaction of foreign countries had been underestimated.

Much of the difficulty in grasping the facets of reality is due to the variety of efforts and the problems of information which characterise our fragmented world.

We should note, however, that aviation is *basically a technology* after all, and that technology, by nature, *tends to divide* more than to unite. Raymond Aron has raised the question whether technology is not responsible "for an inequality among peoples which is at once less open to question and less acceptable than at any time in the past. Have the new techniques which threaten the old patterns fostered or hindered the unity, or at least the peace, to which men of good will have always aspired?" (*).

The answer may be that to become an instrument of peace and progress, technology has to be submitted to conceptual confrontations which will achieve a common understanding and give rise to *an adequate legal structure*.

That is precisely what was sought in Chicago, in 1944. And nowadays it remains true that the peoples of the world want equitable access to a technology which is important to their economic development and, more often than not, to their survival.

The big question is : considering the difficulties encountered by the Chicago-based regulatory system over the past decades, what are the chances for an international legal order to prevail in civil aviation, at a time when socio-economic gaps among the nations of the world are wider than they ever were before?

*The time has also come to reconsider the role of air transport, in the light of those disparities.* Is air transport to be considered as a trade (in ser-

(*) Raymond ARON, "The Prometheus Dream : Society in search of itself"; *Britannica Perspectives*, vol. II, 1968, p. 152.

vices)? If so : is it a trade everywhere, and under all circumstances? How are we to qualify this proposition? With what criteria will we be able to determine whether air transport has ceased to be a *commodity*?

A *regional approach* to these questions might help us towards a solution consistent with the principles to which a large number of States committed themselves in Chicago.

The Chicago Convention of 1944 has not been seriously challenged for over four decades, a commendable achievement in itself. The philosophy of fair and equal opportunities for all meets the need for compromise between national interests and international organisation.

What this organisation should be in the future is now a matter open to debate, notably at regional levels. Bilateralism may not be the only, nor the best method to implement the broad principles of Chicago. Europe might opt for some form of de-nationalisation of its airspace, possibly deriving long-term benefits from a common attitude. At the same time, the respect for the human environment and the concern for security and the conservation of resources, as well as social considerations require a sound management of liberalism : aviation cannot do without some rules. The huge human and financial investments required for the functioning of the total air transport system demand serious advance thinking. The developing countries have to sort out their priorities. A new international balance of interests should be sought within a legal framework.

We modestly hope that by calling attention to a few facts we may help to foster such reflection before the final turning point.

Basically, the user of air transport is right. He does not care much about all the political aspects, economic complexities and legal niceties. He is interested in a wide choice of services and lower fares : the reliability of the service is taken for granted. *As, indeed, it should be.*

# PART I

# The international conventions

# INTRODUCTION

*"ONE WORLD"* was Wendell Willkie's motto, at the end of World War Two. Within a decade, the Charter of the United Nations, the Bretton Woods and GATT Agreements and other international understandings were to be concluded.

In this context, the Chicago Convention was signed, the International Civil Aviation Organisation was set up, as well as the International Air Transport Association, and the two major aviation powers set the bilateral pattern for the development of international air services under equitable conditions.

The founding fathers of this regulatory regime had a common view of civil aviation as a *unifying* and *pacifying* factor in the evolution of the post-war world.

We will concentrate, in this section, on the basic elements of the major conventions which were the basis of the regulatory regime of international air transport. By way of background information, a brief review of the history of air in public law will be given. This may help the reader to place developments in perspective

# CHAPTER 1

## THE CHICAGO CONVENTION

### 1. The air in public law, before Chicago

The question whether the air was *collective property* ("res communis" in Roman law) or belonged to the owner of the underlying soil ("up to the sky", "usque ad coelum" as the English maxim puts it) has always been a matter of dispute.

The concept of air as a *commodity* emerged in England during the 19th century [2]. It implied some limitations to the right of ownership of the soil. This evolution took place in France as well as in Germany : a *common interest* explained the use of the air [3]. The concept was clarified in United States case law : in 1872, a New York court held that "the rule, or maxim, giving the right of ownership to everything above the surface to the owner of the soil has full effect *without extending it to anything entirely disconnected with or detached from the soil itself* [4]".

The right of *free transit through the airspace* was recognised in the Federal Aviation Act of 23 August 1958 : "There is recognised and declared to exist on behalf of any citizen of the United States a public right of freedom of transit through the navigable airspace of the United States [5]".

With the emergence of air navigation, the philosophy of freedom of the air gained momentum, particulary in private law court cases. The doctrine inspired by the "free sea" gospel of Grotius, rallied numerous excellent writers for whom no other rule but the freedom of commerce in the air could meet the needs of the forthcoming age of aviation.

Others held that social and national interests were atstake, and concluded in favour of the "imperium" of the States over the airspace above their national territories : States should exercise and maintain their sovereignty over the airspace which they were able to control, *as part of their territory*.

The confrontation took place in 1912, at the Paris Conference of the International Law Association.

One year later, in Madrid, a compromise was reached [6]. But the war, in which aviation played a strategic part, corroborated the views of those who saw that national interests were closely linked to civil aviation. The *Paris Convention* of 1919 is a landmark in public air law [7]. National sovereignty, which was, at the time, exalted as an almost spiritual value, became the cornerstone of the regulatory system of international air services. It was not shattered at the end of World War Two, when state representatives convened again to consider the future of international civil aviation in a worldwide perspective.

## 2. The context of the Chicago conference

The world was still at war in 1944. The Conference concluded its work at a time when General von Rundstedt launched his offensive in the Ardennes. The devastating effects of the conflict were on everyone's mind.

Aviation had payed a large part in the destruction. Its technology had been considerably developed and its manufacturing capacity tremendously increased — particulary in the United States and the United Kingdom.

The question was : could aviation serve the cause of peace as efficiently as it had served the cause of war?

How could civil aviation foster the peaceful and harmonious development of relations among all peoples instead of becoming an instrument of domination of the strongest over the weakest?

In other fields as well, the Allied United Nations were in search of a political foundation for organised peace, post-war settlements and reconstruction : under the roar of the flying Fortresses, few matters seemed more vitally urgent than civil aviation.

Fifty-six governments were invited to the Civil Aviation Conference, which, at the time, amounted to the entire world, with the exception of hostile countries (the Axis powers) and Argentina. The USSR declined the invitation and fifty-two delegations showed up.

## 3. Striking a Balance

The United States, *major power number 1*, hosted the Conference from a considerably reinforced position, both politically and industrially. It had every reason to seek a revision of the rigid doctrine of absolute sovereignty and hoped that the time was ripe for a more liberal approach, if not for total freedom of the air.

It was realistically prepared for some compromise, but not at the expense of the possibilities for American carriers to expand.

*The other big power*, the United Kingdom, found itself in an excellent negotiating position, although somewhat on the defensive. Its fleet was less versatile than that of the United States, due to the concentration of its war effort. Compared with the US with its Transport Command's capabilities and numerous transport aircraft, the United Kingdom had little but experience to offer, exhausted as it was by an effort sustained so much longer. It proposed the establishment of an International Air Authority, which would licence operators, determine and allocate frequencies, and fix tariffs. The doctrine of State sovereignty, still very much favoured among participating countries, would be preserved.

One position "called for international ownership and operation of all international air services" [8]. At the other extreme, the United States did its best to create the conditions for a multilateral exchange of liberal air traffic rights [9].

In a short period of time, the Conference was able to strike a balance between the interests of all and to reach a compromise between the ideas of the champions of liberalism and the advocates of regulation.

Not much of a compromise, some would say : the Conference failed to achieve what had been most ardently expected, a consensus on a system to exchange the "freedoms of the air" among free nations. But major principles had been agreed upon; an institution would be formed to monitor developments in accordance with those principles.

If only technically, the meeting was a success. "By today's experience and standards in international decisionmaking and drafting of legal texts, the Conference achieved an awesome result by the drafting, adoption and opening for signature of one major convention, three agreements, a standard form of bilateral agreements for provisional air routes and the text of twelve draft technical annexes.

This result probably represents a record achievement in the history of drafting of international legal rules, and the Chicago Conference must be considered to be the most successful, productive and influential international conference ever held". (Michael Milde, writing in 1984) [10].

Beyond this record achievement, the Chicago Convention provided a politically acceptable formula [11].

## 4. The Chicago Convention and Agreements

The following instruments were adopted in Chicago and opened for signature :

— the Convention on International Civil Aviation;
— the Interim Agreement on International Civil Aviation;
— the International Air Services Transit Agreement;
— the International Air Transport Agreement;
— Draft of Technical Annexes A-L.

### I. — CONVENTION ON INTERNATIONAL CIVIL AVIATION (THE "CHICAGO CONVENTION")

The Convention was signed in Chicago on 7 December 1944. It entered into force on 4 April 1947, the date of registration of the 26th instrument of ratification or adhesion.

#### a. Basic principles

#### 1. Sovereignty

"Each State has complete and exclusive sovereignty over the airspace above its territory." (Art. 1).

This principle had been recognised in international custom [12]. Its implications are multiple : physical (air navigation), but also economic (authority over the conditions of the service).

Within the meaning of the Convention, the "territory" is limited, both laterally and by superior limits [13].

No national sovereignty exists above high seas and non-appropriated lands.

#### 2. Equal opportunities

International air services must be established *taking due account of the equal right of all States to participate in the traffic.* (Preamble).

#### 3. Absence of discrimination

The laws and regulations of the air established by a Contracting state must be complied with above its territory by aircraft of all Contracting States, "without distinction as to nationality". (Art. 11). This provision applies to admission, departure of aircraft to and from the territory of the State concerned, or the operation and navigation of aircraft while within its territory.

### 4. *Non-interference*

The Contracting States are free to designate the national companies which will operate air services.

These general rules apply to air transport principles of international public law [14].

### b. *Scope of application*

The Convention establishes the rules for the use of *civil aircraft*. (Art. 3, a).

State aircraft (utilised for military, customs or police purposes) are governed by the Convention generally : for instance, overflight requires special authority from the government of the State concerned. (Art. 3, c).

### c. *Limitations of sovereignty*

The principle of sovereignty set forth in Article 1 received specific limitations in certain areas.

1) The States are committed to observe the *international regulations governing air navigation*. As a consequence, the rights of governments to regulate air navigation above their territories are not absolute, but subject to international rules.

2) In principle, *a liberal regime* is envisaged *for non-scheduled flights :* Article 5 of the Convention provides that such flights ("not engaged in scheduled international air services") ("shall have the right ...") must be authorised, subject to some limitations.

States may :

a) require landing;

b) for reasons of safety, impose prescribed routes or require special permission;

c) impose "regulations, conditions or limitations", as considered "desirable", on the privilege of taking up or discharging traffic.

3) The principle of freedom is *reversed* by Article 6 in the case of *scheduled flights :* no scheduled international service may be operated *unless* with the "*special permission or other authorization*" of the State concerned, "*and in accordance with the terms of such permission or authorization.*"

The same rule applies to overflight and landing rights.

Article 6 did not imply the formal *exchange of traffic rights* through *bilateral agreements*, but the practice developed and Article 6 was ultimately considered as *"the chart of bilateralism"* [15].

4) The various commitments related to the institution and the functioning of the *International Civil Aviation Organisation (ICAO) in pursuance of the objectives set forth by the Convention* constitute restrictions to the absolute sovereignty principle.

They are spelled out in the Second and the Third Parts of the Convention.

5) Among the main obligations contracted by States under the Convention are those relating to the *nationality of aircraft.*

Aircraft have the nationality of the States in which they are registered. Every aircraft must have a nationality, and not more than one.

### d. *Regulation of scheduled and non-scheduled international services*

A problem raised by the distinctive regime imposed on scheduled and non-scheduled services arose due to the absence of definitions.

The *bilateral system* (possibly a lesser evil) was generated by Article 6, as indicated above, *for scheduled services only.* Non-scheduled services remained subject *to unilateral permission.*

The disparity would have consequences for the development of charter operations at a later stage, and would justify the comment that the Chicago Convention suffered from a serious shortcoming in this respect.

The question of definitions deserves some explanation.

*What is an international scheduled air service?*

Article 6 of the Chicago Convention refers to "scheduled international air service", *without defining the word "scheduled".*

"Air service" means any scheduled air service performed by aircraft for the public transport of passengers, mail or cargo". (Art. 96, a).

"International air service" means an air service with "passes through the air space over the territory of more than one State". (Art. 96, b).

Article 5 refers to "aircraft not engaged in scheduled international air services", without providing any further definition.

The need for a definition of an international scheduled air service was recognised as early as 1948 by the Assembly of ICAO [16]. *A definition was adopted by the Council in 1952* [17].

To sum up the elements of this definition, an air service qualifies as a scheduled international air service when the following conditions are met :

The flight must :

a) be performed through more than one State;

b) be undertaken for remuneration, so that all flights are *accessible to the public;*

c) carry trafic between two or several points which remain *identical for the entire sequence of flights*, either *according to a published timetable*, or with such frequent regularity as to make the sequence *a recognisable series of flights.*

In 1952, this definition seemed adequate, but ceased to be so with the emergence of new types of charters which were *programmed like scheduled flights*, advertised in the same way and sold to the general public. They thereby met the conditions of the definition to a degree.

The qualification of « programmed charters » as scheduled or non-scheduled services was left to the discretion of governments, prolonging the legal uncertainty; the panel set up by ICAO's special Conference in 1978 gave up trying to improve the 1952 definition.

## II. — *THE CHICAGO AGREEMENTS*

The *CHICAGO CONVENTION* was supplemented by the *TRANSIT AGREEMENT* and the *TRANSPORT AGREEMENT* (*or "Five Freedoms Agreement"*, to use the name by which this agreement is best known). In addition, a model bilateral agreement was also agreed upon.

The concept of the system was realistic : the general legal framework of the Convention required an instrument which enabled the Contracting States to implement the agreed principles by exchanging, as liberally as possible, the freedoms of the air.

Even though the acceptance of such agreements would be more limited than the Convention's, it would generate a drive towards the universalism of such an exchange of traffic rights.

Unfortunately the effort was not successful. Only the "Transit Agreement" achieved its purpose.

### a. *The Transit Agreement*

The International Air Services Transit Agreement provides for the exchange of "technical" (or non-commercial) freedoms of the air [18].

The following privileges are granted by each Contracting State to the others, with respect to scheduled international services :

1) "the privilege to fly across its territory without landing;

2) the privilege to land for non-traffic purposes ..." (Article 1, Section 1).

Each Contracting State may specify the itinerary to be followed within its territory and the airports to be used. It may impose "reasonable charges" for the use of airports and facilities. (Article 1, Section 4).

Ninety-five States are currently party to this unique instrument for the multilateral exchange of freedoms of the air.

Dealing with non-commercial rights only, it establishes a minimum, but useful basis for this type of exchange.

Transit rights have an economic value, which can be negotiated whenever a State has not ratified or adhered to the Transit Agreement. Some States have been reluctant to become party to this Agreement, as they benefit from a favourable geographical position.

b. *The Transport Agreement*

The International Air Transport Agreement provided for the exchange of the five freedoms of the air, defined as follows :

*First freedom* granted by a State : the privilege to fly across its territory without landing;

*Second freedom* : the privilege to land for non-traffic purposes (any technical or operational reason, such as picking up a slipcrew);

*Third freedom* : the privilege to put down passengers, mail and cargo taken on in the territory of the State whose nationality the aircraft possesses;

*Fourth freedom* : the privilege to take on passengers, mail and cargo destined for the territory of the State whose nationality the aircraft possesses;

*Fifth freedom* : the privilege to take on passengers, mail and cargo destined for the territory of any other Contracting State and the privilege to put down passengers, mail and cargo coming from any such territory.

(Article 1, Section 1).

Those definitions were to be reproduced, with appropriate alterations, in bilateral air transport agreements. So were definitions and rules with respect to :

*Cabotage* (traffic carried between points in the territory of one State) : Article 1, Section 4;

*Nationality of Aircraft :* Article 1, Section 6.

*Certificates and Operating Permits :* Article 1, Section 5.

Only ten States ratified the Transport Agreement, which never came into effect.

The stumbling block was the issue of fifth freedom rights. At the time, the profitability of long haul routes depended heavily on the possibility of carrying traffic between third countries on the route. The issue was no longer the *granting* of the fifth freedom, but the regulation of *capacity* in relation to the fifth freedom. The pursuit of self-interest by all the participants accounts for the failure, and for the controversial resolution of the basic problem through Article 6 of the Chicago Convention. The exchange of traffic rights would always take the bilateral format in future.

A lesser evil was that such bilateral agreements conform to a model.

### c. *Draft Standard Air Services Agreement*

The draft of a bilateral air services agreement was attached to the main instrument. It was later to inspire the model "Bermuda Agreement", which would set the definitive pattern.

## 5. An evaluation

*The Chicago Conference had important and lasting results*

### a. *Positive aspects*

The Conference was more than a technical success : it was a political achievement. It succeeded in creating a viable framework for post-war commercial air transport. Although it failed to achieve a multilateral exchange of commercial traffic rights, it had a significant impact on subsequent bilateral air agreements.

Basic principles were established : equal rights of access to air transport for all nations of the world, sovereignty of and limitations on its use, nationality of aircraft, etc. The ICAO was set up.

The flexible working methods of ICAO would permit the harmonisation of the rules of navigation, and a high degree of safety would thereby be attained in air transport, once a risky undertaking. ICAO would become a neutral forum where aviation experts would share knowledge and expectations, confront views and avoid, to some extent, the recurrent traps of international politics.

### b. *Shortcomings*

The participants were disappointed at their failure to achieve their main objective. In time, some of the Convention's shortcomings appeared.

### 1) *Absence of positive legislation*

The Convention created mechanisms rather than *legislation*. "Falling short of making law, one had created the institution which would be the guardian of the law, when there would be one" [19]. Nothing equals the rules set forth in a treaty : in time, the emptiness would show.

### 2) *Generality of principles*

Despite its vast ambitions, the Chicago Convention essentially consists of the statement of general principles, providing a framework for bilateral agreements and secondary legislation. In addition, it contains a policy regulation governing international air navigation in broad terms, and the skeleton of a code of conduct which could govern international air transport.

The principles were indeed politically well inspired — which partly accounts for the long life of the Convention. Legally, however, they lacked precision.

### 3) *Weakness of economic guidelines*

While the Convention established adequate norms for the uncontroversial technical standards of air navigation, the guidelines dealing with sensitive politico-economic issues were vague and proved somewhat ineffective at critical times.

As a result, States derived authority from other legal instruments, consistent with Article 1 of the Convention, and sought little guidance from ICAO.

Some legal aspects were conveniently covered, irrespective of the Chicago Convention. With regard to *private law*, there was little danger of States adopting widely diverging views : the 1929 Warsaw Convention had proved dependable. It would be the task of the Legal Committee of ICAO to see to it that international conventions were adapted to changing conditions and that, when possible, new agreements were concluded.

As far as international *public law* of the air was concerned, the regulation of the *non-freedom* of the air by a set of broad principles left a large number of questions totally unanswered, including the arbitration of conflicts which might arise from them.

In the long term, such legal uncertainty exposed the international regime to tensions.

The Chicago Convention failed to moderate the « complete and exclusive sovereignty" of States over their airspace (as part of "their" territories) by a multilateral agreement on the exchange of commercial traffic rights. Consequently, States which signed and adhered to the Convention were inevitably reluctant to concede any power to ICAO which could influence the economic future of their air transport.

### c. *In general*

We have indicated in sufficient detail that, for all its imperfections, the Chicago Convention provided a sound basis for the development of civil aviation in the world. It did not resolve its conflicts, but its objectives were nevertheless ambitious, and the creation of ICAO far-reaching. Equality for all in principle, and safety in fact were solid goals, and achievements followed.

Above all, the Convention was *"an act of faith in civil aviation"*, as Mr. Kotaite, the long-time Chairman of the Council of ICAO has called it [20]. It has "met the need in 40 years use" [21], and the homage rendered at its 40th Anniversary was well deserved [22]. But that is history.

The questions which now remains is what will be the *role of the Convention in the future*, and to what extent will all parts of the world be able to live under its dominance without altering its pattern?

# CHAPTER 2

## THE BERMUDA AGREEMENT

An Air Services Agreement was signed on February 11, 1946, at Bermuda, by the United States and the United Kingdom [23].

## 1. Importance

In a joint statement, the signatories proclaimed their agreement on a standard pattern for all further air transport treaties which they would conclude. In fact, it established a model for all, or almost all air transport agreements concluded among ICAO Member States during the following years.

The Bermuda Agreement was a prototype.

## 2. Form

The importance of the treaty was emphasised by the "Final Act" of the bilateral Conference, which set forth a number of general principles. In later bilateral agreements, those principles, as well as the definitions contained in the agreement, were to be reproduced in somewhat different forms, although they remained substantially the same for a very long time. The same subjects would be taken up as main topics of understanding. The format of the Annex (route schedules) would be observed, although the drawing up of the routes would gradually change.

## 3. Background

Predictably the two countries whose doctrines had conflicted the most during the Chicago Conference endeavoured to reconcile their views on the exchange of commercial traffic rights and the modalities thereof.

This compromise was seen as a duty incumbent on "the two leading aviation powers of the world" [24]. Hence the necessity for them to attain a conceptual compromise beyond the mere pragmatic arrangement which they might otherwise have reached.

The UK had great bargaining power, as it controlled the widest range of cities with which to trade traffic rights on air routes worldwide.

Yet the basic philosophy of the Agreement is liberal, as reflected notably in its capacity clauses.

As the major aviation power, the United States might have pressed its point with more energy, especially, with regard to pricing philosophy, so close to the heart of liberal economists.

The compromise was on principles as well as on trade advantages, and it can be concluded, on analysis, that the signatories behaved responsibly.

We may certainly criticise the Agreement for its shortcomings (and we will do so occasionally). But at the time when, and in view of the background against which it was drawn up, the "Bermuda plan" appeared satisfactory : *it raised hopes that, notwithstanding the failure at Chicago, a multilateral agreement for the exchange of traffic rights might be within reach after all* [25].

## 4. General contents

Regardless of the distribution of subjects between the body of the Agreement and the Final Act, the following chapter headings appear :

— Definitions of the freedoms of the air;
— General principles : fair and equal opportunity, etc.;
— Capacity clauses;
— Clause on the establishment of air fares and rates;
— Legal and administrative clauses (customs exemptions, arbitration, consultations, termination, etc.);
— Routes.

We will briefly review some of the main topics under those headings.

## 5. The Bermuda Capacity clauses

Probably the most noteworthy provisions of the Bermuda 1 Agreement are those relating to the provision of capacity by the designated carriers of the Contracting Parties.

The principles are the following :

1) The capacity offered "should bear a close relationship to the requirements of the public for such transport". (Final Act, para. 3).

2) There should be "a fair and equal opportunity for the carriers of the two nations to operate on any route between their respective territories". (id. para. 4).

An early observation made on this much-discussed provision is that "the words 'fair' and 'equal' would be conflicting for in this case neither 'fair' would always be identical to 'equal' nor would 'equality' always be 'fair'". (Adriani) [26].

3) "The interests of the air carriers of the other government shall be taken into consideration so as not to affect unduly the services which the latter provides on all or part of the same routes". (id. para. 5).

4) The primary objective of the air carriers is "the provision of capacity adequate to the traffic demands between the country of which such air carrier is a national and the country of ultimate destination of the traffic". (id. para. 6).

This means, in effect, that third and fourth freedom traffic called *"primary traffic"*, carried on a certain route, *must always be more important than fifth freedom traffic* or, more generally, than traffic originating from or destined for third countries. The proportion of each category of traffic was not defined mathematically and remained controversial, just as the concepts themselves, which lacked clarity, gave rise to some arguments.

The principal effect of the Bermuda capacity clause is to offer the designated carriers the *freedom* to determine their production on any given route, *subject only to an "ex post facto" review* by the aeronautical authorities of the Contracting States. There should not exist, under a pure "Bermuda type" air transport agreement, any predetermination of capacity. We will see that this law has not been observed. However, the designated carriers are bound by the rules set forth in the capacity clause, and the aeronautical authorities may be called upon to verify compliance with those rules. They will, obviously, have a role to play at the stage where timetables are submitted by carriers for approval, but the consultation process provided for in other provisions of the air transport agreement frequently permits an exchange of views on the actual implementation of the capacity principles.

In other words, the free determination of capacity by the carriers is not *exempt from government control*. Such control, may only be exercised, however, after the time required to evaluate the development of the traffic on the services offered by the designated carriers of the two Contracting States.

This observation, on the fundamental liberalism of the Bermuda-type capacity clause, deserves to be made at a time when the Chicago-Bermuda system is being relaxed and liberalised : it is probable that it is the extension of government interference in the processes beyond the rule of Bermuda, which has imposed rigidity, rather than the rule itself.

Not that the rules were legally clear to begin with. They were open to diverging interpretations. For instance, the attempt was made to relate the various types of air traffic allowed to be carried, but this was done in such general terms that "states not only disagree about the acceptable proportion of fifth freedom traffic to third and fourth freedom traffic, but are not even in agreement on how to identify the traffic".

When making this observation at an early stage (1959), an American author, Albert Stoffel, commented : "Like many reasonable general principles, these principles can work only when both sides are in general agreement on their meaning. However, as is so often the case in international affairs, geographic location, the relative development of civil aviation, national aviation, commercial importance, political prestige, and many other criteria are applied by each country, resulting in widely divergent views concerning the capacity principles" [27].

This may be a comment made from an historical perspective, rather than a judgment *on the Bermuda agreement*. But from that same perspective, it is not easy to find a better analysis or to imagine a more effective compromise.

Many years later (1978), when new ideas on capacity regulation had been developed, the ICAO set up a "Panel on Regulation of Air Transport Services", with the task of re-formulating standard capacity clauses and identifying the relevant criteria. The model Bermuda 1 capacity clause was finalised with very few alterations. One of the members, Joseph Gertler, commented : "The developments in the Treaty practice of states after 1946 have brought about little modifications of the original text but in many cases profound changes in the Bermudian philosophy, mostly in the direction of more or less hidden predetermination of capacity. "And Gertler joins the writer of the present work to ask the question "whether Bermuda-type agreements *are still Bermudian*" [28].

An abundant literature exists on this crucial question of the bilateral division of capacity between States which was envisaged at the Bermuda Conference [29]. Without question, the formula has worked for a long time.

In conclusion, the Bermuda capacity clause was probably the closest approximation attainable to a balanced regime : its vulnerability lay less in the language of the bilateral clause than in bilateralism itself.

## 6. Tariffs

Routes, capacity and prices are inter-related aspects of the exchange of traffic rights. While routes refer to the material content of such an exchange, capacity and tariffs are economically co-substantial and a necessary part of any consistent regulatory system.

The post-war ratemaking function for scheduled international air services was carried out by IATA Traffic Conferences on the basis of the tariff provisions in bilateral air transport agreements. This reference provides the legal basis for the compulsory intervention of IATA in the multilateral process.

The mandate of IATA has been expressed in somewhat different terms along the years, but bilaterals generally followed the same patterns, achieving *multilateralism* through *bilateralism*.

One exception is the "International Agreement on the Procedure for the Establishment of Tariffs for Scheduled Air Services ", signed in Paris, July 10, 1967. (Cf. below : Chapter III, 1, f, 1).

The pricing philosophy and the procedures are the subject of a detailed clause.

This tariff clause may be summarised as follows :

1) Fares and rates must be discussed and determined *by the designated carriers, preferably through the machinery provided by IATA*, on condition of their final approval by the civil aviation authorities of the Contracting Parties.

The governments, having recognised the benefits attached to an harmonised and integrated pricing system for international air transport, have made in *mandatory* for airlines to coordinate their tariffs and at least to *try* to reach an agreement on fare structures applicable to services in which these fare are included.

Only the concertation is mandatory, not the agreement itself. An agreement within IATA should be reached "whenever possible", and the airlines are under no obligation to achieve results.

2) In the case of no agreement being reached within IATA, *the designated airlines* will seek an agreement *among themselves*.

*Note :* Due account must be taken of tariffs used by other carriers on the same routes, sections of the same routes and neighbouring routes, thus establishing an obligation to coordinate international fares and rates to the greatest possible extent, whether or not the coordinating machinery of the IATA is used.

Here also, the airlines have to harmonise tariffs among themselves : they do not necessarily have to agree.

3) In the case of no agreement being reached among designated carriers bilaterally, the *governments* of both Contracting Parties will take up the matter and meet in order to determine the tariffs to be applied on the routes concerned.

4) The airlines have to submit their proposed tariffs to their respective national aeronautical authorities for *approval*.

It follows from these principles that *the States have not relinquished their power to decide on air tariffs*, but merely delegated a certain amount of this power to their designated airlines. The final word rests with the government authorities, who may *approve or disapprove*, totally or partially, the tariffs submitted. Both governments of the Contracting Parties have to approve the tariffs. (This system is therefore called the "double approval" regime, as opposed to more recent clauses.)

For the United States, the Bermuda Agreement involved a substantial renunciation of the principles of a liberal *pricing philosophy*. This concession was traded for the almost unrestricted *capacity* regime. The double approval regime for tariffs was endorsed by the United States for the first time. This compromise reflected, internally, the uncertainty of US lawyers as to statutory powers of the Civil Aeronautics Board, an autonomous federal agency, in this matter. Congress ultimately denied the CAB the right to decide tariffs, and confined its powers to the approval of fares and rates arising from airlines' agreements.

The CAB was granted authority to confer anti-trust immunity to the Traffic Conferences of IATA and to pricing agreements reached as a result of these conferences.

On February 19, 1946, the Civil Aeronautics Board approved the IATA machinery for one year; the approval was renewed annually until 1955, when it was made permanent [30].

More recently (1978), the CAB announced its intention to withdraw all anti-trust immunity from IATA's ratemaking machinery; to what extent this intention became effective and the consequences of this attitude will be reviewed later in this book.

At the time, the IATA system appeared to be an adequate response to the apprehension of those who wanted to avoid a war of tariffs in the air, and it was greeted as such by President Truman.

Ironically, the worst price war was to take place under a regime of government intervention which was intended to abolish it forever.

## 7. Designation of the carriers

An important aspect of the arrangements between countries is the process of market access, as recognised in Chicago. This matter includes the assessment of the number of air carriers which each government is entitled to designate to operate services, and the definition of the conditions with which carriers must comply.

Clearly, competition increases with the number of competitors. But not all countries were willing to allow an unlimited number of airlines from the other party to compete with their own (depending on their own strength in this respect). A potential imbalance would require an actual "quid pro quo".

The United States itself had, just before the war, retained in principle the concept of the *"chosen instrument"* (designation of a carrier for each route). But several "chosen instruments bills" were defeated in Congress and the Administration finally decided that two carriers could be authorised to operate *to all major points abroad*.

The Federal Aviation Act of 1958 established the very important principle : that it was in the public interest, and in accordance with public convenience and necessity, to ensure "competition to the extent necessary to assure the sound development of an air transportation system properly adapted to the needs of the foreign and domestic commerce of the United States ..." (Section 102, d).

On February 18, 1959, the President declared that the Administration was committed to the view "that *public interest requires competitive flag service at the earliest possible date on all international air routes serving major United States gateways"*.

These developments illustrate the importance of the concept of multi-designation of carriers as a key to market access and the difficulties to which it may give rise.

The designation itself, whether of one or several airlines, is subject to conditions which must be met to the satisfaction of both Contracting States : *designation is thereby made a bilateral process.*

Basically, the conditions are that the carrier concerned established that its *"substantial ownership"* and *"effective control"* rest in the hands of the State of designation or of nationals thereof. Once again, no mathematical criterion was furnished to help prove "substantial ownership" : *a minimum of 51 % of the shares is generally accepted* as satisfying this condition [31]. "Effective control" relates, as a matter of factual evidence, to participation in the executive bodies in control of the company's management.

The application of a designated carrier may be turned down by the other State, if the latter is not satisfied that these conditions have been adequately met — or if the applicant carrier does not comply with applicable legislation.

The ownership and nationality of the aircraft used do not fall within the conditions of admission within the clause.

*Note :* The "substantial ownership and effective control" clause is part of the key regulation governing *access to the market.* (see below : II, 3, e).

## 8. Routes

The Route Schedules form an Annex to the Agreement. This format was retained in subsequent bilateral agreements on account of its greater flexibility. Aeronautical authorities may agree, with little formality, on a modification of the Annex which, in all other respects, is regarded as part of the Agreement.

What is a *route?* As distinct from an air navigation itinarery (airway), a route is a series of points which may be served by a scheduled international air service. Of necessity, points in the territories of both Contracting States must be included : other points will be "intermediate points", if situated between the points in the Contracting States' territories, or "points beyond", in other cases.

With reference to points beyond, traffic rights are specified : "beyond rights" are the rights granted in a bilateral air agreement for carriers of one or both parties to fly to a point in the country granting the right and beyond to points in any other country, or, in its more restricted version, to a single other country or groups of countries.

The United States adopted the policy of defining the routes broadly and of refusing to grant "beyond rights" to foreign carriers, while obtaining them for their own.

At the time of Bermuda, the United Kingdom agreed on the broad type description of routes. The reason was to gain experience. "The United States attempted to make its routes as general as possible to give its carriers leeway in setting up economically sound service patterns which would reflect the public need for air transportation".

Most other countries did not have "the equipment, manpower, and other resources necessary to fly the routes which they obtained from the United States" [32].

The American concept of "beyond rights" was, and has remained consistent with the view that the United States "constitutes a natural terminal market rather than a natural stop-over market as do many European and other countries". But "the beyond rights obtained abroad by the United States carriers permitted them to carry a considerable volume of fifth freedom traffic". (Albert STOFFEL, Supervisory Foreign Affairs Officer, Aviation, Department of State) [33].

As a result, and due to the obvious imbalance of power and, occasionally, to complementary interests (as in the case of the Marshall Plan, as far as Western Europe was concerned), the United States obtained extensive "around the world" air routes, with fifth freedom rights available on all sectors. In one instance (the US/France bilateral), this early formulation of routes required an arbitration award to clarify the pattern of a route.

## 9. Conclusion

From then on, the bilateral exchange of traffic rights would be made possible and relevant agreements would, generally, be tailored to a similar pattern.

This pattern was a combination of bilateralism and multilateralism, which laid the foundation for a checks and balances system. The exchange of fifth freedom rights implies extension beyond the bilateral framework. At airline level, multilateralism was fully developed as the proper setting for international ratemaking through the machinery of IATA.

The predictability of the regulatory system was considerably increased.

The general rules of the game would be known :

a) with respect to market access : how governments would designate carriers;

b) with respect to capacity : each designated carrier would be able to supply capacity according to its own judgment (subject, however, to governmental review, a proviso which was to be seldom applied);

c) with respect to tariff-fixing : through mandatory multilateral or bilateral consultation, the results of which would be submitted to governments for approval.

This complex, but balanced system would complement the Chicago Convention.

However, the discussion on the merits of bilateralism has continued. The participants in the Chicago Conference of 1944 already agreed on the shortcomings of bilateralism "due to the bargaining and competition wars to which it gave rise" [34]. The issue was not one which the Bermuda partners could solve.

Looking critically at the compromise, we realise that it probably aggravated the effect of the principle of sovereignty. As a result of Bermuda, States tended to interpret the latter as a *right of ownership* of traffic originating in their territories (if not of traffic destined for and/or transiting through their territories).

Indeed, the Bermuda Agreement, in replacing the unattainable multilateral air transport agreement, conveyed to some the impression that *States were to share properties rather than allocate markets.*

For instance, the new rule of primacy of the "natural" (third and fourth freedom) traffic over fifth freedom traffic served to corroborate this view. The organised interference of States in capacity and tariffs, their advantage in those matters and in the designation of airlines, did nothing to discourage the trend.

In that sense, the Bermuda Agreement, for all its merits, contained the germs of the disease which was to affect the regulatory regime at a later date.

*Remark :*

There have been other conventions of interest to public law, but these are beyond the main scope of this book (cf. Appendix 2). We shall focus on the evolution of the regulatory system and its main structural aspects relating to the economic activities of air transport on the international scene.

PART II

The institutions

The universal ambition of all the participants of the 1944 Chicago Conference led to the creation of the International Civil Aviation Organisation. The founding fathers unofficially supervised the subsequent institution of the International Air Transport Association.

Although IATA was, and still is, a private organisation, the context of its institution makes it part of the historical setup decided upon by the international community after World War Two. Moreover, from the legal standpoint, the reference to IATA in the tariff clauses of bilateral air transport agreements justifies its inclusion in the mechanism oft he public law system governing international air transport. We will, therefore, focus mainly on those two institutions.

However, a general overview should also include regional organisations and the reader should be given a brief view of how national authorities are normally structured to deal with international air transport.

# CHAPTER 1

## ICAO

### 1. Source

The constitutional terms of the International Civil Aviation Organisation are contained in Part II of the Chicago Convention.

The Convention itself formed the organisation. (Art. 43).

### 2. Relation to the general obligations of the Convention

Among the various commitments undertaken by States party to the Convention, there are several provisions which relate to their recognised obligation to keep their own regulations uniform, to the greatest possible extent, with those established "from time to time under this Convention". (Art. 12).

The States agreed to establish an adequate international institution with the aim of simplifying and standardising their technical, legal and economic regulations. (cf. Articles 12, 22, 28, 37, 38 of the Convention).

They did not invest this instrument with supernational power at the expense of their own sovereignty : the organisation is largely *associative*. The legal commitments of the adhering States stem from the Convention. However, ICAO has *regulatory* powers, *legislative* and *jurisdictional* functions with respect to the achievement of its objectives.

### 3. Objectives

The Organisation was established in order "to develop the principles and techniques of international air navigation and to foster the planning and development of international air transport". (Art. 44).

We should note that the "technical" (air navigation) and "economic" (air transport) aspects of civil aviation are considered to be on an equal footing among the aims and objectives of ICAO under Article 44 of the Convention.

The objectives to be achieved are the following : to

"a) ensure the *safe and orderly growth* of international civil aviation throughout the world;

b) encourage the arts of aircraft design and operation for peaceful purposes;

c) encourage the development of airways, airports, and air navigation facilities for international civil aviation;

d) meet the needs of the peoples of the world for *safe, regular, efficient and economical air transport;*

e) *prevent economic waste caused by unreasonable competition;*

f) ensure that the rights of contracting States are fully respected and that *every contracting State has a fair opportunity* to operate international airlines;

g) *avoid discrimination* between contracting States;

h) promote safety of flight in international air navigation;

i) promote generally the development of all aspects of international civil aeronautics". (Art. 44) (emphasis added).

## 4. Registration and Legal Capacity

The Organisation is based in Montreal, following an agreement with Canada concluded in 1951. Regional offices have been established in Paris, Dakar, Cairo, Bangkok, Mexico and Lima.

The Organisation enjoys, in the territory of each Contracting State, "such legal capacity as may be necessary for the performance of its functions. Full juridical capacity shall be granted wherever compatible with the constitution and laws of the State concerned". (Art. 47).

The ICAO has been a specialised organisation of the United Nations Organisation since 1947.

## 5. Composition

The Organisation is made up of an Assembly, a Council, "and such other bodies as may be necessary" (Art. 43) — in effect, certain Commissions and Committees, which have become permanent.

### a) The Assembly

The Assembly is the *sovereign* body of ICAO. Member States have an equal right to be represented in the Assembly and each is entitled to one vote (Art. 48, b). Decisions are taken by a majority of the votes cast. (Art. 48, c).

The meetings of the Assembly take place at least once every three years.

The Assembly decides the general policy of the organisation, votes on the annual budgets and determines financial arrangements, reviews expenditure, approves the accounts, delegates powers to the Council, refers matters to commissions, considers and proposes to States modifications or amendments to the Convention, and generally deals with any matter within the sphere of action of the Organisation not specifically assigned to the Council (cf. Art. 49).

## b) *The Council*

The Council is the *executive* body of ICAO.

It is responsible to the Assembly.

It is composed of thirty-three Contracting States elected by the Assembly.

The election is held in different categories according to the three following criteria :

1) the States of chief importance in air transport;

2) the States which make the largest contribution to the provision of facilities for international air navigation;

3) the States (not otherwise included) whose designation will ensure that all the major geographical areas of the world are represented on the Council. (Art. 50, b).

The decisions of the Council require the approval of a majority of its members. (Art. 52).

The Council administers the finances of the Organisation, submits annual reports to the Assembly, appoints the Secretary-General and members of permanent commissions, holds a general responsibility to implement the objectives of the Organisation. (Art. 54 and 55).

## c) *Permanent Commissions and Committees*

The *Air Navigation Commission* studies technical questions. The *Air Transport Committee* deals with the economic aspects of international air transport.

The *Legal Committee*, which was set up by the Assembly (not by the

Convention), drafts conventions of international air law and advises the Council and the Assembly on legal subjects. The *Committe of Collective Aid to Air Navigation Services,* also set up by the Assembly (in its first session), allocates contributions, where needed, to acquire collective equipment for navigational assistance.

The *Financial Committee* should also be mentioned.

## 6. Main functions of ICAO

### A. — REGULATORY FUNCTIONS

The powers of ICAO are primarily of a regulatory or quasi-legislative nature : they consist of the development and revision of the Annexes to the Chicago Convention.

Although the Contracting States are not bound against their will, the procedures followed give ICAO an important role in the production of the standards and recommended practices that form the Annexes and become binding to all ICAO Member States as part of their obligations under the Convention itself.

In relation to air navigation, the definitions of the standards and recommended practices are the following. (By substituting a reference to international air transport, the same definition applies to this latter sector, but, broadly speaking, this procedure is used for "technical" matters more readily than on economic subjects).

### 1. *Standards*

A standard is "any specification for physical characteristics, configuration, material, performance, personnel or procedure, the uniform application of which is recognised as *necessary* for the safety or regularity of international air navigation and to which Contracting States will conform in accordance with the Convention; in the event of impossibility of compliance, notification to the Council is compulsory under article 38 of the Convention" [rr].

### 2. *Recommended practices*

A recommended practice is "any specification for physical characteristics, configuration, material, performance, personnel or procedure the uniform application of which is recognised as *desirable* in the interest of safety, regularity or efficiency of international air navigation, and to which Contracting States will endeavour to conform in accordance with the Convention" [35].

The compulsary nature of the two categories of norms is different legally, but in practice most are made part of the domestic laws and regulations of the Contracting States. The objective of uniformity is thereby achieved to a very large extent, without prejudicing the rights of national governments to raise justified objections.

## 3. *Procedure*

The flexibility of the system is increased even more by the procedure of adoption of the Annexes to the Convention or of amendments thereto. This procedure is as follows :

Within three months of the adoption of the norms by the Council, the texts amending the Annexes to the Convention are submitted to all Contracting States for approval.

No State may be forced to accept, and at this stage, a double possibility to have the proposal rejected still exists.

a) Either a State may decide to maintain some differences between the international standard and its own legislation, in which case it has to notify the Council of its attitude and provide full information on the differences and explanation of its reasons;

b) or a majority of States may disapprove the international standard despite its previous adoption by the Council. This second level verdict may still result in the standard being rejected.

The first instance only results in the rejection of the standard by the dissenting State.

## B. — LEGISLATION

ICAO prepares international conventions in international air law. However, these conventions must be adopted by diplomatic conferences following international practice.

## C. — JURISDICTION

The Council of ICAO has jurisdiction to decide on conflicts of interpretation or application of the Convention or of its Annexes. (Article 84 of the Convention) It may also arbitrate conflicts relating to questions of civil aviation. (Bilateral agreements often contain arbitration clauses to that effect.)

## 7. Annexes

The ICAO regulations are embodied in the Annexes to the Chicago Convention, which are republished from time to time. The standardisation of the norms and their constant adaptation to changing conditions are necessary to the maintenance of safety in international civil aviation.

The 18 Annexes deal with the following subjects :

1. Personnel Licencing;
2. Rules of the Air;
3. Meteorological Service for International Air Navigation;
4. Aeronautical Charts;
5. Units of Measurement to be used in Air and Ground Operations;
6. Operation of Aircraft;
7. Aircraft Nationality and Registration of Marks;
8. Airworthiness of Aircraft;
9. Facilitation;
10. Aeronautical Telecommunications;
11. Air Traffic Services;
12. Search and Rescue;
13. Aircraft Accident Investigation;
14. Aerodromes;
15. Aeronautical Information Services;
16. Aircraft noise;
17. Safety;
18. Safe Transport of Dangerous Goods by Air.

## 8. A comment

The work of ICAO has often been praised, with good reason.

Le Goff wrote : *"We do not believe that there can be a more beautiful rational achievement than the elaboration of standards in matters of air navigation, performed by ICAO ..."* [36].

## 9. ICAO and air transport

Under the terms of Article 44 of the Convention, ICAO has been entrusted with a number of economic tasks and with missions either of a political or general nature so as to encompass all aspects of international air transport.

However, the difficulties of taking concrete steps to pursue such objectives as "orderly growth of international civil aviation throughout the world". (Art. 44, a) "economical air transport" (Art. 44, d), the prevention of "economic waste caused by unreasonable competition" (Art. 44, e), or the avoidance of "discrimination between contracting States" (Art. 44, g) are manifest.

The Organisation lacks the statutory power to impose measures on Contracting States in a number of areas where, in fact, the Convention itself has left these States with full authoritiy of decisions, and subsequent arrangements have established the quasi-discretional powers of governments in dealing with economic factors.

However, ICAO is an incomparable forum. Better use might have been made of it for in-depth discussion of the problems of international air transport at the time when these were emerging as potential threats to some of the major objectives of the Convention.

By proceeding with recommendations, ICAO might have been in a position to redress a certain number of erroneous courses, when the symptoms were still controllable.

It is not, however, as if the Air Transport Committee had not done its work : emphasising certain facts, establishing working groups, underlining certain trends, assessing perspectives and seeking definitions (when confronted with the unexpected growth of charter services), essentially, though, producing statistics and drawing the Council's attention to various relevant factors.

The Member States did not seriously come to grasp with the realities of the problems of air transport until the latter had reached a critical stage.

In the seventies, the Council reflected on the procedures by which governments could influence the fare-fixing machinery and appointed a "panel of experts for the establishment of international fares and rates". (Resolution A 21-26). The panel conducted surveys of international fares and rates and regional differences, studied tariff enforcement and other practical aspects of the pricing problems facing the air transport industry [37].

The Organisation, following those and other studies, produced a "standard bilateral tariff clause" [38], which did not entirely achieve its purpose of harmonisation.

Not until 1977 did the *first Air Transport Conference* [39] generally review the problems facing the air transport industry. Working groups were set up and remained active for several years. A second (1980) and a third (1985) special Air Transport Conference were held with the same objectives of bringing about concrete, if only partial, solutions.

*Conclusion :* The role of ICAO in the economy of international air transport has been considerably less effective than in technical matters. The difference is inherent in the legal set-up and linked to the political intricacies of the regulatory system.

On the other hand, ICAO has dealt continuously with the far from negligible economic aspects of air transport operations, such as airport and navigational charges, telecommunications, airport facilities and so on.

CHAPTER 2

## IATA

Although the role played by IATA in the regulation of international air transport has been a controversial one in the last few years, we should attempt to view it with the serenity, if not the cynicism of the historian. Moreover, in changing times, there is no telling in advance what the role of an institution like IATA will be in the future, although it appears to be a fair guess that such a role will inevitably be different from what it was in the past. IATA itself has changed to an extent that makes its description difficult.

Anyway, "sub specie historiae", there is no question that IATA, following the guidelines of the governments, has rendered considerable service to international civil aviation [40].

## 1. Objectives of IATA

The International Air Transport Association was founded in Havana, in April 1945.

Its "aims and objects" are :

"1) to promote safe, regular and economical air transport for the benefit of the peoples of the world, to foster air commerce, and to study the problems connected therewith;

2) to provide means for collaboration among the air transport enterprises engaged directly or indirectly in international air transport service;

3) to cooperate with the International Civil Aviation Organization and other international organizations." (Article III, Articles of Association).

## 2. Membership

The composition of IATA confirms its implied relationship with ICAO : active membership is reserved for air transport enterprises which operate international scheduled services "under the flag of a State eligible to membership in the International Civil Aviation Organisation as provided for in Chicago in 1944". (Article IV (2), Articles of Association).

*Note :* The Chicago Convention and the subsequent international agreements have clearly linked together governments and airlines represented in both ICAO and IATA. Understandably, in a number of cases, including commercial and tariff issues, airlines were considered to be better equipped than governments to make judgments and seek cooperative solutions.

Whereas some forty airlines were members in the beginning, the membership reached 151 on January 1, 1987.

## 3. Head Office

The Head Office is maintained "in the city in which the headquarters of the International Civil Aviation Organization is located" (Article II, Articles of Association), which is Montreal.

IATA has a second establishment in Geneva.

## 4. Legal Statute

IATA is a private law cooperative association with Canadian status. The Royal approval of a specific law instituting IATA was granted in December 1945.

## 5. Changes in structure and membership

Originally, only scheduled airlines (international as active members and domestic as associate members) were elegible.

Charter carriers were later made legally eligible, but did not take advantage of this possibility.

Important structural changes resulted in the separation of tariff coordination activities and corporative activities.

*Note :* The current text of the bylaws results from an amendment of September 16, 1986 to the Articles of Incorporation and the Rules and Regulations including the Provisions for the Conduct of IATA Traffic Conferences (16th edition, May 1986).

## 6. General Meetings, Standing Committees, Director General

a) *General Meetings*

"The ultimate authority of the Association is vested in the General Meeting, composed of representatives of the active Members of the Association". (Article VII (1), Articles of Incorporation).

A majority of the active Members constitute a quorum. Each active Member has a vote.

b) *Executive Committee, Standing Committees*

The Executive Committee is elected by the General Meeting. It carries out the executive functions of the Association. (Article VII (2), Articles of Incorporation).

Other standing committees are :

— the Legal Committee; (status revised in 1988);
— the Traffic Committee;
— the Technical Committee;
— the Financial Committee.

Other (advisory) groups include those dealing with so-called "aeropolitical" matters, medical, facilities, security, charges, public relations and other matters of interest to the industry.

c) The *Director General* runs the Secretariat and implements the general policies.

## 7. Traffic Conferences

The Traffic Conferences, probably the most original creation of IATA, grew to be increasingly important and autonomous with the years.

They concern themselves with all international air traffic matters involving passengers, cargo and mail, particularly the following :

1) Analysis of operating costs;
2) Fares, rates and charges for passengers and cargo;
3) Schedules;
4) Approval of Agencies and their administration.

Seen from outside the organisation, the main task of the Traffic Conferences is obviously the discussion and conclusion of tariff agreements.

Each Traffic Conference corresponds to a particular geographical area.

Joint meetings are held "for the purpose of determining fares, artes and related matters between points within one Traffic Conference area, and points within one or more other Traffic Conference areas". (Article VI, 1, Provisions for the Regulation and Conduct of the IATA Traffic Conferences).

Traffic Conferences take their decisions independently, within the scope of their competence.

## 8. Clearing House

The Clearing House is a small and efficient unit that permits quick financial settlement of accounts among airlines. Some airlines which are not members of IATA are allowed to participate in the Clearing House system.

## 9. Activities of IATA

*The activities of IATA must be viewed against the background of the overall public law system.*

Its tariff coordinating functions in particular are related to intergovernmental arrangements and relevant domestic laws.

### a) *Tariff coordination*

IATA only deals with one of the three main regulatory factors of international air transport : tariffs. Market access and capacity remain within the jurisdiction of governments.

Tariff Conferences are responsible for the *coordination* of fares and rates. The word "coordination" is a modernism used to avoid the earlier connotation of conspiracy and to reflect more accurately the present activity of the Conferences.

The legal foundation for the meetings is the provision of the bilateral agreements under which governments agree, with some variations, to their designated parties discussing and agreeing on fares and rates, thereby establishing common points for submission to their respective governments. The governments are supposed to grant the relevant exemptions from national anti-trust laws, whenever required.

Not all bilaterals require a multilateral coordination of tariffs in IATA.

But the usual condition is that account should be taken of tariffs applied on the routes concerned or sections of those routes by other air carriers. A basic requirement has therefore been, in effect, that *airlines attempt to establish, by consensus, similar tariffs on similar routes.*

A number of technicalities complicate this attempt at coordination. The rules for *air fares* (passengers), for instance, differ from the rules for *cargo rates*. Not only *levels*, but also *conditions* have to be specified. The rules governing the relationship between airlines and *sales agents* also have to be defined, again differentiating passengers and cargo agents.

Moreover, besides tariffs, dealt with by Traffic Conferences, the committees and working groups of IATA had to deal with various related problems, such as the development of conditions of carriage, remittance of incomes in certain countries, market integrity, cross-border sales, etc.

The *Traffic Conferences Resolutions* constitute the body of IATA laws. They are enforceable. A *Breaches Commission*, for airlines, and *Arbitration Boards*, for agents, were set up to act with full jurisdiction on tariff violations.

A *Compliance Director*, reporting to the General Director, was in charge of the investigation and the prosecution of offences. (The Breaches Commission and the Compliance Department have now been dissolved). The task has proved to be overwhelmingly difficult. The disappearance of the compliance activities of IATA, once so intensive, reflects not only the changing environment of the industry, but also the incapacity of the industry itself to abide by its own rules and to prevent price-cutting.

It must be borne in mind that, if ever a cartel existed, it did not work. Competition not only existed, but became uncontrollable. To their own dismay, airlines committed and encouraged innumerable tariff malpractices in the market-place. They undermined their own profitability, bitterly complaining about competitors whom they themselves persistently emulated.

In the early eighties, when the situation appeared all but hopeless, IATA attempted to change its approach.

The compliance activities were replaced by regional programmes of voluntary restraint.

The "yield improvement programmes", "market clean-up boards" and other equivalent bodies set up locally were often delegated authority by civil aviation administrations.

Once government bodies were involved, the nature of the exercice changed somewhat.

The observance of approved tariffs sometimes became a condition to obtain operating permits. Alternatively, national laws made any tariff violation of that nature a criminal offence entailing penal sanctions. (The compatibility of such legislation (in France) with the provisions of the EEC Treaty has been challenged and the European Court of Justice ruled on the issue in its so-called « Nouvelles Frontières" decision of 30 April 1986). Vis-à-vis national law, the legality of self-imposed discipline, preventing downward flexibility in pricing, has been denied by an administrative court's decision in Australia. (We refer to these developments later in this book, notably in Parts V and VI).

For all practical purposes, IATA has lost its grip on compliance. And the days of self-discipline, if there ever were any, are counted. The mechanism of ratemaking itself has changed radically. Members of IATA may choose not to participate in Traffic Conferences; those who have decided to participate are never obliged to do so. Traffic Conferences are more in the nature of an exchange of information and views, resulting at best in a juxtaposition of bilateral agreements. The unilateral filing of innovative fares by any Member is authorised after closure of the Conference, and the tariff in question may be made part of the "multilateral" agreement ...

Under current conditions, IATA has become, in a sense, "a Spanish inn", which travellers are still happy to find in the countryside, but which will not provide them with much more than comfortable housing. There can be no doubt, however, that, in the past, the ratemaking machinery of IATA did serve its purpose.

It will probably continue to serve some purpose in the future, depending on the policies which different countries and parts of the world will decide to follow in matters related to the multilateral coordination of air fares.

b) *General cooperative activities*

IATA acts as a laboratory and a link with governmental organisations on matters of general interest to civil aviation.

It also acts as a professional organisation for the protection of the interests of its members. To these belong safety, security and airport facilities, to name only a few .IATA monitors closely the security conditions prevailing in airport and classifies them according to their efficiency in anti-terrorism prevention; its suggestions in this field are being listened to by national authorities and followed up by the powerful International Federation of Airlines Pilots, the IFALPA. Simplification of airport formalities is constantly advocated by airlines' representatives through IATA.

Unquestionably, the predominant achievement of IATA is the inter-lining system, the full benefit of which could not have been achieved without multilateral coordination of tariffs.

## 10. Conclusion

It is interesting to ponder on the motives international airlines may have had to cooperate, in particular in tariff matters, through IATA. It would be simplistic to regard it as a cartel. The situation of interna-tional airlines is unique in more than one respect. The mere necessity of a global outlook and worldwide interdependence implies that regular meetings cannot realistically be avoided among members of this commu-nity. Nowhere is the trend towards internationalism so genuinely spon-taneous and, if one may say so, pragmatic.

Right from the start, the airlines found they had a practical interest in fighting national protectionism. The first Director General of IATA, Sir William Hildred, once declared : "Any organization dealing with transport and communications must fight national pride, national cupi-dity, national prejudice and national selfishness" [41].

And, to quote Le Goff : "The activities of IATA are placed under the sign of clear and simple internationalism in worldwide air trans-port" [42].

There was no question at the outset but that airlines would seek internationalisation of air transport. More often than not, governments followed policies inspired by their national carriers, who then turned virtuously to their colleagues with the claim that they were acting accor-ding to the "will of the prince". (One could elaborate endlessly on the relations between governments and "their" airlines, and we will refer to the subject at times.)

On the other hand, an unfortunate characteristic of our time is the increasing involvement of politics in the economic life. This phenomenon has also marked international air transport. Whereas ICAO could not entirely avoid politics, IATA may have appeared as a haven, a fraternity devoted to business.

In addition to possible idealistic motivations and the nice sensation of belonging to the inner circle of the influential, the benefit of IATA for the major airlines lay in the fact that they could establish for themselves the *norms of competition* in tariff-related fields and that they were able to do this for a number of years. The ability to plan services under relatively stable conditions, at least as regards prices, is a condition for the large investments required in the airline business — a permanent underlying consideration. In this context, IATA was viewed as an instrument of *competitive stability*.

In fact, the airlines relied on their governments for traffic rights and capacity, and on IATA for tariffs : in essence, they were seeking stability.

That the motivation for cooperation included a mixture of idealism and cynicism is not surprising : managers were, after all, required to make airlines profitable. Governments bore their share of duplicity : they expected IATA to play its role and also carefully measured the degree of economic independence left to the airlines, which the long arm of the law could reach at any chosen moment. One example of this, relating to IATA, is the possibility of withdrawing immunity from national anti-trust laws as granted to the Traffic Conferences — a possibility, as we will see, which was put to use. Moreover, the outcome of the Traffic Conferences (the tariff agreements) has been increasingly subject to government reservations and reviews. The times when governments rubber-stamped IATA agreements have long gone.

Recent developments as well as past experience suggest that IATA might be difficult to replace, but also that its role may change on the international scene. The number of airlines seeking membership has increased worldwide; an easy guess is that small and third world airlines will gain unfluence in and through IATA and the last word has not been said on this subject.

# CHAPTER 3

## REGIONAL ORGANISATIONS

"All agree that an effective form of world organization for air purposes is necessary. This does not exclude regional organizations having a primary interest in the problems of their particular areas". (Adolph Berle, Chairman of the Chicago Conference, 1944).

Article 55 of the Convention reflected the concern to grant regional organisations their role : ICAO never underestimated the need for coordination at regional level, but undertook to control the effort. The ICAO Secretariat made it a policy to assist regional intergovernmental bodies, officially recognising that the problems peculiar to a region can be adequately handled by government agencies of the countries directly involved.

These bodies evolved independently from ICAO. The trend towards regionalism in air policies has increased the political importance of some of these organisations which are potentially capable of playing an even greater role.

*Airline associations* were also set up regionally and, separately from IATA, acquired influence with inter-governmental agencies. *Airports* established regional concerns as well. In some cases, agencies were created to deal with *air navigation problems*.

We shall consider the major inter-governmental agencies as follows :

— the European Civil Aviation Conference (ECAC);
— the African Civil Aviation Commission (AFCAC);
— the Arab Civil Aviation Council (ACAC);
— the Latin American Civil Aviation Commission (LACAC).

We shall then briefly review other relevant organisations, in particular, airline and airport associations.

## A. — REGIONAL INTERGOVERNMENTAL ORGANISATIONS

## 1. ECAC

### a) *History*

This organisation was created by the Council of Europe, in 1954, following a recommendation of its Assembly [43]. The Council of Europe was founded in 1949 by ten States, and later expanded to eighteen States. ECAC is currently composed of twenty-two States [43].

The original purpose assigned to the Conference convened by ICAO, as conceived by the Council, had been, interestingly, to consider the possibility of establishing an association of airlines to operate air services between Member States more efficiently through close cooperation.

The Conference met in Strasbourg, with seventeen countries taking part, and decided to establish a permanent organisation which would continue the work of the Conference : review developments of intra-European air transport in order to promote coordination better utilisation and orderly development of such air transport, and consider any special problems in this field [44].

The first session of the new organisation, ECAC, was held in Strasbourg between November 29 and December 16, 1955.

ECAC is presently a very active organisation.

### b) *Relationship with ICAO*

Although an entirely separate agency, ECAC works closely with ICAO and benefits from its support both financially and administratively. (Partial financial support and Secretariat).

### c) *Nature*

ECAC is consultative in nature. It formulates recommendations concerning common policies or practices which States should incorporate in their regulations. Subject to approval by Member States, ECAC is a common negotiating body which may finalise agreements with third countries or implement resolutions involving such countries or other organisations.

### d) *Constitution*

The Organisation of "ECAC" is established through its Constitution and Rules of Procedure" [45].

The Constitution provides for a triannial Plenary Conference at which officers and Committee Chairmen are elected, programmes and budgets for the subsequent three-year period are approved, and recommendations, resolutions or other conclusions are adopted [46]. In those years when no Plenary Conference is scheduled, intermediate sessions are held. These sessions may adopt recommendations, regulations and other conclusions, and approve the work of the Conference established by the Triennal Session [47].

"If it appears necesary or urgent to convene a Special Intermediate Session the President shall do so" [48].

The delegates to ECAC are members of the civil aviation administrations of Member States.

The bodies are :

a) the Plenary Conference (in triennal or intermediate sessions);
b) the meetings of Directors General of Civil Aviation;
c) the Coordinating Committee;
d) the Standing Committees.

These bodies are assisted by the Secretary of the Conference.

The four standing committees are :

— the Economic Committee for Scheduled Transportation;
— the Economic Committee for Non-Scheduled Transportation;
— the Technical Committee;
— the Facilities Committee [49].

The decisions of the Conference and of the Standing Committees are taken by a majority of the votes cast by the States represented.

e) *Objects*

"The objects of the European Civil Aviation Conference ... shall be to :

a) review generally the development of European air transport in order to promote the co-ordination, the better utilization and the orderly development of such air transport.

b) consider any special problem that may arise in this field." (Art. 1, 1 of the Constitution).

*Remark*

It has been rightly observed that "during the past few years ECAC seems to have concentrated its efforts more on the political attitude of Western Europe towards third countries than on co-operation and harmonisation of air traffic within Europe" (Diederiks-Verschoor) [50].

However, since 1983, ECAC has been active and influential in the area of regulatory reforms of intra-European air services, perhaps under pressure of political events in the EEC.

ECAC must, indeed, take into account the "importance and interest of the subject to a large number of Member States and to other European organizations". (Art. 1, 2 of the Constitution).

The specificities of air transport in Europe create difficulties in several areas, which ECAC has continuously explored [51].

f) *Activities*

A. ECAC has managed to coordinate policies of Member States in a number of technical and operational matters.

It monitors the evolution of scheduled and non-scheduled services to and from and within Europe. Areas such as intra-European air services, tariffs, interchange of aircraft, and many others were covered by *recommendations*.

B. In some instances, ECAC even succeeded in drawing up *multilateral agreements* among its Member States. We shall summarise two of these :

1) *The Multilateral Agreement on Commercial Rights of Non-Scheduled Air Services in Europe, Paris, 30 April 1956.*

As expressed in the Preamble, the Policy of Member States is the following : "Aircraft engaged in non-scheduled commercial flights within Europe which do not harm their scheduled services may be freely admitted to their territories for the purpose of taking on or discharging traffic".

Despite this amplification of the liberal principle or Article 5 of the Chicago Convention, the Agreement has been qualified as "relatively insignificant" [52]. Indeed, it did not effectively measure up to the expectations it had raised.

It constituted some interesting progress towards harmonisation of policies and had some liberalising effects. If one views the charter policy of European States between themselves globally, it has been reasonably liberal. Whether this was due to the Multilateral Agreement or not remains uncertain. The compatibility of this Agreement with sometimes cumbersome rules may also be somewhat puzzling. The text of the Agreement has been protectively construed. The automatic approval of flights, which represents an abandonnent of sovereignty, was already limited in the text and was further limited in its interpretation.

The Agreement specified that the "regulations, conditions or limitations" provided for in the second paragraph of Article 5 of the Chicago Convention would not be imposed on aircraft engaged in :

a) flights for the purpose of meeting humanitarian or emergency needs;

b) taxi-class passengers : flights of occasional character, offering a seating capacity of more than six passengers, no part of that capacity being re-sold to the public;

c) flights on which the entire space is hired by a single person; ("own-use charter");

d) single flights, no operator or group of operators being entitled to more than one flight per month between the same two traffic centers. (Article 2, 1).

2) *The International Agreement on the procedure for the establishment of tarifs for scheduled air services, Paris, 10 July 1969.*

The ECAC Member States decided to unify, through this multilateral agreement which was open to accession by all UN Member States, the principles and procedures for establishing tariffs for scheduled air services.

In the Preambule, it is specified that "wherever possible use should be made of the procedures of the International Air Transport Association".

None of the principles of the Agreement is basically different from the classical tariff clauses evolved from the Bermuda model but the Agreement suppressed the variations which had developed in numerous bilaterals, especially with respect to procedures, and instituted a system which would apply in the absence of bilaterals.

The effects of the Agreement are described in Article 1, as follows :

"The present Agreement :

a) shall establish the tariff provisions applicable to scheduled international air services between two States, parties to the present Agreement;

i) when such States have no bilateral agreement between them to cover such services,

ii) when such a bilateral agreement exists but contains no tariff clause;

b) shall replace to the tariff clauses in any bilateral agreement already concluded between two States, parties to the present Agreement for so long as the latter remains in force between the two States".

C. ECAC succeeded on several occasions in coordinating the positions of its Members vis-à-vis third countries. We should note one such agreement, concluded recently, for its significance and side-effects :

*The Memorandum of Understanding* (on air fares for scheduled services over the North Atlantic) *between ECAC States and the United States, Washington, 2 May 1982*[53] *.

ECAC organised the negotiation; twelve of its Members originally signed the Memorandum.

This arrangement was concluded after a long period in which no IATA agreement had been possible on the North Atlantic because of the policy of the United States. It made it possible, at least for a time, to re-immunise IATA tariff coordination activities from US anti-trust laws. It also contributed to a certain stabilisation of tariffs over the North-Atlantic; at the very least, the authorities and airlines concerned were able to talk to each other and move towards a certain order of things in the pricing area. This order was even innovative : the Memorandum introduced a new concept in the pricing philosophy of European States — the concept of *zones of flexibility*.

A *zone* is defined by upper and lower limits established by a percentage of a reference fare. Within those limits, the government authorities automatically approve (or refrain from disapproving) any fare launched by an airline, irrespective of the terms of the bilateral agreement in force between the countries concerned.

Above or below the zone limits, the provisions of the bilateral remain applicable.

This mechanism is described as follows in the Memorandum of Understanding :

"In applying the provisions of the relevant bilateral air services agreements or arrangements, the Parties shall, during the period this Under-

---

* Renewed for limited periods, not yet permanent.

standing is in force, approve or, as the case may be, refrain from notifying dissatisfaction with, specified fares filed by the carrier of another Party in accordance with Article 2.3) within specified pricing zones constructed as set out in Annex II". (Art. 3, 1).

Moreover, it is important to note, as reflecting a principle of US legal philosophy, that participation in multilateral tariff coordination can never be made a condition of approval of any fare. (Art. 2, 1).

*Note :* ECAC later examined the conditions for an adaptation of the concept of zones to the intra-European context, which originated new EEC proposals in the pricing field and led to the acceptance, by a majority of ECAC Director Generals, in December 1986, of a draft Multilateral Agreement on Tariffs and Capacity (cf. p. 111 and following).

## 2. AFCAC

### a) *History*

The AFCAC has been a specialised agency of the Organisation for African Unity (OAU) since 1978 [54].

It was based upon a Conference held in Addis Abeba, in January 1964, and founded in 1969.

The constitutional convention became effective on June 11, 1972 upon the adhesion of twenty States. Thirty-nine States are currently members of AFCAC [55].

An interesting development is the establishment by AFCAC, in 1980, of the basis of the African Air Tariff Conference (to be formally set up by a Treaty).

### b) *Nature*

AFCAC is a consultative body and its conclusions and recommendations are subject to acceptance by each of the governments. (Constitution, Art. 2).

### c) *Objectives*

a) To provide the civil aviation authorities with a framework within which to discuss and plan all the required measures for coordination of and cooperation between all their civil aviation authorities;

b) To promote coordination, better utilisation and orderly development of African air transport systems.

(Constitution, Art. 3).

AFCAC is particulary requested to establish plans for air services within and outside Africa, to study possible standardisation of equipment and integration of the policies of governments regarding commercial aspects of air transport. (Constitution, Art. 4. 1).

d) *Cooperation*

AFCAC works in close cooperation with OUA, ECA, ICAO. (Constitution, Art. 4, 2).

e) *Organisation*

Ordinary plenary sessions are convened once every two years. Extraordinary sessions may be convened by the Bureau and *must* be convened upon the request of two-thirds of the Members.

f) *Activities*

All activities are geared to the solution of problems specific to African air transport.

1) *Air services network*

AFCAC has worked out a plan for the *optimal development* of air services in Africa. The plan includes an improved structure of intra-African networks and flight frequencies, as well as the right for all African operators to use fifth freedom rights on intra-African sectors.

It was adopted at political levels.

2) *Integration of African airlines*

A series of objectives were assigned to AFCAC : the creation of multinational African airlines was part of this plan [56].

Short and long term objectives included :

— optimal utilisation of technical and training facilities;
— reduction of operating costs; improvement of return on investments, in general;
— creation of jobs requiring a high degree of technical proficiency.

The strengthening of relations between African States was a political aim and, ultimately, the creation of new multinational airlines in Africa was to help achieve that aim, as well as accomplish all the other objectives. To date, however, AFCAC has not brought about the required consensus in concrete terms.

But cooperation has been improved in some of the above-mentioned areas.

### 3) *Personnel training and exchanges*

The policy of AFCAC includes *training* of aviation personnel "in all disciplines affecting aeronautical activity" : pilot training centres were, for instance, established.

The standardisation of training methods is aimed at harmonising the procedures for the *issuance of personnel licences* and at *promoting a programme of personnel exchanges*, as part of the cooperation between African States in this particularly important field. In the same context, AFCAC seeks to harmonise procedures for the issuance of *airworthiness certificates*.

### 4) *Tariff matters*

AFCAC was instrumental in establishing the convention which gave birth to the African Air Tariff Conference.

The decision in this matter was political. (Resolution CM/Res. 739 on Civil Aviation in Africa of the 33rd ordinary session, OAU Council of Ministers, July 1979).

### g) *African Air Tariff Conference*

The Conference is composed of airlines registered within OAU Member States (or eligible for registration), with States (OUA, ACAC) being observers and individually committed to certain obligations within the Convention which established the Conference [57].

Its aim is to act *"upon all tariff matters relating to scheduled services of concern to its members"*, as well as to *"study, advise and coordinate"* *tariff matters relating to non-scheduled services "of concern to its members"*. Finally, it should act as negotiating machinery.

The Convention will come into force after the deposit of the 25th instrument of ratification or approval.

It was signed on 12 December 1982, but the ratification process has been extremely slow.

Nevertheless, it is an interesting development in the changing world of civil aviation. It implies the *political view that worldwide tariff coordination no longer responds adequately to the specific needs of air transport in Africa, not because multilateral coordination is the wrong solution, but because it should be carried out differently* [58].

On the other hand, for the African States, bilateralism would damage the interests of the region.

The establishment of fares through bilateral negotiations is "not likely" to permit "the optimum development of air transport in Africa".

It should also be noted here that the "African Airlines Association" is requested under the Convention "to implement the establishment of the said Conference and to organize and coordinate its activities in accordance with the provisions of the Convention". The airlines are thereby placed in charge of the implementation of any programme developed along the lines defined by the governments.

## 3. ACAC

### a) *Constitution*

The *League of Arab States* took the initiative of establishing the Arab Civil Aviation Council in 1965 : the Agreement to that effect came into force in October 1967 [59].

Arab countries not members of the League can be admitted to ACAC on the decision of two-thirds of the Members of this organisation.

### b) *Objectives*

Its objectives are :

a) the achievement and maintenance of harmony between the scheduled and non-scheduled services;

b) the regulation of capacity;

c) good coordination on tariff matters, taking into account the views of countries with airlines that are not members of IATA; and the creation of a common policy on enforcement of approved tariffs;

d) technical and economic cooperation in the Arab world, including joint planning of route networks and establishment of cooperative and training centres;

e) the promotion of cooperation in matters related to air transport facilities and air security.

### c) *Activities*

### 1) *Traffic rights*

ACAC was instrumental in the establishment of the Arabic Services

Transit Agreement. An Arabic Air Transport Agreement is in preparation.

The concern about Arabic air space has been constant : recommandations have been issued to exchange extensive traffic rights and to prohibit the exploitation of such rights, or the combination of services, between Arabic countries by third country airlines.

2) *Multinational airline*

ACAC was also instrumental in working out an agreement to set up a Pan-Arab Airline.

To date, one airline (an all-cargo carrier) has been created jointly by two Arab countries and exercices combined traffic rights, owned by Iraq and Jordan. But joint training of airline personnel and standardisation of equipment through the Arab Airlines Association have been pushed to a degree which permits interchange of aircraft and some integration at a later stage.

3) *Routes and airports*

ACAC achieved results in the coordination of route and airport facilities, as well as in the field of technical and training cooperation between the civil aviation authorities of Member States.

4) *Rules of the Air; Air Law in general*

ACAC has codified national regulations in the form of a "Uniform advanced Aviation Law", which was adopted by Member States.

# 4. LACAC

a) *Constitution*

The *"Comissión Latino-Americana de Aviación Civil"* was established by a Treaty signed in Mexico on 14 December 1973, which entered into force on 12 October 1975, upon ratification by 12 out of 27 Latin-American countries.

Twenty countries have currently ratified, or adhered to the treaty [60].

The nature of LACAC is consultative.

b) *Objective*

Much like other regional organisations, LACAC aims to promote orderly development and better utilisation of air transport within the region.

The Latin-American region is defined by the Treaty as including South America, Central America (Panama and Mexico), and the States of the Caribbean.

### c) *Activities*

*The work programme* of LACAC consists essentially of the same range of activities carried out by ICAO, but on a regional basis. The organisation works towards the application of ICAO norms and regional plans for air navigation facilities. It has supplemented ICAO traffic statistics and other relevant data by monitoring air traffic to and from Latin-American countries, as its policy is largely to restore the balance of production in favour of Latin-American carriers.

The problem appears to be that, in the past, third country airlines operated the majority of flights to and from the region and used fifth freedom rights within the region, i.e. between LACAC countries. In the seventies, it was found from LACAC statistics that "seventy percent of all airlines which use the Latin-American air transport system do not belong to the region" [61].

The policy adopted in principle by Latin-American countries has been geared to the restriction of intra-Latino-American traffic rights to airlines registered in one of the subscribing countries.

The actual success of these policy recommendations depended on the extent to which Member States were able to introduce appropriate clauses in their bilateral agreements with third countries.

The protection of regional and neighbouring traffic dates back to the policy recommended in 1959 by the first Regional Conference of Civil Aviation (Art. 7, Rio de Janeiro), and in 1960 by the second Conference (Art. 7, Montevideo); it was initially adopted by countries like Argentina, which later developed their own policy that was nevertheles no less protectionist in tendency. But the overall policy, embracing a number of different problems, was defined in numerous meeting of the *Confederación Inter-americana de Transporte Aéreo* (CITA). When LACAC took over, it developed recommendations and positions or common attitudes in a number of areas, in particular tariff issues and deregulation.

Several attempts have been made to unify Latin-American air law through a "Código Aeronáutico Americano".

## 5. Conclusion

For several reasons, regional organisations have not, so far, made a significant impact. They suffer from internal lack of coherence and their nature is consultative. However, in the landscape of world aviation, they exist as possible places from which new concepts may emerge. They are well positioned to foster the development of regional policies. This evolution should be monitored very carefully in the future.

B. — REGIONAL PROFESSIONAL ASSOCIATIONS

*Regional airline associations* worth mentioning are :

in Europe :

AEA : (Association of European Airlines), formerly EARB (European Air Research Bureau), (1973), an influencial organisation representing the major scheduled airlines from EEC and non-EEC Western European countries, plus JAT (Jugoslavian Airlines) and Malev.

The AEA has intelligently contributed to the definition of a new European policy, although part of its membership has remained understandably conservative.

ACE : (Association des Compagnies Aériennes de la CEE), the active representative of independent carriers from the EEC countries, (1980) has pushed, persistently towards a free market.

ACCA : (Air Charter Carriers Association) (1971).

ERA : (European Regional Airlines Association), an active group, which picks up momentum from the political trend towards more regional services in Europe. Its list of members (March 1986) includes :

18 regional airlines and other aircraft operators;

17 manufacturers of aeronautical material;

12 airports;

 6 others.

in the United States :

ATA : (Air Transport Association), (1936), the well-established and influential group of scheduled US carriers;

NACA : (North American Carriers Association) (1962) was particulary influential at the time of the "supplemental" carriers;

in Africa :

AFRAA : (African Airlines Association) (1979), the active association of carriers from AFCAC countries;

in the Middle-East :

AACO (Arab Air Carriers Organisation) (1965) (1968 : re-organisation), effective in carrying out cooperative tasks;

in Asia :

OAA : (Orient Airlines Association) (1966).

in Latin America :

AALA : (Asociación Andina de Líneas Aéreas) carriers from Chile, Bolivia, Peru, Equador, Venezuela, Columbia;

AITAL : (Asociacion Internacional de Transportadores de América Latina) (1980) (South America and Mexico).

## C. — OTHER REGIONAL ORGANISATIONS

Other relevant organisations include regional groups of *airports*, for example : the WEEA (Western European Airports Association) (1950, Brussels).

*EUROCONTROL* deserves analysis in another context. It is an exemplary adventure in sophistication, weakened by politics. Created in 1960, by Belgium, the FRG, France, Luxembourg, The Netherlands and the UK, the "European Organisation for the Safety of Air Navigation" was supposed, according to the Convention, to "strengthen their cooperation in matters of air navigation and in particular to provide for the common organisation of the air traffic services in the upper air space". In fact, its effective task shifted from partial autonomous organisation of the air space to a (well-equipped) joint agency, mainly engaged in collecting navigation fees.

# CHAPTER 4

## NATIONAL INSTITUTIONS

The primacy of international over domestic law is altogether certain and total, which does not imply, however, that all texts adopted by ICAO are *"per se"* applicable in national laws and internal regulations. Moreover, numerous matters are subject to the exercise of national sovereignty. So are all matters related to the organisation of air transport, technically and operationally, the creation and maintenance of infrastructure and facilities, as well as the wide area of administrative jurisdiction and the implementation of government policies regulating air services, within the limits set by international law.

National policies necessarily influence, to various degrees, the evolution of public international law.

The matter being complex, civil aviation experts often have a say, if not a final word in those developments. It is, therefore, appropriate to regard them as part of the international organisation, as the same people appear to play a part on the wide international scene, the regional scene, and at the national level.

Civil aviation authorities are, in general, organised as follows :

1) *Centralised administrations*

In several countries, the original set-up was unified in all matters relating to aviation and was the responsibility of the Minister of Defence. This structure has almost entirely disappeared. But, in some cases, an administrative body remains which is entrusted with all regulatory tasks under the Minister responsible for civil aviation.

2) *Double-branched administrations*

A number of governments have separated the *technical* functions (in-flight and ground security, qualification of crews, airworthiness of aircraft, airports, navigation aids) from the *economic* and *administrative* or *policy*-making functions.

### 3) *More complex systems*

Whether or not the executive agencies report to the same Cabinet Minister, the international implications require delicate coordination. A *consultative* body is sometimes formed to provide this coordination and/or give advice on politically sensitive issues, including bilateral negotiations. Such an Advisory Council exists, for instance, in Brasil ("Cernai").

A clear distribution of complex functions can be seen in the United States : the *Civil Aeronautics Board* exercised a certain jurisdiction, alongside the *Federal Aviation Administration*, the *Department of State*, the *Department of Transport* and the *White House*.

The CAB was an independent agency, reporting to Congress. The Federal Aviation Act of 1958 (Section 102) adapted a concept already to be found in the 1938 Civil Aeronautics Act : a Board would be appointed to promote "adequate, economical and efficient services" by air carriers "at reasonable prices, without unjust discrimination". The CAB reviewed carriers' applications, delivered "certificates of public convenience and necessity", allocated air routes, regulated air fares, and generally exercised regulatory authority over domestic air services, from the administrative and economic point of view. Its powers over international air services, including foreign carriers, were somewhat more restricted. They were, nevertheless, substantial.

The CAB was dissolved in the process of deregulation, and the remaining domestic functions were transferred to the Department of Transport.

The FAA is another agency involved in the regulation of air transport which survived deregulation. It is a separate agency within the DOT, whose Administrator is directly responsible to the Secretary of Transportation. Section 601 of the Federal Aviation Act provides that safety of flight of civil aircraft shall be promoted through "minimum standards governing the design, materials, workmanship, construction and performance of aircraft, aircraft engines, propellers and appliances". In addition, the FAA is to establish reasonable rules and regulations and minimum standards governing inspection, servicing and overhaul of aircraft etc., maximum hours or periods of service of airmen, and all other «practices, methods and procedures necesary for safety and national security". It issues certificates to carriers, personnel, airport operators and certifies aircraft. The FAA shares safety responsibility with the National Transportation Board (NTSB).

Essentially, FAA has authority over safety and assignment of navigational space — although the line is sometimes blurred between that power and that of the state and local authorities to control noise, condemn property adjacent to airports, and enter into local leasing agreements.

The control of air safety is unaffected by deregulation.

The *State Department* is naturally involved in the international aspects of air politics and diplomacy, and the *President of the United States* has the final word on US policy decisions in international aviation matters.

# PART III

# The acquisition of commercial rights

# CHAPTER 1

## METHODS OF ACQUISITION

Traffic rights are, in a sense, *the commercial stock of airlines*. The latter have to rely on traffic rights, not only for the planning of their operations and sales, but for the day-to-day performance of their services. Yet traffic rights, essential as they may be to airlines, do not "belong" to them : they *"belong" primarily to States*.

Governments are generally the *granters* and the *holders* of traffic rights, with variations according to the forms their concessions may take and according to national laws and regulations. The holder of the authority to operate a charter flight will be the operating carrier — somehow at the same level as the holder of an operating permit for scheduled flights. But, in the final analysis, States deal with each other and settle their accounts between themselves.

It is somewhat paradoxical that this asset of the airlines, comparable in importance to their fleets, largely escapes their control. That this primary right, the national licence to operate, remains under the control of the government is only natural under the Chicago-regulated system. But the acquisition of international rights is more debatable. They are never acquired or maintained by airlines alone, and they are frequently withdrawn for reasons unknown to them. They are the ultimate sign of sovereignty and the core of bilateralism.

Admittedly, in practice, the efforts of the airlines to obtain the landing rights they seek often play a decisive role in their acquisition. The airlines' own behaviour sometimes accounts for the loss of these rights (and not infrequently for their development through interline cooperation). Formally, the methods of acquisition of commercial rights (leaving aside the rather different technical liberties), were the following :

a) *administrative decisions :* the basic process of *licencing* is in principle valid for all types of air operations, based on the principle of sovereignty and the requirement of permission to fly set forth in the Chicago Convention. The level of *full traffic rights* is reached for domestic or cabotage flights. Unilateral rights can be granted by administrative decisions relating to international non-scheduled or even scheduled services.

b) *bilateral air transport agreements :* such agreements are the normal pattern for the exchange of rights for international scheduled flights; they also occasionally serve to exchange non-scheduled rights.

c) *multilateral agreements :* e.g. the 1956 Agreement on non-scheduled flights in Europe.

With respect to these general schemes, we should note the following :

1) In many, but not in all countries commercial air transport is subject to a licencing system.

The licence may relate to flight-operational and therefore purely technical aspects : in this form, the system is general. But a licence may also be issued in relation to the economic and transport-political aspects of air transport.

The distinction rests upon the legal difference between *traffic rights* and *operating rights*, in that the latter implement the former : their formal source may be different; their autorities distinct; and their conditions of another nature.

2) In principle, and in most cases, *non-scheduled flights* are submitted for unilateral approval of the countries concerned; *scheduled flights* are subject to bilateral exchanges of rights.

3) *Civil aviation authorities* intervene at all stages of all those processes; however, bilateral air transport agreements provide for rights of recourse through consultation or arbitration.

# CHAPTER 2

## UNILATERAL GRANTING OF TRAFFIC RIGHTS

### 1. Scheduled flights

In principle, scheduled flights are the object of *bilateral agreements*.

However, in certain circumstances, airlines apply directly to the civil aviation authorities of a foreign State. They may wish to operate in the territory, or overfly the territory of such a State. Overflying permission may be granted without a bilateral pre-requisite. Scheduled flights may be unilateraly authorised, in accordance with Article 6 of the Chicago Convention.

Prior to the conclusion of a bilateral agreement, a temporary authorisation may be granted *in advance* of an exchange of traffic rights between the countries concerned. Authority will also be granted in expectation of, or in response to, the granting of reciprocal rights. Situations can exist, as is the case between several European States, under which civil aviation authorities approve the schedules of each other's carriers, in the absence of any treaty or agreement between their countries.

As a point of law, it is our opinion that no difference exists, as far as the involvement of States is concerned, between a situation in which the bilateral agreement has been *formalised* and one in which it has not, insofar as it can be established that States *are* exchanging rights in favour of their mutually recognised undertakings. In other words, *a consensus between States, even a tacit one, underlies the mutual granting of traffic rights*, and a certain role is played by international practice in the matter.

This confirms the more general opinion that *scheduled* rights are normally *exchanged* between governments.

### 2. Non-scheduled flights

In keeping with the diverging philosophies of Articles 5 and 6 of the Chicago Convention, the situation is reversed in the case of non-scheduled flights.

Here *the rule is unilateralism.*

True, a landing permit is *not* legally required under the terms of Article 5, provided its conditions are met. Moreover, States should not prescribe the route to be followed except, as provided in Article 5 (1), over regions which are inaccessible or deprived of adequate air navigation facilities. States should not prescribe the airports to be used for non-scheduled flights except, again as provided for under the Convention, in the case that operators may be required upon entering or leaving the country to land at and depart from specified customs airports.

Relevant provisions of the Convention are Articles 10, 68 (applicable only to scheduled international air services) and 96.

Nevertheless, operating permits are frequently required, a practice already in use in the early fifties.

The main characteristic of the regulatory regime of prior permissions is its complexity, a result of the variety of national legislations with respect to landing rights and charterworthiness rules.

Bilateral agreements dealing with non-scheduled services are rare and mostly ineffective.

A significant exception is the *Multilateral Paris Agreement of April 30, 1956* [62]. The Council of Europe, at the level of the Committee of Ministers, decided on the principle, and the European States through ECAC (the European Civil Aviation Commission) confirmed the consensus in 1954 : "non-scheduled commercial air services could be allowed freedom of operation within Europe without prior permission from governments *if such services did not compete with established scheduled services".*

The initial Conference which established the ECAC indeed set itself the objective of greater freedom for intra-European air transport which does not encroach upon scheduled international air services.

This broad principle gave birth to the Paris Multilateral Agreement, of which the scope and conditions could be interpreted restrictively. In fact, the States involved were quick to recover a great deal of the powers they had formally relinquished through the Paris Agreement of 1956, all but forgotten today.

This is but one more example of the departure from the freedom granted in theory to non-scheduled services by Article 5 of the Chicago Convention. In practice, States have been given the possibility of subjecting this freedom to certain restrictions and they have made good use of it [63].

## 3. Bilateral air transport agreements

Bilateral air transport (or air services) agreements constitute by far the most important source of law with respect to all conditions for the exchange of traffic rights and the operation of services between countries. Their number is not known with precision : several thousands have been concluded; they are frequently re-negotiated.

With very few exceptions, they deal with scheduled air services.

### a) *Status*

Air transport agreements are treaties in the terms of the national constitutional law of most countries.

There are significant exceptions. United States domestic law distinguished between treaties and international agreements other than treaties. Under the Constitution, the President has the power to conclude treaties, provided two-thirds of the Senators present agree. (Article 2, section 2) But the President of the United States may also use his own authority as Chief Executive and sign other international agreements, which are called "executive agreements". The fact that the President could dispense with the approval of Congress has some consequences for the status of the agreement as part of the domestic law of the country.

Executive agreements do not supersede domestic law, such as the anti-trust Act. This situation was to create an international legal conflict in the famous "Laker case", in 1984-85. According to non-US lawyers, the distinction between treaties and executive agreements is purely domestic and "in no way affects the character, and still less the legal validity, of such agreements as international treaties, by whatever name called" [64].

Although in the instance just referred to, the United Kingdom questioned the legal foundation of a particular theory of exclusion, UK legislation itself precludes the direct application of rights derived from air transport bilateral agreements. By virtue of the Air Navigation Order of 1950 (Article 80), a foreign airline is required to hold a *permit* granted by the Secretary of State before it can make use of traffic rights.

In other words, traffic rights granted under international law need to be translated into domestic law. The Secretary of State may deny an application for a permit from a foreign airline entitled to operate a route under a bilateral agreement. The UK government would, in that case, be in breach of its obligations under international law "but not under domestic law, and the designated airline would have no remedy in the courts of the United Kingdom" [65].

It is held, nevertheless, that it is possible for British courts to exercise a measure of judicial review over the decisions of the Secretary of State.

### b) *Negotiation and conclusion of bilateral agreements*

National delegations generally consist of representatives of civil aviation authorities, the Ministry of Foreign Affairs and air carriers who, in several instances, are only members of the delegation in an advisory capacity. Delegations usually conclude "ad referendum". The provisional entry into force may be stipulated, as from the signature by governments. Clauses frequently submit that definitive entry into force of the agreement depends upon notification of the fulfilment of constitutional requirements.

Constitutional *ratification* practices differ, and may occasionally delay the implementation of the agreement.

However, as a rule, the flexibility built into the system of bilateral agreements is such that although formalities can be used as delaying tactics, the beginning of operations seldom falls behind schedule for merely legal reasons. The agreements include safeguard provisions in that respect.

### c) *Contents of bilateral agreements*

Bilateral air transport agreements consist of the text of the agreement, its annexes and any other document specified as part of the agreement and treated as such.

Not all of these documents are public. Registration with ICAO is mandatory for all countries which adhere to the Chicago Convention. However, only the texts of the agreements are usually registered, with their annexes, excluding confidential memoranda.

The difference between the agreement itself and its annexes is important as far as flexibility is concerned : routes may require frequent changes, for instance. These are modified by consensus of the aeronautical authorities, whereas the agreement itself can only be amended by the Contracting Parties themselves. The involvement of governments implies a political decision, an exchange of notes, and the process of ratification were required.

Let us review the main points :

1) The *Agreement* includes, essentially :

a) *definitions of the terms* used in the text, in particular, the freedom of the air, as exchanged;

b) a clause on *designation of the carriers;*

c) a clause on *capacity;*

d) a clause on *tariffs*;

e) clauses relating to *operations :* these clauses are kept to a minimum among countries which are members of ICAO; nowadays, however, airport *facilities* are dealt with together with operational provisions;

f) operational and financial provisions relating to *immigration, customs, tax exemptions, office establishment;* nowadays, an important item of reference is the *remittance of transferable revenues;*

g) a clause concerning periodical *consultations* between aeronautical authorities in order to review from time to time the application of the agreement and a clause providing a procedure to *amend or modify* the text of the agreement;

h) clauses of a legal nature spelling out the rules of *arbitration, termination, entry into force* and *registration* (with ICAO, for ICAO Member States) of the Agreement.

2) The *Annexes* include :

a) the *route schedule*, describing for each Contracting Party the itineraries on which the agreed services may be operated between their respective territories;

b) sometimes (frequently, nowadays) the indication of the authorised *frequency* of services.

3) *Additional documents* may include exchange of *confidential letters* or stipulations of *agreed minutes.*

d) *Bilateral agreements as a public law regime*

"Being treaties, within the meaning of international law, they constitute the formal expression of government's tutorship, as far as domestic law is concerned" [66]. This observation by Folliot reflects the differences that may exist between countries, as far as control of the State over airlines is concerned, hence the extent to which States effectively rule the regulatory system based on bilateral agreements.

The degree of control over some or all regulatory factors varies considerably according to specific domestic law governing the airlines, and their respective legal status. However, the agreement constitutes a treaty, and differences in airlines' national status will not affect it, not the rights and obligations derived from it. Worldwide, bilaterals form the framework of the operation of air services and the expression of the will of governments to retain jurisdiction : whether and to what extent they effectively exercise this jurisdiction is another matter [67].

In any case, a significant role is left for the airlines to play and governments never would or could occupy the entire scene. It is part of the public law system that the implementation of bilateral agreements through the operation of agreed services is in the hands of the *"designated airlines"* (once, not insignificantly, called "instruments").

The *agreements among airlines* therefore complement official bilaterals and often become inseparable from them. This set of private law agreements should be considered as part of the overall regulatory system established by the set of public law air transport agreements.

This is not to underestimate the role of governments. They bear exclusive responsibility for the policy principles of the agreement, the conditions of access to the market, the allocation of routes and the distribution of capacity. Indeed, among the three major regulatory indicators, only tariffs are chiefly in the hands of the airlines. Historically, it does not make too much sense to point to IATA as having generated the restrictions on competition which were imposed on the airlines through IATA, under the terms of bilateral agreements. Governments approve air fares and take responsibility in that field as well.

At the same time, the airlines are seldom absent from the policy-making stage and their advice is listened to by States of which they are the flag carriers. In fact, the system could only work through a continuous interaction of public and private acts and initiatives, a unique blend characteristic of air transport.

The rejection of a laissez-faire competition system in favour of more predeterminist policies has been a clear example of the influence of airlines in the field of capacity. Traffic restrictions were imposed quite logically, given the system, by the party whose airline carried an insufficient share of the traffic (less than forty percent, according to Wheatcroft, for a country operating under a Bermuda type agreement). The division of economic benefits between airlines, decided by governments under a Bermuda type agreement, is necessarily inspired, directly or indirectly, by the airlines themselves.

An analysis of other components of the bilateral exchanges will further substantiate this view.

e) *Market access*

The key to the main door of the air transport market is held firmly in the hands of the governments.

They can adopt the policy of their choice as to the *designation* of the carriers which will exercise national rights. That policy will depend on the specific situations in which governments find themselves : some will require particular routes to be operated by one carrier, but will designate two or more on some other routes : multidesignation does not necessarily correspond to a desire to relax control or increase competition.

In that sense, the emphasis placed on multidesignation as a sign of market deregulation is ill-founded. The issue is whether the absolute right of governments in this field will remain unchallenged, or whether *some degree* of *automatic access* is conceivable. A Directive of the EEC creates a limited automatic access of this kind.

The *substantial national ownership* clause (already part of the Transit and Transport Agreements of 1944) was rendered bilateral by the Bermuda Agreement : in line with the relevant clause, each Party can exercise some control on the criteria applied by the other. The rationale of the clause is to prevent a situation in which a carrier, deprived of legitimate ties to a State or nationals of a State would still benefit from the rights obtained by this State : the assumed or fictitious "nationality" of the carrier *would divert the consensus* reached between the Contracting States. The Chairman of the UK delegation at Chicago, Lord Swinton, explained :

"Everyone shall know with whom they are dealing, and if an airline is registered in a particular country, it is a national airline and *not something quite different, masquerading under an assumed nationality*" [68].

One problem related to the issue, which was not envisaged in Chicago nor in Bermuda, is the situation in which a designated airline *leases* equipment and crews from another airline registered in a third country. It has been contended, for policy purposes, that a systematic use of a lease contract to operate agreed services may circumvent the will of the Parties as to the traffic rights exchanged. Unless it is reflected in a multilateral treaty, preceding the relevant bilateral air transport agreement, such a policy would have no legal foundation. The conditions of designation laid down in bilateral agreements are *strictly* applicable : any unilateral addition to those conditions would contravene the agreement, legal comity and security. Every Contracting State has the guarantee that it may verify the application of the relevant criterion set forth in the clause of designation of the bilateral agreement.

There is a broader aspect to this problem of nationality. A protectionist construction would hamper the possibilities of operation of some developing countries, and contravene the principle of equal opportunities.

Moreover, the cooperation between airlines to set up international operating instruments, irrespective of the nationality of aircraft, should be encouraged in the interests of all concerned. The problem of barring flags of convenience from international air transport could only be solved by a sweeping liberalisation of the conditions of market access. In the present situation, it does not serve the interests of the weakest countries, nor of the public at large to add to the restrictive conditions already prevailing.

Bilaterals also contain provisions relating to *national laws and regulations*. One formulation, usual in early post-Chicago agreements, is the following :

"The aeronautical authorities of one contracting party may require an airline designated by the other contracting party to satisfy them that it is qualified to fulfill the conditions prescribed under the laws and regulations which they normally apply in conformity with the provisions of the (Chicago) Convention to the operations of international commercial air services" [69].

Besides, the designated airlines have to comply with *local laws*. It is customary in bilateral agreements to require aircraft of the designated airlines to be operated in compliance with the laws and regulations of the grantor State for entry into or departure from its territory, or for operation and navigation within its territory; local laws and regulations must apply regarding the movements of passengers, crew and cargo carried on board such aircraft.

In general, the dual right of governments to grant operating permits and to designate carriers has been maintained as an untouched privilege of sovereignty in civil aviation matters.

Following the distinction made above, licences can be merely operational or transport-political. Operating licences are understandably the responsibility of governments. The aeronautical authorities have to control the airworthiness of aircraft, the qualification of the crew, the insurance coverage of carriers and verify the conditions of fitness they have imposed on applicants. States merely exercise their duties and fulfill their obligations under the Chicago Convention and ICAO regulations when they proceed with such controls and take responsibility for their findings.

The logic of economic licensing and designation is more debatable from the international standpoint.

There is more than mere national interest to take into account, and the decision, whether or not to grant a licence, should certainly be based on more than the criterion of fitness : in most cases, the question boils down to maintaining the principle of reciprocity in bilateral exchanges. But more can be at stake : licencing can support a different kind of international policy. A licencing policy may, for instance, be used to work out a deregulation.

The bilateral aspect of *licensing* is *designation*. The main factors behind the designation to fly routes under a bilateral agreement are the fitness of the operator (a matter investigated at the stage of the licence), commercial criteria in relation to public interest considerations, such as the network to be built, (also a determining factor of a licencing policy), and international considerations of different kinds. While those factors are primarily national (in normal circumstances), the international context may change. The choice between national undertakings may become more difficult, even legally speaking, where pluridesignation becomes the rule; even more so, where automatic approval of foreign designated carriers has been agreed among certain countries. (As in the European Community, in matters concerning inter-regional air services). States are essentially committed to facilitate international air services and develop international civil aviation.

All these specific characteristics of market access policies bear on the question of how national national airlines need to be. There are incongruities attached to the cult of sovereignty; at a certain point, what Aurelio Peccei called the real interests which this cult serves and its long-term costs are lost sight of.

f) *Capacity sharing*

I. *Discussion of the formula*

Another area where the responsibilities and activities of governments and airlines are closely interrelated, and sometimes confusingly overlap, is the area of capacity.

As indicated earlier, the States establish the principles which govern the capacity to be served by their designated "instruments", and determine the sharing formula in broad terms. However, it would be both difficult and ineffectual for the air carriers involved to implement those rules without talking to each other. Capacity sharing agreements are frequently concluded between designated carriers on a route simply to sort out the problem effectively. Whether such agreements are entered into separately, concurrently with commercial agreements, or made part of the latter is immaterial. Another question is whether the conclusion of such arrangements is *imposed* by the governments, a condition deemed unacceptable by the EEC Commission in its proposal for a common European air transport policy. (Memorandum nr. 2, see infra 111). But the Commission recognises, in its proposal, that a *non-compulsory* capacity-sharing agreement should be exempted from the prohibition laid down by the Treaty of Rome. (Article 85, 1).

The *arithmetics* of capacity are left to the airlines. Such is the logic of the system. The governments make the policy, which the airlines implement. At governmental level, "air transportation should not be approached in an arithmetical spirit but whith wide open eyes for the needs of the air carriers *and* those of the travelling public". Van der Tuuk Adriani continued : "That the authors of the original Bermuda principles limited themselves to broad lines and refrained from going into too precise details is an act of wisdom that cannot be overestimated" [70].

Nevertheless, some figures make guidelines for governments who, more often than not, retain a *50/50 entitlement*. This construction of the fair and equal opportunity clause and of the national primary capacity criterion rests on the concept that traffic generated by a State somehow "*belongs*" to that State. Commentators from developing countries (and others) will find this "an equitable and practical solution for the apportioning of capacity" [71].

Yet the "fifty-fifty" division *is not an established principle of international law*, and remains controversial.

## II. *Discussion of the "sixth freedom" question*

As an issue related to the "primary capacity criterion", the so-called "*sixth freedom*" issue has also been controversial among governments.

The reason may be the lack of a legally recognised definition of sixth freedom traffic. Even though the proportion to be observed between *primary* and *secondary* traffic was loosely defined, at least the relevant traffic was identifiable. But the rule left no room for a certain reality : traffic with third countries is not necessarily confined to recognised fifth freedom traffic — i.e. traffic carried between countries B and C, named in the bilateral air transport agreement between countries A and B. *Sixth freedom traffic is "traffic between two foreign countries via the country of the airline carrying that traffic"* [72].

It is not the recognised right to use, *but the actual use* of the geographical possibility to carry traffic between two countries other than the one of which the aircraft has the nationality, through the territory of the latter. At an airport located as an intermediate stop, the operator connects two services which he is entitled to operate at this airport *by virtue of two different traffic authorisations.*

It is therefore inaccurate to allege an illegal fifth freedom, where two legitimate traffic rights are merely combined. It has been contended, however, that the combination itself constitutes an abuse of the rights which have been conceded separately : none of the conceding third countries had envisaged the throughflight possibilities, which amount to a *new* commercial right.

The physical capability of combining third and fourth freedom traffic not only corresponds to a genuine natural resource without contravening any international rule, but it in fact implements an obligation to promote international air transportation by providing the best service ("in specie", offering a wider choice of options to the public). The founding fathers of Chicago and Bermuda certainly never envisaged policy decisions which in effect would diminish or suppress freedom of choice between existing services. Passengers would be penalised by not being alble to use an available commodity that might best suit their needs.

One fails to see which public interest concept would be hurt in such a case [73]. Furthermore, a carrier would have no valid reason to refuse access to its flights.

III. *"National traffic" as a basis for capacity entitlement*

The sociological aspects of international air transport make it unduly archaic to construe the old Bermuda rules *as nationalistic by nature.* The businessman nowadays travels to one or another city on a continent almost indifferently, according to his business schedule, and may well depart from the continent at another airport than his airport of arrival.

He does not care about legal restrictions, built on Bermuda rules which he may never have heard of in the first place.

Basically, this situation highlights the intellectual flaw inherent in the underlying nationalistic philosophy behind many of the political attitudes in matters of capacity. Never has "primary" traffic, in the sense of Bermuda, been meant to refer to "national" (why not "ethnic"?) markets. It would be practically impossible to identify such "national" traffic, let alone monitor it, and the only criteria retained in the definition of commercial freedoms are related to the place *where the traffic embarks or disembarks.*

Some States tend to appropriate air traffic as a national resource. Professor Wassenbergh has rightly fought this concept on many occasions, as the cornerstone of bilateralism and of increasing protectionism in international civil aviation. He has conclusively demonstrated that the principle of appropriation is contrary to the Bermuda concepts and may not be held as a principle of international air law [74]. This line of reasoning leads us of course, into questioning the wisdom of apportioning capacity among a number of countries involved in bilateral relations.

A limited number of bilateral "liberal" air transport agreements have departed from the general line of Bermuda and post-Bermuda capacity clauses and related policies. The European Community also endeavours to reduce the requirements of States in capacity matters and relax their control.

However, it is useful to recall that, following an examination of capacity clauses in use, a Special Air Transport Conference of ICAO has given status to bilateral provisions providing for predetermination of capacity.

In this difficult and sensitive area of capacity, more than in other fields, schools of thought are clearly in conflict, as national interests dominate.

g) *Fare fixing*

1. *Classical clauses : "double approval" system*

As long as the Bermuda tariff clause determined the standard agreements, with some minor variations, the bilaterals worked together consistently to produce a *worldwide integrated tariff system.* IATA was instrumental in providing the forum, the rules, the outcome and even the policing of such a system.

The provisions for government approval of fares, detailed as they might be and though at variance with each other, seldom materially affected the entry into force of agreed fares; for a long time, none of these clauses provided for unilateral filing of fares by an airline. All, of course, retained the possibility that tariffs could be refused or that approval of them could be withdrawn at the request of civil aviation authorities. The respective roles of public authorities and air carriers were therefore relatively well defined.

In Europe, the 1967 International Agreement on the Procedure for the Establishment of Tariffs for Scheduled Air Services replaced and unified the tariff clauses of existing bilaterals [75].

Within the general concept which we referred to earlier, *airlines are under an obligation to consult with each other*, preferably within IATA or directly through the carriers designated to operate on the same route, in order to arrive at common tariff proposals. Airlines then have to *submit* the *agreed fares for approval* to their respective aeronautical authorities.

If agreement on such proposals cannot be achieved at airline level, public authorities themselves will have to negotiate and set the tariffs. No tariff can come into force unless it has been duly approved by the aeronautical authorities *of both States concerned*. The system is therefore called : a "double approval system". The approved tariffs are *enforced* by the authorities.

2. *Liberalising clauses : "country of origin" and "double disapproval" systems*

The progressive liberalisation of air transport in some countries has given rise to different concepts.

These concepts have been formulated in a number of modern bilateral agreements and memoranda.

The relevant clauses depart from the double approval regime without conceptually reaching the extreme logic of economic liberalism which leaves the setting of prices to market forces : governments wish to retain a right of control on a certain degree of price fixing, at least in the territories under their control. As a result, the double trend has been to remove the obligation for the airlines to coordinate tariffs and to restrict the right of disapproval to the pricing of traffic originating in the territory of the disapproving country.

The modalities are the following :

a) The *rule of the country of origin*, derived from the practice of charter price approval, consists of the automatic recognition of the tariffs set by any airline for trafic originating in another country : the right to approve fares remains formally organised, but is *restricted to outbound traffic.*

Each Contracting State relinquishes its right to disapprove fares and rates approved by the other.

b) The *double disapproval* system is at the other extreme of the spectrum from the double approval regime. Under this provision, the proposed tariff is deemed to be approved *unless both aeronautical authorities disapprove it* within a fixed period. This system is favoured by the United States.

The difference between the two systems is in fact very slight : directional fares cannot long resist the competitive forces in the marketplace.

The United Kingdom has, since 1984, successfully negotiated bilateral arrangements that include provisions of either one or the other kind, while allowing certain nuances and escape clauses. While in the 1984 UK-Netherlands arrangement an Amsterdam-London tariff could not be disapproved by the UK authorities, but still required approval by the Netherlands, provision was made for consultations if either of the authorities considered a proposed tariff to be "predatory" [75]. With Belgium, Luxembourg and again the Netherlands (1985), the double disapproval regime includes a provision to the effect that "if one authority considers a tariff filed by an airline of the *other* country to be predatory, there would be consultations but the tariff would still come into effect unless, following such consultations, both authorities disallow it" [76].

h) *Disputes and arbitration*

The settlement of disputes has always been a difficult feature of air transport agreements.

The arbitration clauses derived from the Bermuda model never proved very effective in the volatile field of air transport : following unsuccessful consultations between the States involved, the Council of ICAO would hear the parties and present a non-binding report, by way of an arbitration award. This procedure is very cumbersome and non-conclusive. The material jurisdiction of the Council extends, however, beyond the interpretation or application of the agreement to tariff issues and conflicts related to the route schedules contained in an Annex to the agreement.

Other formulae hardly proved more effective. Arbitration awards were rendered in a route case in 1963, and, in the same year, in a matter of interpretation of the agreement. In 1984, a capacity dispute was resolved by arbitration, under a simplified procedure involving a single arbitrator [77].

The reason for this general abstention must be found in the nature of the bilateral regime, which leaves no place for a superior organisation, or does so only in appearance.

Among procedures provided for in arbitration clauses, a classical international arbitration formula is often proposed, with alternative recourse to the Council of ICAO; a frequent modern clause spells out the designation modalities of a college of arbitrators : each Contracting State designates a member, and the two, in turn, together elect a third member.

Finally, the parties sometimes decide to rely on "customary rules of law".

We should note that the *periodical consultations* clause has proved to be more effective, in preventing conflicts than the arbitration clause in settling them.

## 4. Conclusion

It would be ill-advised to draw conclusions at this stage on this essential subject. But we may perhaps already pinpoint a few findings.

The methods of acquisition of commercial rights are different : they are mostly unilateral in the case of non-scheduled services, bilateral in the case of scheduled ones, but they all reflect the fact that "civil aviation has become a part of the "face" of the State" [78].

A bilateral confrontation may be resolved by an exchange of unilateral concessions. The liberalism of Article 5 of the Chicago Convention is adulterated by state practice. There are good and bad reasons why no country has been found willing to abandon regulatory intervention in capacity allocation and airline pricing across the board for any length of time. The truth of the matter is that there is little difference in the nature of bilateral powerplay.

Even legally speaking, it makes little or no difference whether or not a bilateral arrangement receives the dignity of a formulated treaty.

To a certain extent, the pattern of bilateral agreements has a soothing effect on antagonistic interests, if only because a treaty implies a certain degree of stability, and emphasises the integration of aviation interests in overall international relations. Most of them are concluded for an indefinite period, to be denounced at twelve months notice. In fact, the weapon of denunciation, being political, is used only after due consideration, and the prospect of an abrupt cessation of air services between the two countries is dissuasive. It happens that situations where the twelve months notice is running are deliberately used to pressure the partner into a more amenable attitude, without anyone believing in the final rupture. In other words, the formalities of bilaterals serve as brakes on the infernal machines of latent and rampant conflicts in air relations. Moreover, many of the provisions of bilateral air transport agreements clarify the rights and obligations of the parties concerning specific aspects of air service operations. Finally, the content of these agreements is flexible : their terms can sometimes accommodate different interpretations; the routes are modifiable without too much formality; additional instruments — even minutes of meetings — may, for a time, amend or interpret in effect some of their major provisions. It is already obvious at this point in our analysis that the evolution of ideas can bring about radical changes in regulatory concepts which, nevertheless, fit the bilateral air transport agreements like gloves.

But for all their advantages on practical grounds, bilateral air transport agreements do little more than illustrate and crystallise a straight confrontation of national powers.

The system contains the possibility of progress, but experience has demonstrated that it could equally well regress.

Instead of this two-sided nationalism, consideration should be given once more to multilateral exchanges of traffic rights, along with some de-politisation and de-nationalisation of the treatment of the airline industry.

Clearly, such a concept could not depart, any more than bilateralism does, from the philosophy of international air transport as a service to the international community.

# PART IV

# The evolution of the regulatory system

# CHAPTER 1

## GENERAL REMARKS ON THE EVOLUTION

*The regulatory system of international air transport was not absolutely rigid* in the minds of its founding fathers : it had a certain degree of built-in flexibility which permitted it to accommodate economic and technical developments. They felt that on the one hand, all nations of the world ought to be able to participate in such developments; on the other hand, some common principles should guide the States in their endeavours to regulate this activity.

*In order to achieve legal certainty, political attitudes should be co-ordinated.* It was not envisaged that political attitudes would disrupt the system and lead to legal uncertainty.

Yet, certain signs of weakness existed at the outset.

a) *The Chicago system was conceived as essentially international, but did not produce the adequate legal instrument*

Failure to reach agreement on an instrument to exchange rights multilaterally condemned the whole system to rest on the narrow and fragile basis of unilateral abandonment of sovereignty. This fact has been recognised [79].

But it was hoped that international law would continue to progress, as nations would increasingly realise that their common interest lay in a coherent set of rules governing a general exchange of rights to fly across borders. The Bermuda plan fed this illusion, together with the efforts of ICAO, which continued for a number of years to establish a multilateral framework for such a sweeping exchange.

Bilateral agreements would contribute and impose their individual significance. "The time has passed", Bin Cheng wrote after Bermuda, "when these treaties could be regarded as merely *ad hoc* and temporary arrangements between individual States without any general significance. Like the man-made canyons of Manhattan, these agreements are no longer isolated skyscrapers but form a new skyscape in international law. A well-delineated law of international air transport has emerged ..." [80].

Other internationalists, like Le Goff, expected that air law would in future be shaped less by national legislations than « thanks to the initiatives of free international groups and to the action of international governmental organizations »[81].

This great hope, based on nothing but the acute knowledge of the missing link between the theory of law and the practice of politics, has not, so far, materialised.

b) *A regulatory system based on the assumption of voluntary abandonment of prerogatives by sovereign States has a built-in weakness. It may permit the development of the activity in favourable circumstances, but it is bound to degenerate when diverging interests prevail.*

As soon as the regulatory system designed to develop the international legal order was subjected to tensions, it was predictable that national interests would easily overcome any consensus that might exist. Bilateralism is based on a mutual interest to compromise and is exposed to the resurgence of particularism, despite the formal standardisation of the agreements.

Internationally recognised norms serve to accommodate national interests, to a certain extent and under a certain set of circumstances. The Bermuda regulatory principes are admittedly flexible. Given the tribulations of the world economy *and* of the regulatory norms, it is, after all, a noteworthy achievement and quite surprising that the system itself was not more deeply shaken. Not only did bilateral agreements differ more and more *on substantive issues*, they all drifted furhter and further away from the original Bermuda model — without necessarily renouncing the Bermuda forms.

Tariff agreements in IATA gave all the appearance of a multilateral process giving equal rights of participation to all airlines. They were settled according to regulations. Yet increasingly restrictive conditions were imposed, and governments increased their reservations to the tariffs submitted to them by participating airlines. On the other hand, the observance of the approved tariffs often became nominal.

c) *The system left open the regulation of non-scheduled services*

The founding fathers had some excuse for not considering charter flights to be a significant sector of air transport and therefore worth definition : in 1944, they could only think of air taxis, rescue and other emergency flights, some own-use cargo charters, none of which seemed to warrant a particular regulatory regime. Freedom in principle entailed little risk of damaging competition. (Had they realised the potential importance of non-scheduled flights, they might well have reconsidered the implications of Article 5 and written it differently!)

As a consequence, however, "a growing gap was created between the legal structures and the actual functioning of international air transport" (Michel H. FOLLIOT) [82].

CHAPTER 2

## THE GOLDEN AGE (1946-1962)

a) *General circumstances*

Between 1946 and 1962, the average annual growth rate of air traffic in the world was approximately 20 %, reflecting the growth of the gross national product in western countries and the volume of global world exchanges.

The monetary system remained relatively stable; the inflation rate did not exceed two or three per cent worldwide.

The continuous technological progess in aeronautics allowed for a regular increase in the capacity provided on the market and for the improved comfort and rapidity of aircraft, while flight safety received particular attention, both in the air and on the ground. These changes occured gradually; none of them upset the terms of the deals in which States exchanged traffic rights or airlines negotiated their tariffs and their programmes. During the whole period, for instance, fifth freedom rights remained important for the profitability of the international routes.

When operating at cruising speed, the Chicago-Bermuda regulatory system performed as efficiently as probably any system would have done, given its quasi-ideal circumstances.

The regulatory institutions adapted themselves painlessly to the developing aviation world. States organised their administrations to handle civil aviation separately from military aviation. ICAO developed international rules and conventions. IATA worked out Traffic Conferences agreements.

b) *IATA*

The fifties were years of rapid development for most airlines, including the European airlines.

Networks operated in fifth freedom stimulated air traffic between several regions, and the airlines became interested in a tariff structure covering the interconnection between their respective networks, for the sake of common growth and facility.

Interline sales benefitted the carriers and the travelling or shipping public equally. Such sales largely depended on a common tariff structure.

IATA member airlines negotiated the levels and conditions of tariffs in Traffic Conferences, sometimes aggressively, but generally successfully. If a Conference (an interregional set of routes) remained "open", failing to achieve a consensus, such failure was felt to be inadmissible and remedies were consistently sought.

The unanimity rule offered sufficient protection for the minority at a time when the total membership did not exceed sixty companies. It was implicitly admitted that the eight or ten senior members had a special voice, but this voice was subdued, as was suitable in a well-to-do club. For IATA was a club, more than a cartel in the strict meaning of the word. Conditions of membership were restrictive, fees were high, positions honourable. Members were supposed to abide by the rules as gentlemen.

It might happen, however, that members would be found to be in breach of Traffic Conference Resolutions. On such occasions, they were tried by a tribunal of honour, called the "Breaches Commission". Soon, a body had to be set up for investigation and prosecution (the "Enforcement Office", later the "Compliance Office") which reported to the Director General. The Office acted on its own initiative or on complaints by other members. In an arbitrary capacity, the Breaches Commission has created an abundant jurisprudence in interpretation of Traffic Conferences Resolutions. The precedents and the "Informal interpretations" provided on occasion by the DG formed a body of genuine IATA law of its own. In the first years, tariff violations were rare and often unintentional. The Commissioner would explain the point at issue, dismiss the complaint, issue a reprimand or impose a fine. Such fines, in the end, especially when cumulative, could reach huge amounts in US dollars.

The fashionable appearance of the process did not imply any naïveté. From its first decisions, the Breaches Commission imposed a rule of objective responsibility, called the "any device" principle : any device by which a discount had been granted to the public on a fare or rate agreed by IATA automatically involved the airline on which the carriage had taken place, irrespective of the intermediary who had actually transacted the business. In principle, the member airline was held liable for the actions of its agents. But travel agents, acting in their own capacity under the terms of the IATA approval conditions, could also be tried before an Enforcement branch of the Compliance Office. Another set of rules was established for that purpose. This whole situation shows that, for all the credit granted to its honourable members, IATA entertained no illusions about the practives in the market-place; it also shows that, to a certain extent, competition never died under the system, whether fair or unfair.

To clarify how the system worked, *minimum* levels of fares and rates and conditions applying to them were imposed under Conference agreements. Sales *above* those levels, or performed with more rigid conditions, were not prohibited; but sales *under* those levels, or on looser conditions, were necessarily illicit, regardless of the processes used to attain the result.

It is generally considered that the Breaches Commission fulfilled its task quite adequately during the period under review.

From experience, the author would not make the same comment about later developments, when the compliance system could no longer cope with the extent of the malpractices in the industry.

IATA often maintained a low profile, but generally speaking its activity developed harmoniously. To take but one example, the IATA Legal Committee took quite a few initiatives and worked together with the ICAO Legal Committee towards developing international conventions in matters ranging from carriers' liabilities to the prevention of illicit seizure of aircraft.

In all fields of airline activity and air transport related matters, such as security, facilitation of formalities at airports, navigation aids, carriage of dangerous goods, etc., the cooperation between IATA and ICAO was examplary.

IATA's great contribution to the internationalisation of air transport, in the most practical sense of the terms, is in the field of *standardisation of airline documents*, of procedures for the exchange of tickets, and quick settlement of interline accounts. That a passenger can move around the world on one ticket and change airlines according to his needs *without additional charges or bureaucracy* is obviously a crucial achievement. In a period of rapid traffic growth and on extended networks, it was especially important that airlines cooperated introducing a full interlining capability within their operational system.

This implied that the *conditions of carriage* be uniform — another achievement in itself — and that a *reference currency unit* be conventionally recognised. The integrated interlining system based on multilaterally agreed fares levels and conditions in turn fostered the development of the airlines' route networks.

The global result has been widely recognised as a success of the air transport system founded on cooperation.

To take the words of Ross Stainton, then Chairman of British Airways, at a Convention in New York in 1979 :

"By the 1960's the scheduled airlines had constructed by far the most comprehensive transport system the world had ever seen. Never before could so many journeys be so conveniently and quickly arranged and made over such distances, between so many cities across so many frontiers, by so many routes, with so lavish a choice of departure times. Just as intended in 1944, this huge integrated interlinked system made and makes a powerful contribution to peace and prosperity" [83].

c) *The classical age of Bermudianism in bilateral air transport agreements*

It is needless to stress that the first post-war period was favourable to the conclusion of agreements tainted with sweeping liberalism, but carefully written to meet individual aspirations.

The moral undertaking to standardise the conditions of exchanges was also omnipresent.

Therefore, with the few exceptions of a number of "pre-determinist" agreements (South Africa was one such country adamantly opposed to the Bermudian philosophy of capacity), and taking into account the particular situation of East European countries, not yet members of ICAO, numerous bilateral air transport agreements were concluded along the model of Bermuda 1. They tended to ressemble each other, as far as the structure and the text of the agreements were concerned.

One of the clauses that underwent substantive changes was the tariff clause, which was eventually simplified and clarified — but nevertheless, at a certain point, deserved standardisation in Europe, because bilaterals began to be at serious variance with each other.

The description of the routes, in the Annex to the agreements, evolved from a sweeping enumeration of regions and countries (the United States favoured "around the world" route descriptions), to the precise identification of all points allowed to be served on the specified itineraries.

The United States had valid reasons to prefer a broad description of the routes; in Bermuda it had to bargain every precise point obtained with the United Kingdom. While such a vast potential market, supported by an extensive network, did not call for the granting of „beyond rights" to other countries, the development of US airlines required the possibility of freely combining stops in foreign countries.

From this point of view, the geopolitical situation during the first post-war decade suited the interests of the United States, who could well afford to negotiate traffic rights with "Empires" or vast zones of influence, conglomerates of States and possibly communities like the emerging European Community.

Similarily, "the US considered the five freedoms critical because of their great impact on improving the economic status of US airlines by permitting greater flight freedom thoughout the world and allowing US planes to carry more foreign passengers" [84].

The conception which the United States had of the description of routes and traffic rights influenced the terms of bilateral arrangements in this respect to a considerable extent in the fifties. We have already quoted Albert Stoffel, who explained the process thus :

"In most cases the foreign country concerned went along with our desires largely because they were too involved with straightening out their economies at home and did not have the equipement, manpower, and other resources necessary to fly the routes which they obtained from us. It became a standard practice, for example, for the United States to describe its own routes as being from the United States, as a whole, to specified points in the foreign country and similarly the foreign routes were described as from that country, as a whole, to specified points in the United States ... Later, however, as aircraft operating ranges were extended and trans-Atlantic hops could be made non-stop from several points in the United States, the value of the descriptions of the routes granted to the United States became evident" [85].

Certainly, in the course of the period under review, a number of new factors awakened awareness of the far-reaching implications of Bermuda-type agreements. Newly independent nations entered into such agreements, knowing little at first of their own possibilities for using reciprocal rights. Onroute rights for major or established carriers, operated in fifth freedom, were to become valuable third and fourth freedom rights for emerging national carriers of the countries concerned. Those developments resulted in more States entering into Bermudian agreements, rather than the modification of such agreements. The competition gradually increased, while its terms remained superficially unchanged. The introduction of jetliners, by the end of the period, not only made it more difficult to achieve a balance of interests regarding capacity and marketing advantages, it also decreased the value of some fifth freedom rights and increased the value of point-to-point routes. Politically, the dismantling of imperial or Colonial/post-Colonial powers reduced the value of routes obtained, in particular by the United States.

Perhaps the economic criteria of the value of routes should have been reviewed from time to time, on the occasions of periodical consultations between aeronautical authorities or of fully fledged bilateral negotiations.

The United States might have set the example and helped to establish standards, instead of remaining exceedingly cautious in all these matters. In fairness, however, we should note that the U.S. did not press other nations to re-negotiate each time its own routes lost value or ceased to be pertinent.

Generally, the steady development of international air traffic on scheduled services and the prevailing stable market conditions helped the governments and the airline industry to cope with political and technological developments, while remaining effortlessly within the regulatory system established in Chicago in 1944.

The fact, however, that tariff discussions eventually showed a tendency to harden and that bilateral negotiations and agreements became more precise and to the point as they proliferated, reflects an increased awareness of the value of the terms of the exchanges in a competitive environment.

# CHAPTER 3

## THE EMERGENCE OF DISRUPTIVE FACTORS
## IN THE SYSTEM (1962-1975)

a) *Some signals*

In 1962, a Traffic Conference of IATA, held in Chandler, *failed to reach agreement*.

The fact was unprecedented. It showed that the system was creaking, and the noise it made was heard.

The competition of charters, which emerged as a counter-power, coupled with monetary instability, created an uneasy feeling within the IATA membership. The sense of solidarity about tariffs had begun to erode : some felt much more exposed to the danger than others and were prepared discreetly to reconsider their pricing policies, or even their operating policies as exclusive scheduled carriers.

Initially, they advocated *within IATA* an agressive policy towards the new competitors. Others advocated an open rate situation, and, failing to convince their colleagues, created such situations and then adopted their own policy in the sectors left open.

IATA was still arguing that its multilateral tariff system was the "cornerstone of international cooperation" : "We have no choice", — an expert commented, — "but to realise the fact that, with time, this stone has considerably eroded — a process familiar at least to archaeologists" [86].

It would not be accurate to interpret the *disruptive factors* as signs of *recession*. Some of them were, on the contrary, clearly indicative of market expansion, such as the progress of mass long-haul tourism. But all concurred, for different reasons, to diversify government policies and create reflexes of defence with the result that, failing to provoke concerted action, the established airlines could only react to outside pressure in a less and less coordinated manner.

On the whole, the position of scheduled airlines on the market regressed, and their yields diminished in sectors where they had to engage in price wars.

Two figures are indicative in this respect :

1) Between 1962 and 1972, the portion of the total air traffic taken by charter carriers grew from 2 to 19,9 %.

As scheduled carriers increasingly engaged in charter traffic themselves, the new distribution of air traffic became even more apparent.

2) On the North Atlantic, in 1960, 88 % of the passengers travelling on scheduled services paid the normal published fare. In 1973, 75 % of those passengers used promotional fares, basically designed to overcome charter prices.

The trend clearly was to make a rule of the exception, and to confuse scheduled and non-scheduled markets at the level of products and prices.

On the most important air routes of the world, in terms of volume of traffic, the average true fares were in practice aligned, with the exception of first class fares, to charter prices. How long would IATA discussions on normal economy fares be much more than academic? Would cut-throat competition change the rules of the game?

b) *The major developments*

The major developments which prompted the desperate reaction of scheduled airlines and led to a gradual disorganisation of the Chicago-Bermuda regime are the following :

1. The progress of charter operations;
2. Over-capacity;
3. The multiplication of scheduled airlines;
4. Changes in the world economy.

It is interesting to observe the underlying evolution which precipitated those developments.

1. *The progress of charter operations*

A number of reasons concurred, at the end of the fifties, to encourage the chartering of aircraft.

Essentially, as far as passenger traffic was concerned, longhaul tourism became organised for groups by specialised operators; as for freight, professionals had begun consolidating goods of different origin and nature.

At the beginning of the trend towards mass tourism by air, the regular airlines had endeavoured to cope with this new traffic within their own possibilities by setting up branches or subsidiaries. The charter activity, being seasonal, could be organised within a pool of equipment and benefit marginally the overall operation of the airline.

However, due to their self-imposed restraint, the scheduled airlines did not devote sufficient efforts to that weak — though admittedly developing — sector, and they left gaps wide open for new entrants in the market of tourist transportation.

The *economic* gaps corresponded to the *legal* vacuum left by the Chicago Convention, aggravated by the practice of bilateral agreements in the field of scheduled air transport. Charters were "terra incognita".

Soon, some governments felt the pressure of domestic lobbies which made it politically untenable for them to resist the expansion of democratic tourism simply for the protection of national airlines who were unable to meet public demand in this new field.

Countries on the receiving end of tourist traffic also tended to open up to charters, and to welcome the additional revenues in foreign currency.

Some governments therefore granted liberal rights to charter companies of their own or of a foreign nationality, such concessions being of necessity unilateral. As the bilateral regime was almost exclusively geared to the exchange of scheduled rights, no technique existed by which a *comprehensive exchange* of air traffic rights might have been organised in an homogeneous legal framework.

As a result, certain bilateral situations became unbalanced.

Traffic rights, as well as tariffs escaped the regulatory system, though to a varying degree. Corrective measures were adopted by IATA as long as the tariff distortion remained controllable (restricted, for example, to North-South European axes). But this caesed to be the case once the North Atlantic "boulevard" was affected.

The new opportunities to expand their global participation in the air transport market did not escape the governments of the countries most particularly concerned with the new traffic generation.

"In allowing more operating rights to charter carriers and interfering with the scheduled traffic, the governments did not lose sight of the objective to increase the national participation in international air transportation", Wassenbergh pointed out [87].

It is not really surprising that the power game was developing along new lines, as the opportunities arose. Meanwhile, some underlying concepts were dying away, slowly but surely.

An accelerating factor in the US, with respect to charter flights, was, unexpectedly, the Vietnam war or, more precisely, the end of it. At the disengagement phase, the Pentagon was badly in need of transportation capabilities in addition to the US Air Force. The "supplemental" carriers which then emerged to fulfill those tasks were set up in view of these contracts, with prospects in the avenue of mass-tourism.

Moreover, US aircraft manufacturers were eager to place orders for the newly conceived jumbo-jets. Potential tour operators realised the future role of these high density aircraft.

Once reconverted from their military commitments to civilian work, these carriers "supplemented" scheduled transportation, affirming that they were fit, able and willing to perform services that scheduled airlines could not offer.

They lobbied the Congress, the Administration and public opinion in order to obtain operating permits which would allow them, in the most flexible conditions, to operate international non-scheduled services. They claimed that they would thereby considerably enhance the position of the United States in the world air transport market.

Later on, they pressed the US authorities to insist on favourable operating conditions and ensure some stability for their permits. The Administration should negotiate to that effect with third countries. By so doing, it would not, according to these carriers, harm the interests of established scheduled US carriers, whose markets would not be affected.

The Administration could no more grant the request of the newcomers than deny it outright. The interests of scheduled airlines had to be protected : the designated instruments of bilateral agreements were responsible for the performance of services recognised as being in the public interest and convenience, under the terms of the Federal Aviation Act.

The US scheduled carriers contended that there was only one market in aviation, and they could not legally be deprived of their position in that market : "hit and run" carriers would erode the revenue and thereby degrade the profitability of the industry.

This controversy presaged the debate which later would develop at a much larger scale around one essential question : is it possible to preserve the economic viability of the scheduled services *while favouring the introduction of low fares?*

After all, the modalities of introduction of low fares were more or less immaterial : under the pressure of the charter flights, which it authorised, the US Administration felt compelled to address the issue of tariffs in scheduled transportation.

The CAB retained discretionary powers of appreciation over the prices used in charter transportation : it also reserved the right to consider the conditions of charterworthiness set out by IATA. The declared intention was to preserve the competitive position of scheduled airlines. Moreover, the pricing policy reflected in IATA Resolutions would be scrutinised and submitted, as the case might be, to reservations and refusals. From this moment, in the United States, *the pressure towards liberalisation of air fares was on.* The US carriers within IATA ceased to be unconditional partisans of strict fare structures, as they realised that orthodoxy, once confronted with liberal charter rules, would open a substantial segment of their market and cause their current position to deteriorate.

Indeed, the CAB decided on very liberal charter rules. The scheduled airlines complained, but saw no solution but to lower their own prices on the low fares travel market, hoping to discourage their charter competitors. The price war had legal cover through the government approval system of IATA agreed fares, and life could be made difficult for supplemental carriers. The Chairman of Capitol International declared that "one of the major problems facing the supplemental industry is the cutthroat rate war tactics of the scheduled airline industry and the proliferation of discount fares, group rates, illegal rebates and their below-cost operations, all in the name of competing with the supplementals bulk traffic "[88]. The allegation of predatory pricing was not sustained in court.

Certain supplemental carriers did not survive this initial confrontation and some foreign charter carriers suffered the same fate, being dependent on US-originated traffic. As a rule, however, the charter industry flourished under the new conditions. It was able to operate at a much lower cost than the scheduled airlines and charter carriers organised themselves to carry bulk traffic in high density aircraft at a load factor approaching 100 %.

The *reaction* of the scheduled airlines was slow to emerge, partly due to the cumbersome IATA machinery. The US Administration triggered off a mechanism of *government orders* or *government reservations* which short-circuited, to some extent, the classical tariff-approval procedures. For instance, tariff conditions were removed or added following decisions by the CAB. Some civil aviation authorities engaged in the process of issuing *special on-route fares* for some categories of traffic and reserved for third and fourth freedom carriers on the relation concerned. These fares became bilateral — if only through a matching process. The country at the other end of the route could indeed either reject the tariff approved or decided by the other party, or it could, in turn, issue a matching order in favour of its own national airlines. In fact, these *"point-to-point" fares*, reserved for national carriers, were seriously disruptive to international competition.

From the North Atlantic the charter phenomenon, and its consequences on scheduled tariff structures, spread to other routes and other parts of the world. There was a public demand for low fare leisure transportation by air. European tour operators were prompt to pick up the concept and build the product. *"Inclusive tours"* included the air fare, accommodation, local surface transportation and amenities. Such package tours were sold at record prices, not only to traditional tourism resorts around the Mediterranean, but to the Middle and Far East. Destinations in South East Asia also became popular.

To match these developments, the scheduled airlines developed several promotional fares within IATA, by whose conditions they did not always abide; nor did they always obey the rules for dealing with tour operators and sales agents. Illegal discounting started plagueing the industry. Scheduled airlines also continued to compete on their own and with increased resources on the charter market. To do this, they set up and developed subsidiaries on a large scale and sometimes in a confusing manner. For instance, the major British airline, BOAC formed a charter subsidiary company bearing precisely the same initials. This daughter airline soon enjoyed a specific regulatory regime which appeared to have been tailored to its needs. The new framework included very liberal though exclusive charter rules. It became increasingly evident that the entire regulatory apparatus in these areas was getting out of hand, over-reaching itself to keep up with the developments on the marketplace.

The new set of rules in the UK had to do with the so-called "exempt charters". According to this concept, some flights were permitted to be chartered, and seats were sold to the general public on board such flights irrespective of the conditions set forth by IATA in its once sacrosanct Resolution 045. Thus the UK finished off the kill which the US had started. Resolution 045 was a lame duck anyway, and the way was now paved for the "Sky-Train" and other experiments, oblivious of legal categories. Regular, if not scheduled, high frequency flights, advertised and open to the travelling public at large, made little difference *in practice* to scheduled operations and actually spread the low fare system to India, South East India and beyond (upsetting the structure of the imperial "kangaroo route" to Australia).

The interaction of the factors involved here is easy to comprehend : the regulatory system was put under severe stress.

## 2. *Overcapacity*

The concept of capacity in air transport does not belong to an exact science. It is impossible to determine objectively the conditions of an adequate offer of production, hence the critical levels are indiscernible and under or overcapacity are equally debatable.

On routes between two countries, capacity is defined by reference to ton/kilometres offered and carried during a given time : the ratio provides a *load factor*.

These notions may appear to be relatively clear in terms of economics and arithmetic, but the corresponding regulatory aspects are far from lucid. No standard *criterion* is recognised. Segments of the air transport market differ widely from each other; factors determining a satisfactory level of capacity within the terms of the Bermudian agreements vary with the itinerary and the type of traffic (in airline language, the "traffic mix") carried on the route considered.

It would therefore be simplistic to rely on a particular load factor as *the* criterion that the requirements of public transportation are met adequately in other instances. The discussion of the figures remains possible in many instances.

In others, the situation is clarified by its extremes. Following the introduction of jumbo jets and supplemental carriers on the North Atlantic, there was a time when all the routes in that area were flown with overcapacity as the average situation. As far as the scheduled airlines were concerned, excess production occurred irrespective of any additional capacity they supplied or restrictions they committed themselves to : as a consequence of an *overall* overproduction, their load factor fell anyway and they were the ones to fly more empty seats.

As more carriers become equipped with jumbo jets, they inevitably employed them on the high traffic density routes. The result was that the number of seats offered — frequency remaining constant — was roughly doubled on the North Atlantic in a matter of two years. Even allowing for a lower critical load factor on jumbos than on other jet planes, the lowering of fares undermined the profitability of those routes.

The United States remained consistently faithful to the concept of freedom to provide services, all through the worst turmoil on the North Atlantic. At no time did it envisage limiting the frequencies in bilaterals, thereby restricting the development possibilities of US operators.

Had the problem of overcapacity been dealt with differently, it is doubtful that it could have been brought under control : *the cause of the trouble was itself beyond the system.*

### 3. *The growth in the number of airlines*

After World War Two, the means of production were concentrated among a handful of national airlines. At the end of the sixties, some seventy scheduled carriers occupied the arena.

Several new countries joined the aeronautical community. A first group was formed by former enemy countries, a second group involved East-European airlines, and the most numerous group of new-comers included the flag carriers of emerging independent countries. Air traffic was increasing at a steady, impressive rate.

New entrants enjoyed facilities to purchase US-made aircraft from American financing institutions. Crews and staff could be recruited without too much difficulty. In the political (United Nations) and legal context (the Chicago Convention), market access was encouraged.

*Note :*

At the Chicago Conference in 1944, 52 countries had been represented : the current membership is 152. (In 1978, it had reached 142).

The IATA membership, as indicated earlier, climbed from 40 to 151 (the current membership).

The government of the new applicant country was not deprived of negotiating weapons. Enjoying the State's exclusive sovereignty over its airspace, it might, for instance, choose not to ratify the Transit Agreement, thereby forcing countries interested in transit rights to negotiate them. A well-situated country had an immediate advantage in this respect. (I remember having heard Professor Roger Nys, on the open esplanade of the Law Court building in Kinshasa, telling the future diplomats of Zaire that their interests would not be served by ratifying the Transit Agreement and why.) Anyway, foreign airlines probably served airports on the new entrant's territory : reciprocal rights were readily available. Non-aeronautical arguments could be used. Foreign countries were sometimes benignly inclined at the early stages of independence ...

New bilateral agreements of course added to the number of competitors. It was not merely a matter of the number of airlines, but of shrinking fifth freedom rights, as more third and fourth freedom operators arrived on the stage.

Fifth freedom rights were losing importance anyway, due to the increasing operating range of aircraft, which would make multi-stop services less attractive in the forthcoming decade. Because of both losses of rights and changing route patterns, bilateral agreements had to be re-negotiated all around. For some carriers, this posed a challenge. Fifth freedom rights had been very important for them : they now had to radically reconsider their strategy.

Unfortunately, this whole process of diplomatic activity generated new forms of nationalism in air transport. While the years immediately following the Bermuda plan more or less allowed the dream of internationalism to continue, the crowded scene induced each participant to guard his share of the market or to gain a place in the sun by all available means. National interest became the key word — the more so because, as we have seen, the rules of the game were changing. The centrifugal force at work was augmenting. To carry the flag in the air became a sign of recognition, and prestige a principal reason to set up an airline, even at the cost of subsidising it.

## 4. *Changes in the world economy*

The period under review was one of major economic changes. The main factors are well known : monetary instability, linked to inflation, the corresponding increase in production cost of industrialised countries, the first energy crisis and the beginnings of recession, notably in Europe, with consequent effects upon labour and the social situation at large.

The monetary factor was of particular importance. The Chicago regulatory system relied heavily, though implicitly, on the currency exchange rate keeping relatively stable — or being subject only to a limited instability.

In the seventies, two problems began seriously to hamper the airlines' capacity to accurately forecast their profit ratio. On the one hand, the value of their yield in any given country was difficult to predict due to erratic variations on the currency market and, on the other, the airlines faced extreme difficulties, in some countries, obtaining remittance of their local revenues. Such transfer blocks jeopardised the profitability of operations and reduced to nothing the rights and advantages obtained by a carrier under the bilateral air transport agreement concluded by its government. Yet such factors were beyond the control of aeronautical authorities, let alone of airlines.

Admittedly, disparities in the monetary system affect all sectors of world trade. However, international air transport is particularily vulnerable to these; developing countries need to spend huge amounts in strong currency for the purchase of aircraft, for spare parts and maintenance costs; debts are expressed in US dollars; margins of profitability are often thin and can be eroded in a very short time on small monetary differences; transactions are concluded on the thin edge of profits and losses; governments are often blind to all the complex issues raised by the financial aspects of air transport, which are beyond the province of aeronautical authorities.

Scheduled air services are supposed to operate with a certain stability. Such stability is threatened by unpredictable monetary variations.

The energy crisis and the recession that consequently hit the Western world raised operating costs while reducing the purchasing power of the population, and slowed down the expansion of both passenger and goods traffic worldwide. The airline industry entered a very difficult phase.

## 5. *Two facts, by way of conclusion*

1. "Even before the deep discount fares first proposed in the summer of '78, the minimum cost of crossing the Atlantic by reserved scheduled service for the average American has dropped from 207 hours work in 1957 to around 40 hours. The situation for the European is even more dramatic : — from 580 hours down to 70" (Knut Hammarskjöld, D.G. IATA) [89].

2. "Operating profits from the international scheduled services of the members of IATA fell from 10 % in 1965 to barely 2 % in 1970" (Ross Stainton, Chairman of British Airways) [90].

Mr. Stainton added in comment : "Both figures are remarkably poor for an alleged cartel!".

# CHAPTER 4

## THE INTERNAL DISMANTLING
## OF THE REGULATORY SYSTEM

To all appearances, the public law system remained intact.

ICAO pursued its activities, particularly in providing the assistance required to extend navigation and infrastructure aids to new regions, a costly and often difficult endeavour. IATA also performed useful tasks; Traffic Conferences, possibly more agitated and numerous than usual, were often conclusive.

Bilateral air transport agreements, though more often re-negotiated, were also concluded in a greater number than ever, which might pass for a sign of health. Nominally, the tariffs remained stable, with the the only signs of erratic behaviour on the North Atlantic. But they were only premonitory signs. The global growth rate of air traffic, given the recession, remained more satisfactory than in many other economic sectors.

Yet the system was under pressure; the role, and soon the nature of international cooperation in civil aviation was at stake.

## 1. ICAO and the Governments

"The best way to make a cooperative system work is to have one group of people, the airlines, pursue normal sensible business objectives (like the satisfaction of customer needs, adequate profit, sound and stable employment prospects, and the efficient use of resources) and to make another group of people the alert guardians of the community's interests, responsible for preventing the emergence of co-operation's less beneficial side-effects, internationally as well as in the domestic field" [91].

This analysis by the Chairman of British Airways at the time, Ross Stainton, was correct in essence : the system could only work through the cooperation between airlines, and provided the governments maintained a strict control over the results of this cooperation, bearing in mind the public interests for which they were responsible. The "less beneficial side-effects" (perhaps an English understatement) on the public, due to excessive restriction on competition, were to be prevented, suppressed or at least minimised by "alert guardians", the governments.

The implication was that States accepted clearly defined obligations to abide by some rules and would see to it that those same rules were followed in turn by industries under their control.

The Chicago Convention provided such a set of rules, in the form of principles — which were sometimes too vague, as we have noted earlier. The economic aspects, as we have also noted, were covered by particularly imprecise terminology. It was to be expected that, under heavy skies, there would be some evasions from the responsibilities recognised in more glorious times.

The governments tended to deal with short term problems in purely bilateral relations : essentially, traffic rights and capacity control, of which most took an increasingly restrictive view. They generally paid little attention to tariffs during most of the critical period, except to express some "reservations" — often at the request of their own carriers. A collective examination of the economic developments in the regulatory context was not undertaken. ICAO committees tackled a few specific problems and otherwise contented themselves with producing statistics. Only in 1977 did ICAO convene a Special Air Transport Conference.

## 2. IATA

Before the airlines had realised that the crisis they were entering was more than a growth crisis, they found themselves entangled in heavy and cumbersome machinery to solve their pricing problems in IATA. This procedure had become necessary because of the increase in the number of members, but it was fed by growing uncertainly and dissent. Traffic Conferences which, at the beginning, disposed of their agendae in a few days now dragged along almost continuously throughout the year.

Airline experts who had originally represented their marketing management and defended clear-cut policies, now ended up forming a group of permanent negotiators, the issues often being too technical to be grasped by laymen, and the trade-offs so complicated that they were lost sight of even before the outcome was made public.

Air traffic had diversified. The category of cargo goods, for instance, had proliferated. The segmentation of the market called for regulations on definitions, levels and conditions. The Tariff Manual of IATA ended up containing no less than 330.000 tariffs and rules to construct 2.000.000 of them.

When airline representatives arrived back at their headquarters from Conference meetings, more often than not they began seeking government reservations to the Resolutions they had voted and invented devices to bypass some agreed fares. From year to year, tariff malpractices increasingly plagued the industry, corrupting its morale and ruining its profitability.

The fines imposed on violators by the IATA Breaches Commission were anything but dissuasive; their amounts became quite imposing, yet they gave only a feeble, almost symbolic idea of the true degradation of the market.

## 3. Bilateral Agreements

The diplomacy of the air underwent even more dramatic changes. An academic reading would not discern any difference between the bilateral air transport agreements of that period from earlier ones, but optically balanced exchanges, despite the classical form, hardly reflect the ultimate deal. It was not the form that changed, but the spirit.

There was a lot of shrewd diplomacy in air transport agreements : one of the few genuine bilateral matters left for States to negotiate. On some occasions, despite protests to the contrary, non-aeronautical advantages were bartered; superior political interests played a role in the outcome of negotiations which might otherwise have failed on mere technical grounds.

The change in the economic content of bilaterals came with increased production' the proliferaton of competitors, the narrowing of profit margins and the aggressive competition shielded by governmental interests.

As well as legal formalism, the discussion frequently dealt with critical commercial issues which, ultimately, had to be solved among companies. In basic scenarios, official talks were suspended so that airlines could sort out their differences and reach a consensus on their own. The result was reported separately from the official agreement. The heads of government delegations referred, in a confidential paper, to the agreement among airlines which, in effect, conditioned the life of the treaty.

The limitation of frequencies is a good example of diminishing scruples about repudiations. In the beginning, such a limitation would never have been recorded in an official document : it was blatantly contrary to the philosophy of the Bermuda-type capacity clauses. But soon, such restrictions were published in the Annexes, a clear case of contradiction.

Other inconsistent clauses restricted the traffic rights exchanged in the main body of the Agreement. The latter may have been written in the five freedoms of the air; nevertheless, the fifth freedom was removed from the operation of certain routes, unless a commercial agreement re-established it, by an inter-airlines consensus, for its duration.

In this flood of agreements of all kinds, combining public and private law concepts and rules, it is sometimes difficult to ascertain which supersede which. Questions may arise, for instance, as to the cancellation delay, should airlines abruptly terminate their arrangement while schedules have been approved for the current season of operation.

Even third and fourth freedom rights are sometimes subject to cooperative conditions — which amount to little less than confidentially voiding the essence of the intergovernmental agreement. Such a process is also likely to raise some legal difficulties.

The problem addressed in such cases is one which we might call : the position of *the least interested party*. Whenever a State which was party to a bilateral agreement had no intention of exploiting the possibilities offered, its bargaining strength was increased and it could impose conditions on the other party. Such conditions might consist of the conclusion of commercial agreements, based on the concept of equal entitlement to the services of the designated airlines of the contracting parties. An obligation to "compensate" the non-operation by the least interested party rests upon the "single-track" carrier, as long as the latter operates unilaterally. Partial *compensation* may similarly be imposed to redress the balance in the case of uneven capacity provided by the most interested airline.

Incidentally, it is clear that the "fifty-fifty" capacity share is normally favourable to the least interested party.

Various forms of direct or indirect "royalties" have thus been introduced as confidential conditions for the actual exercice of traffic rights, defined and set forth as granted in the bilateral air transport agreements. The commercial and other cooperative arrangements concluded may appear, upon analysis, to have been imposed by the respective governments upon their airlines; but the inspiration behind those conditions derives from the commercial requirements or financial appetites of the airlines.

In any event, barriers were set up that reflected the worst side of bilateralism, its mediaeval side.

Among the most protectionist and restrictive practices set down in confidential agreements and duly sanctioned, stamped and adopted by governments are the quotas imposed on the exercise of traffic rights. In such systems, not only is the frequency of services limited by rule, but a definite number of passengers and/or a specified volume of cargo are imposed upon the designated airlines.

A quota can be more or less taxing. Under its most restrictive form it is imposed upon each service separately. This means that the number of passengers per flight is actually a ceiling computed on each and every service and may never be exceeded.

A "cumulative" quota, however, is an average per flight which is calculated on the basis of a certain period of time, generally one month : an occasional excess figure has to be compensated on the following services within the period under review.

But, in any case, once the quota has been reached, it leaves no alternative to the carrier but to refuse to transport passengers, even those duly booked on a flight, arriving at the registration desk. By a reproachable fiction, a flight may be deemed to be "full", when operating uneconomically with empty seats.

It is legally debatable whether the carrier has grounds to refuse boarding permission on account of a traffic restriction which is not apparent in the relevant published documents, such as timetables, notices or advertisements.

Another restrictive practice is related to the condition of equal sharing of capacity, which sometimes results in the imposition of commercial agreements to be concluded between the designation carriers. When more than 50 % of the actual proceeds are demanded, Professor Wassenbergh speaks about "the imposition of tolls, ... a far cry from Grotius. It is even a far cry from flag discrimination in shipping and from the UNCTAD code" [92].

One has to recognise, however, that the freedom of trade and the true community of nations advocated by Grotius, as well as the "mare liberum", the concept of which he succeeded in imposing, have only materialised up to a certain extent and are currently threatened by the evolution of the world economy. The unfortunate evolution of aeronautical bilateralism towards ferocious trade-offs may be just one more syndrome of the same illness.

It cannot be denied that air transport was the object of intense competition among enterprises, in a strictly regulated environment, although some considered it to be the *wrong kind of competition*. But for all that met the eye of a good observer, the air market-place looked increasingly like Adam Smith's "great mercantile republic". It remained for political theories to emerge and shake the protected positions from which airlines fired at one another.

## 4. Regionalism as a Defensive System

While bilateralism allowed the airlines to entrench their firing positions behind governmental bunkers, governments in certain parts of the world tended to create what Michel Folliot called "the second form of regionalism, the defensive union". The negotiating capabilities of the governments of a region would be enhanced, each within its own particular dealings with third countries, if a common understanding could be reached among the countries within that region on a number of basic principles and attitudes.

Referring to such typical examples of "defensive union" as the "Arab cabotage" policy and the pressure exercised by States belonging to the CLAC on airlines, mainly European, enjoying intra-Andean fifth freedom rights, Folliot commented in conclusion that : "despite the strength of regional interests, union is not always possible" [93].

An example was given by ECAC, which sought for years to establish and negotiate with the United States a common policy on charter services over the North Atlantic. This effort culminated in a Memorandum of Understanding which some Member States either remained reluctant to sign or immediately betrayed by making separate arrangements, on more favourable terms, with the United States.

The sixteen European signatories of June 1975 were to recognise unashamedly, in 1977, that a common policy was unattainable.

But then, the difficulty with Europe is that it can be identified from far away, but blurs into a mist at closer range. Thirty jealously preserved domains under so many different social systems correspond to different perspectives and to countries that may find themselves in positions which may change and antagonise friendly neighbours overnight. The problem is the lack of a long term view. A common defensive attitude can trigger off a coherent reaction; yet it takes time to adjust to the necessity of making such reactions permanent.

## 5. The Relaxation of Charter Rules

Charter flights are distinctive in that they are not made available to the general public. This criterion was identified in ICAO as early as 1952, when scheduled international services were defined.

Other features could be blurred, but the above condition of non-availability to the general public appeared clear cut and easy to monitor. This condition was essentially distinctive and easily recognisable.

However, charterworthiness rules became sophisticated as time went on and confused the issue by adding freedom to restrictions.

IATA itself produced modified versions of its Resolution 045, which had been clear in its original 1948 version. This resolution on charters contained the insidious notion that a so-called "affinity group" could be eligible for charter service. The concept of affinity is flexible. How can one ultimately prove the affinity of a group of persons gathered (or gathering?) to travel together, ranging from a party of parishioners going to Lourdes to would-be visitors of the Rajastan, and from a football supporters' club to war veterans and academic researchers? And what about an aircraft where several of such groups would be found together? The basis for a legal judgment was not easy to re-trace in such a variety of situations.

As rules were drawn up for study groups and "special events" travellers, new concepts became necessary to deal with the mixture of groups on the same flights : "part-charters", "co-mingling" of groups, and so on. If all this confusion proved the difficulty of applying the ICAO definition of 1952, it also illustrated the ingeniousness used to meet the challenge of competition and achieve a gradual relaxation of charter rules.

With the introduction of the loose conditions of "Advance Booking Charters" (ABC) and "Travel Group Charters" (TGC), the road was open to "public charters" being offered in the United States under virtually the only condition that the product must emanate from a qualified tour operator. Other conditions had indeed become so artificial to a point where it no longer required a devious mind to circumvent them.

Logically, once the concept of affinity had become theoretical, charter flights for non-affinity groups began to develop. Whether or not they qualified for this name under one of the new categories (TGC or ABC or VARA on the North Atlantic) ultimately became immaterial. In Europe, such formulas were successful, but in the United States the experiment conducted in 1973 proved inconclusive, which induced Senator Cannon to propose a complete liberalisation of charters. In July 1973, the CAB authorised US and foreign charter carriers to accept "inclusive tour charters" (ITC) without prior approval, in third and fourth freedom, all restrictions having been lifted. This evolution led to public charters. The United States attempted to negotiate bilateral agreements specifically devoted to non-scheduled flights and providing for fifth freedom rights.

One of the reasons for this policy was the difficulty encountered by the US supplemental carriers in obtaining stable and predictable operating rights : the delays experienced in obtaining these were often excessive. The carriers complained of discriminatory treatment. The Chicago Convention gave them no protection.

But a handful of bilateral arrangements would not solve the problem. The disparity of the legal systems was the real cause.

Some attempts were made to achieve a certain compatibility between rules applicable to scheduled and non-scheduled services. It was possible, in theory, to reduce the distance between the capacity rules, the pricing principles and the compliance with these rules in both fields.

But, in fact, the regimes of the two types of service drifted further apart and the guidelines became a question of national policy.

No amount of national legislative inventiveness could reconcile the diverging interests. It became clear that :

a) competition was exercised on the same market, roughly speaking;

b) its conditions were uneven, sometimes to the advantage of one group, sometimes of the other;

c) liberalisation of the charter rules could harm scheduled services, without necessarily giving equal chances to charters.

CHAPTER 5

THE EXTERNAL FACTORS :
NEW TRENDS AND FACTS ANNOUNCING THE PRESENT

From 1975 onwards' the centrifugal tendencies accelerated and the tensions endured by the Chicago-made regulatory system became critical for the international community.

This situation developed against a background of profound economic degradation following the energy crisis, notably with respect to growth rate, social conditions, level of income, energy costs, security of financial transactions and monetary stability. In aviation terms, overcapacity and tariff wars resulted in a general decrease in yields, while traffic began stagnating and operating costs, particularly fuel costs, escalated.

In this context, some bilateral relations reached breaking point. Exemplary as always, the relationship between the former Bermuda partners was the first to undergo a fundamental revision.

## 1. The Denounciation of the Bermuda Agreement

The United Kingdom had, for some time, judged the North Atlantic congestion to be unbearable.

The United States having, notwithstanding the Bermuda Agreement, increased production by launching off-agreement charter carriers who took up 27 % of the traffic and escaped all commonly agreed regulations, had in addition used the broad privileges of the Bermuda capacity clause to throw even more capacity on the market : its powerful scheduled airlines were determined to crush supplemental competitors at all costs (including those which the British carriers would bear ...).

Well aware of the likely effect of this policy, the United States had taken steps, including the authorisation, exempt from anti-trust law, for US and foreign carriers to hold bilateral capacity talks geared to the reduction of excess capacity. A case in point had been the British. But British airlines considered the formula to be inconclusive at airline level.

The US Administration undertook to challenge the capacity mounted by KLM, Sabena, SAS and Swissair as excessive in relation to the natural traffic of these carriers. The dispute bore on sixth freedom.

Such actions, as recognised since by the Americans themselves, were without legal basis. They did not succeed in diverting the attention of the British from their own problems.

More to the point were the efforts deployed to achieve a multilateral agreement on charter services in the North Atlantic market, between the United Kingdom, the United States and Canada.

But this result was not achieved. (The Bermuda 2 Agreement would contain the commitment to the idea : "while continuing their efforts to achieve a multilateral arrangement for charter air services in the North Atlantic market" ... (the Parties shall) "apply the following bilateral provisions to charter air services". Art. 14).

There was no reason to allow the situation to deteriorate any further : the United States sent out the first signals of a liberalisation which meant additional freedom to produce capacity.

A Declaration by President Ford announced that the United States would exclude an equal division of market shares with foreign countries, and would favour conditions of free competition : "because the efficient carrier should be awarded for its efficiency and the consumer should benefit from the innovative, cost-based services that result from competition".

In June 1976, the United Kingdom notified its intention to terminate the Bermuda Agreement of 11 February 1946.

The psychological effect of the denunciation was considerable.

## 2. Negotiation of a Difficult New Deal : „Bermuda 2"

The two parties found themselves back on the starting blocks of 1946. But the world had changed, and they themselves were changing The twelve months of negotiation left them with different conceptions from those they had had at the beginning of the talks and which they had defended, sometimes with success!

However, contrary to their stands in 1946, thirty years later they did not feel as if they carried the burden of teaching the world a lesson in air law. They wanted to be pragmatic, to bargain with facts rather than theories.

But first, they had to assess the facts, and that took time.

Market access, the relative value of stopping points, routes and frequencies, equipment used, and fifth freedom rights were carefully discussed before being bargained for : to reach a common understanding on economic facts proved difficult and took several months.

The next phase proved equally difficult : the discussion bore on the issue of multidesignation of carriers. The Americans had opted for the designation of more than one US carrier on any route granted to the United States; consistent with their views on the existence of an overcapacity, the British advocated the designation of a single carrier for each state on each route.

They sorted out the issue somehow by some compromises on some routes, the British position being undermined by the decision of a British judge. The action, sometimes referred to as the first Laker case, was brought by Mr. Freddy Laker, who was involved in charter transportation and had vainly applied for authorisation to launch a new type of service, with some of the characteristics of the scheduled and some of the non-scheduled flights : the "Sky Train".

Such flights would be operated on high density routes, with fixed schedules, and made available to passengers with no advance booking, on a "first come first serve" basis. The absence of sales intermediaries and the "no frills" in-flight service would allow for low fare transportation. This new phenomenon played a direct role in the negotiation of the Bermuda 2 Agreement. The English judge involved in the lawsuit brought by Laker ruled that the plaintiff was entitled to obtain government designation on certain routes between the United Kingdom and the United States, concurrently with (traditional) scheduled airlines.

Indirectly, the "Laker phenomenon" laid the ground for further legal action and awoke interest in a promising new type of democratic air transportation service. It served to illustrate the internal contradiction of the regulatory system.

On two routes, the United Kingdom accepted the pluridesignation of carriers.

Nevertheless, the economic interests at stake on both sides continued to hamper the negotiations, with the British pushing forward the idea of an institutionalisation of some concerted scheduling of operations on the North Atlantic. The deadline of the notification delay, June 20, was reached without the compromise being concluded. For the first time, the media and public opinion became aware, concretely, of the scale of the crisis.

This was no mere US/British crisis : it had become a critical issue worldwide, one that might divide the "have's" and the "have nots", and which deserved attention.

The compromise agreement was, however, initialled shortly after the deadline had been passed, and was signed on July 23, 1977.

## 3. The „Bermuda 2" Agreement

The Air Transport Services Agreement [94] did not have the farreaching implications of the Bermuda 1 Agreement.

It reflected a more restrictive tendency, which was duly observed and commented on. It was interesting in many respect : it dealt with charter flights and provided for procedures which could permit new developments on an experimental basis.

But observers soon began to question whether the experiment would effectively take place. The reception was tepid in both countries. Almost immediately, the United States, engaged in a liberalising process at home, expressed their reluctance at implementing a system whereby civil servants would deal with tariff policies and eventually pre-determine capacities, pre-empting free adjustments to market needs.

The impact of Bermuda 2 boiled down to the temporary relief that, at least, a vacuum had been filled. The observers did not expect a great precedent to be established.

The contents can be summarised as follows.

### 1. *Capacity clauses*

The operating programmes of airlines must be exchanged by governments six months in advance of each season of operation. During that delay, the governments may raise objections and consult with a view to re-adjusting the capacities, if needed. The agreed solution is imposed on the airlines. If no solution has been agreed, airlines are not allowed to increase their flights by more than twenty services over their previous summer programme or fifteen over their previous winter programme.

### 2. *Tariff clauses*

Airlines are called upon to consult each other, classically, within IATA; the innovation lies in a consultative mechanism purported to prevent undue blockage of tariff agreements by one or the other party.

The civil aviation authorities are to harmonise their pricing policies through a joint commission on tariffs, composed of government officials only.

### 3. *Charters*

An interesting feature of the Bermuda 2 Agreement is that it contains a section devoted to charter flights.

Although not an innovation in terms of US policy, the bilateral treatment of non-scheduled services came as a welcome relief from the frantic efforts made in Europe collectively to reach a common position vis-à-vis the United States, and by individual countries to strike the best confidential deal with that country.

But the original Agreement contained innovative procedure rather than substance. The complementary Agreement modifiing the liberal Memorandum on charter flights of April 1977 brought material to Bermuda 2 in this respect, as from its conclusion on July 23, 1977. Article 14 of the Agreement was thereby completed and a new Annex 4 attached [95].

Essentially :

— Third and fourth freedom rights are exchanged without restriction; rights to and from third countries are subject to a two nights stopover condition.
— The charterworthiness rules are those of the *country of origin* of the traffic.
— The principle of *fair competition* is recognised.
— Rules of *designation* of the carriers are set out.
— Flight programmes should be submitted in advance.
— *Categories* of charter flights are defined in some detail.

### 4. *Traffic rights*

Traffic rights are described in conformity with the traditional definitions of the freedoms of the air; however, their exact importance is weighed in modalities with such conceptual research and flexibility as to bring interesting innovations to this field.

For instance, the change of gauge, change and combination of flight numbers, and facilities attached to such rights leave no doubt as to the intention of the Contracting States to clarify doubtful aspects of freedoms and, in particular, to recognise and to legitimate the infamous non-existant sixth freedom.

As to the route schedules, they are the end product of the long evolution since Bermuda 1, both in the geo-political sense and of the art of drafting. Here as well, the concern is clarification. The categorisation and tight description of itineraries, as well as the luxury of details in the calendar of use of fifth freedom rights by US carriers, the number of additional gateways in the US open to British carriers, etc. reflect the intricate and tough negotiations which took place, and the diplomatic skill required to finalise them.

5. *General clauses*

The Bermuda 2 Agreement is of some interest, and has established a model in the new or modernised provisions on matters such as financial aspects, security, taxation, etc.

6. *Comments*

A turning point had been reached : if Bermuda 2 had been a new landmark, a more stringent application of the Bermuda 1 principles, amounting to a substantial modification would have become the rule and would have precluded progress of the liberalisation of air transport, at least for a certain time. The comment was, at the time : "Should Bermuda 2 become a model for future bilateral agreements, we would no doubt be moving towards a more stringent system and therefore the deregulation affecting the domestic services within the USA would not reach the international field". (F. Videla Escalada) [96].

# 4. ICAO becomes Aware

The time had come to assess the economic factors which affected the development of international air transport.

At a Special Conference, which took place in April 1977, one hundred and two countries and eleven organisations were represented. The four hundred and fifty delegates and observers formed an impressive assembly, and it would later be recognised that the high level of participation illustrated the *general concern* about the problems related to the economic regulation of air transport in a changing world.

The results of this first SATC (Special Air Transport Conference) may appear to have been limited; however, the delegates conducted a comprehensive overview of the problems and made it clear that they intended solutions to be sought intensively. Some directions were given.

*A.* — The main orientations of the Conference are the following :

1) *The governments are aware of their responsibilities,* under the Chicago Convention, to meet the conditions of an orderly economic development of internal air transport.

The Conference acknowledged the fact that a certain number of factors currently influence the regulatory system and deprive it of its original beneficial aspects.

2) *The governments intend to analyse the situation and seek remedies* for present shortcomings.

3) Realising that one of the shortcomings is the divergence between the regulatory treatment of scheduled and non-scheduled international air services, *governments intend to harmonise their policies with respect to both categories of services.*

*Reasonable possibilities* to use non-scheduled flights should be offered to the public *without endangering the economics of scheduled services.* (Recommendation 2/1-3, c and d).

Indeed, as the Chairman of the Conference, Dr. Guldimann observed, both categories of flights belong to the same system, and it is satisfying to see a global perception prevail.

However, to reach a stable and harmonised system will take time. The Conference invited the Council to examine the following possibilities :

a) to amend the Chicago Convention (Articles 5, 6 and 96, al. a), in order to take into account provisions and regulatory principles governing both scheduled and non-scheduled air transport services, on the basis of their characteristics, as well as the present and future structure of the international air transport market.

b) to revise the definition of "scheduled international air service". (Recommendation 2/1-2).

*Note :* The developing countries were generally in favour of a global approach, and their attitude was pragmatic : they can gain revenues from charter flights, which should by no means be disregarded, but it is essential for them on many accounts to preserve the economic viability of their international scheduled operations.

4) *The coordination of policies at regional level* should be encouraged, as it can bring about positive results with respect to specific conditions prevailing in that region.

5) *In adopting tariff agreements*, each airline operating on a given route or section of route should be given *equal opportunity to participate in the transport market concerned.*

This proposal was moved by developing countries, in an effort to exclude the detrimental "point to point" (restrictive bilateral) fares, which were perceived as discriminatory and contrary to the principe of equal opportunity set out by the Chicago Convention.

Governments should make sure that airlines comply with this principle in practice. (Recommendation 4/13-1-2).

6) *Governments intend to take responsibility in tariff matters.*

The Recommendations of the Conference may be summarised as follows : the era of government passivity vis-à-vis the pricing policies of the airlines is over. From now on (according to Recommendations voted), governments will assist as observers at the Traffic Conferences of IATA, will require submission of fares at least sixty days prior to the date of their introduction, will seek any justification needed from the airlines, and will notify their decisions within thirty days. Once the approved tariffs are introduced on the market-place, governments will see to it that are duly applied.

On the entire spectrum of tariff-related issues, a working group of government experts is being set up, which will issue a report and recommend solutions to the next Conference.

B. — THE MAIN LACK OF ORIENTATION OF THE CONFERENCE WAS IN THE FIELD OF THE EXCHANGE OF TRAFFIC RIGHTS

More generally, the basic legal aspects of the treatment of economic problems were not dealt with to any significant extent, due to everwidening differences in perception.

If there had been a vote, though, there were indications that a large majority of States represented at the Conference would have rallied around a policy of more stringent government control over air transport — hardly a means to bring the countries together and make the governments less selfish in exchanging operating rights. Among the concepts that emerged, the Chairman of the Conference regretted the *claim of each State to reserve for itself half of its international traffic,* definitely anchored and protected. "Competition is left aside", he said, "as the main instrument for the promotion of progress and the optimisation of the offer ...".

Another signal was the easy rallying around the concept of capacity pre-determination.

In the meantime, some countries were seriously considering the benefits of deregulation as a national policy, which might sow the seed of competition and ultimately leave no other law to rule it than the law of the market ....

## C. — CONCLUSION

The international community was unquestionably divided on main issues, except on one point : *that the adequacy of the regulatory system of international air transport was in question.* It would take some time to assess exactly where and how this system required updating and to what extent it required modification, but the task now undertaken would have to be pursued.

The 22nd General Assembly of ICAO decided to convene another Special Air Transport Conference within three years. The decision contained the following whereas clause : "Considering that *the moment has come to recognise that the thirty years old regulatory system should be modernised*" ...

## 5. The Policy of Deregulation of the United States

The first ICAO Special Air Transport Conference took place in 1977. The following year saw the dawn of deregulation.

"The year 1978 was an exciting one for the airline industry. It celebrated the seventy-fifth anniversary of the first powered flight by the Wright brothers and saw the beginning of a period of feverish competition which has drastically changed the industry's way of doing business". (Comments of Dorothy Diane Sandell) [97].

At least (to begin with), in the United States ...

### a) *The US domestic deregulation of air services*

The doctrine of deregulation of the air transport industry belongs basically to US history. Its exportation is a by-product.

Since 1940, the economic regulation of the airlines had been entrusted to the Civil Aeronautics Board. Route control, certification of carriers and regulation of air fares were prerogatives of the CAB, who had authority under the enabling statute to develop its own policies. Every aspect of airline activity, including right of entry, level of competition, pricing and services was government-controlled. The changes in charter rules decided by the Board in late 1975 triggered off a price war in 1977, the year during which Professor Alfred E. Kahn became Chairman of the CAB.

Cornell economist Kahn had a forceful personality and very clear ideas on deregulation. He is sometimes considered as the grandfather of deregulation in air transport. However, the idea had been aired in other places in connection with air transport, notably in Congress. A legislation had been under way since 1974; hearings on the issue were held under impulsion of Senator Cannon in April 1976. After discussion of the bill introduced by Senators Kennedy and Cannon, the Air Transportation Reform Act was passed by the Senate in 1978. The bill presented in the House was conceived somewhat differently, but tended to the same effect; the final legislation signed by the President on October 24, 1978, is called the *Airline Deregulation Act* [98].

Among the main objectives of the new legislation, was « the encouragement, development, and maintenance of an air transportation system relying on actual and potential competition to provide efficiency, innovation, and low prices, and to determine the variety, quality, and price of air transportation services".

The CAB lost the power to exercise its own judgment on the extent to which competition was "necessary" to develop an air transportation system. From now on, the placing of maximum reliance on competitive market forces was considered to be in the public interest, and in accordance with public convenience and necessity.

But the changes of policy imposed on the CAB were radical in all areas where it had previously exercised regulatory jurisdiction : market entry/exit, fares, routes, capacity.

The reason behind this change was the new manner in which the legislator viewed the airline industry. A Congressman had clearly expressed this change of attitude : „Historically, aviation was a fledgling industry which needed help and financial guarantees, and the public needed controls for safety. But we're 40 years from that point and there is no need for the CAB to be overly protective of a $ 100 billion industry" [99].

The logical ultimate consequence of that attitude for the industry was that the CAB itself would „eclipse" and be dissolved at the end of a six-year period, „once the airlines are on their own" ... ("CAB sunset").

But the new doctrine also rested on a fresh approach to the problem of air transport as a public utility — the idea that the relaxation of public constraints and controls over the market-place would necessarily result in an improvement of the service offered to the public. The efficiency required from air carriers would enable them to offer better service at cheaper prices and, at the same time, to make better profits, thus enhancing the benefits of the air transportation system for all concerned. Airline managers would be able to proceed with major changes to their route systems more rapidly than the Administration could do, while adapting those changes to their specific needs.

In a market-responsive system, many of the economic problems faced by the airlines today would be solved. Automatic or quasi-automatic rights of entry and pricing would bring about new situations : as an example, commuter airlines would be able to challenge trunkline carriers for subsidies and eventually, through automatic entry programs, for routes as well. In other words, business would be allowed to developed with reduced government interference, and this development would benefit the service to the public.

Incidentally, in connection with public service obligations, the Deregulation Act comprises a Section entitled "Small Community Air Service", which guarantees continued air transportation for ten years to all cities listed on air carrier certificates on the date of enactment. "Essential service" must be provided by carriers serving those cities.

In fact, besides the declaration of policy, the new Act contained a number of transitional provisions which would gradually lead to the final goal of complete deregulation.

The removal of regulatory controls was coupled with the general safeguard provided by anti-trust laws to prevent and punish anti-competitive practices on the market-place.

b) *The new international doctrine*

It was inherent in the logic of deregulation that its economic advantages were equally available at an international level.

In effect, an „open sky" may well be necessary to derive the full benefits of the domestic liberalisation of air services.

But the development of an international doctrine lacked the consistency and the strong political formulation which domestic deregulation had received.

No less than three agencies had thoughts on the subject : Congress, the CAB, and the Department of State. They followed somewhat different lines and, despite the efforts to coordinate them, the approach remained piecemeal and never acquired complete coherence, even when the consolidated policy statement took form in the 1978 Carter Declaration.

The Department of Transportation acted more or less as a liaison officer and claimed that the United States had to act responsibly, being the chief aviation power in the world.

"The United States has provided, and continues to provide, responsible leadership in the international air transport community. This leadership is required if we are to adapt the international air regulation structure to meet the needs of today's travel and freight markets, and the needs of these markets for the next decade" [100].

Senators Cannon and Kassebaum introduced a bill to be the counterpart of the Domestic Airlines Deregulation Act at international level. President Carter declared the principles of a new policy on August 21 1978 : the International Air Transportation Policy Statement. This policy became law in the *International Air Transportation Competition Act* 1979.

The executive agencies had immediately started implementing the President's policy statement — little worrying about its equivocal legal stature. This meant re-negotiating bilateral air transport agreements. It had been relatively simple to enact a domestic policy, but this policy needed to be shared to prevail internationally.

The psychological problem was serious : how to convince third countries to lift bilaterally agreed safeguards was a matter of finding attractive concessions to trade. Most countries primarily sought to protect the interests of their airlines. They were concerned that the United States no longer retained the policy objective of assuring that essential levels of regularly scheduled services "could be *economically maintained*" (1976 Policy Statement). Would competiton not work necessarily to the advantage of the strongest?

"The US will work to achieve a system of international air transportation that places its principal reliance on actual and potential competition to determine the variety, quality and price of air service ... Especially in major international air transport markets, there can be substantial benefits for travellers, shippers, airlines and labour from increasing competitive opportunities and reducing protectionist restrictions". (1978 Policy Statement). The doctrine did little more, in fact, than transpose the Domestic Airlines Deregulation Act or attempt to translate it into international diplomacy. In doing so, perhaps the Policy Statement (also called the "Carter Declaration") took little account of international implications.

Admittedly, the United States Administration was genuinely prepared to draw the logical conclusions of its doctrine, and offered tempting traffic rights, for the first time, in exchange for liberalising concessions. Yet many countries reacted with suspicion to the "open sky" motto of the American diplomatic offensive.

The so-called "integrated position" of the United States in international air negotiations, according to the Presidential Policy Statement of 1978, consisted of *seven objectives* :

1) to obtain increased possibilities to launch *innovative and competitive fares*, opening up new service options to new categories of travellers and shippers;

2) *to liberalise charter rules;*

3) to allow for a free development of scheduled air services through the *elimination of all restrictions on capacity, frequencies, routes and operational rights;*

4) *to eliminate all forms of discrimination and anti-competitive practices* directed against US carriers on international markets;

5) *multidesignation* of US carriers;

6) *to broaden the access to international passenger and freight markets*, through direct services operated to and from a *larger number of US cities*, and to achieve a better integration of domestic and international air services;

7) *to increase the flexibility of cargo rules*, to simplify bureaucracy and thereby permit the development of competitive international freight services.

To achieve those objectives, the negotiating policy and strategy would be directed towards an *exchange of opportunities* rather than the quest for selfish and short-term competitive advantages for the US carriers only". The US "cannot and does not", — negotiators would say — "seek competitive *advantage*. What we want, and believe is fair, is competitive *equity*".

The new international doctrine of the United States was based on the theory that it would be possible to expand deregulation by the multiplying effect of liberal bilateral agreements : an assumption remote from reality. The strategy followed rested on the simplistic presumption *that a multilateral system can be modified by a sufficient number of carefully selected bilateral actions.*

c) *Weakness of the new international doctrine*

It is obviously not true that a multilateral system founded on an international convention, even though it is implemented essentially through bilateral agreements, can be modified at the will of one State, however powerful : the legal logic has to be consistent.

One shortcoming of the logic in point is the gap between its application to a legally homogeneous industry — in a national domestic market — and its introduction to other distinctive markets, each responding to specific national requirements. As long as the principles of the Chicago Convention and subsequent bilateral agreements remained generally consistent with such requirements (more so than the new guidelines proposed), the tactics of divided efforts would not bring about meaningful results : there might be a cohesion of ideas in the long run, but no spectacular reversal of the trends in air transport agreements.

A similar line of reasoning may be used to criticise the negotiating policy from an economic point of view. A liberal economy, according to Keynes, develops as a model based on the proposition that *the market is a system.* By no means should deregulation be mistaken for anarchy, for what it really brings about is a new type of order, an innovative order which brings satisfaction to those who rely on it and apply the rules of the game. But for the air transportation market to be a system, where the rules of the game called competition could be applied evenly, the nationalistic barriers raised through a dense network of international conventions would have to be removed. Worldwide, the system as it existed before deregulation was a non-market.

In other words, against the background of the galling experience and realities of international air transport, and the legally entrenched nationalism of many countries, political assessment was lacking in Washington. The domestic doctrine had been carelessly transferred to the international scene, regardless of the differences.

Yet, internationally, the new doctrine was not that new, and it bore a striking resemblance to previous exhortations by the US in favour of freedom of the air. The reaction was to be expected. As an authoritative writer, Barry R. Diamond, has observed, "the freedom of the air the United States has long advocated under the Bermuda principles is a special kind of freedom : the freedom of the stronger (in terms of traffic generating capability and bargaining power) to freely compete with the weaker. This Darwinian notion of freedom has understandably not set well with that large body politic of countries which together comprise the category of "the weaker". Like weaker species in nature, these countries have fought back with whatever weapons they happened to have at hand" [101].

Another commentator, R. Thornton, remarked on the long-standing strategy of the United States, from the Chicago Conference onwards, that "while freedom of competition has a ring of justice to it, there is some absurdity in its being espoused by a competitor who has a commanding lead in an industry characterized by strong economies of scale and considerable restriction of entry. As Charles M. Sackrey put it, the US position was "similar to that taken by the proverbial elephant, who, while he danced through the chicken yard, cried : "Everyone for himself"! [102].

Admittedly, more effort was put this time into selling the idea of limited deregulation to countries for which it might have some appeal in relation to particular outstanding bilateral issues. This effort accounts for the number of liberal bilaterals concluded (twenty in all). But the large majority of countries, and the international community itself, reacted negatively to these openings.

Another flaw in the policy concerns what was locigally held to be a safeguard against carriers shying away from competition through competition restraining agreements : the US antitrust laws.

On the one hand, the extra-territorial application of those laws would inevitably create international problems; but, on the other hand, the extent to which such application would be made possible through the "direct effect" doctrine [103] would nevertheless be insufficient to allow for free and equitable competition to take place, as in the domestic market.

"Although US antitrust laws have some extra-territorial effects, in the area of US *international* airline deregulation the US Government cannot act unilaterally, but must act in conjunction with other Governments which may or may not share the US philosophy of the economic regulation of air transport". (P. P. C. Haanappel) [104].

Here again, the misconception is a result of the reasoning. The United States market is homogeneous, while the worldwide market of air transport is far from that. In the United States, a unique executive power exercises authority, one legislation prevails, a Supreme Court arbitrates jurisdictional differences, interstate commerce is regulated, and all air carriers are privately owned. It is therefore possible to regulate the system with an efficiency totally incomparable with that of a fragmented international community of sovereign countries.

This community, still in *"the stone age of bilateral negotiations"* (!) [105], rests on customary international law which includes the principle of national sovereignty in air space.

It is a blunt fact that so far "all endeavours to weaken this citadel of sovereignty have failed" [106]. The only possibility for the United States to export its deregulation doctrine all the way to the "open sky" was to convince its bilateral partners. Predictably, few countries would take chances in aligning themselves with a free market doctrine; and none would relinquish its sovereignty to please America. The first and possibly last result of the American offensive might well have been to revive the old dividing issue of national sovereignty.

d) *The new liberal bilateral agreements*

In retrospect, the characteristic features of each innovative air transport agreement signed by the United States since 1978 are not particullarly important. There were seventeen of them, not including four "partial liberal" agreements.

For a time, observers monitored these agreements with the utmost attention in the belief that they would mark the future like the Bermuda Agreement had done in 1946.

The various nuances of liberalisation were noted and conclusions were drawn as to trends and prospects.

But seen globally, they all reflected the same uncertainties and the same difficulties in reaching clear concepts on pricing or in relation to market access and multiple designation.

No new pattern was emerging. Knut Hammarskjöld would rightly comment : "Such a regime ... evolves in strong contrast to that established by the Bermuda One model, both as regards divergence and controversy on the provisions of the agreements, and in terms of undermining the stability that was obtained on the basis of a largely standardized legal and political infrastructure.

The United States has now recognized the disappearance of a model for air transport diplomacy with the resultant fallback on negotiation on a case-by-case basis. Furthermore, the new bilateral agreements are currently negotiated on a partical and/or provisional basis, implying correspondingly different status" [107].

The US Administration, however, sought uniformety. The Carter Declaration had established in principe that the seven negotiating objectives which it set forth were to be attained *simultanously;* if one of them was not attained, or only imperfectly attained, no grounds would exist for route or other concessions on the US side. But even those countries which agreed to negotiate and conclude a liberalising agreement showed considerable resistance or reluctance with respect to particular clauses and ideas advanced by the US delegations.

The resulting mosaic of systems blurs the objectives and sometimes the issues. For instance, the US policy advocated *free entry* so that markets could become what promoters of deregulation call "contestable", which means that *any carrier can enter at any time*. Failures become immaterial : several more carriers will want to try. Such a philosophy works to the advantage of the *large* against the *small* and could not be shared by partners of the United States. However, their dissent itself took more or less accommodating forms. Similar varied reactions can be found in *pricing* policy principles, which were, nevertheless, the core of the matter as far as the Americans were concerned. They often had to be satisfied with measures going only halfway towards total freedom. A pragmatic attitude indeed consisted of making some headway in particular markets and of hoping for more progress to come with time and the generalisation of deregulating concepts.

The twenty-one agreements present certain similarities, as they all achieve some degree of liberalisation of services in exchange for increased route and other opportunities offered by the United States.

Another reason for not engaging in a detailed analysis of these agreements it the relatively small impact they had on the international situation. Instead of spreading the ideas around the countries involved, the agreements gave rise to more restrictive attitudes in their neighbours and even resulted in concerted regional opposition by several countries in Africa and Latin America. In the long term, however, it cannot be denied that they helped to carry the new ideas further, and in some cases, particularly on the Atlantic markets, tariffs were lowered due to traffic diversions, and the free competition on some markets had a contagious effect.

As far as the relations between the United States and Europe were concerned, the liberal agreements concluded with the Netherlands and Belgium, for instance, must be considered in perspective with other endeavours by the US to expand pricing liberalisation over the North Atlantic, in particular the negotiation of the US-ECAC Memorandum of Understanding on the North Atlantic tariffs.

The list of liberal agreements with references to their most interesting features is available [108].

We will mention the agreements which pioneered the new type of bilateral exchanges.

— *The Netherlands*

The Protocol between the United States and the Netherlands concluded in March 1979 was amended on March 31, 1978.

It concerns scheduled and non-scheduled services.

The section on non-scheduled services confirms a previous agreement on charter flights between the two countries, in which the *country of origin rule* had been recognised.

The clause dealing with this rule is as follows : « Airlines of a Contracting Party ... shall be permitted to exercise those rights in accordance with the rules specified in that Party's designation for the carriage of international charter traffic from its territory on a one-way or round trip basis, or any waivers of such rules granted for appropriate reasons. These rules shall be the charterworthiness rules now or hereafter published by the aeronautic authorities of each Contracting Party."

This clause was extended, for the first time, to the pricing arrangements.

At a later stage of the negotiations, the Netherlands went further on the way towards pricing freedom, but refused to agree on an American proposal which automatically entitled third countries to participate in the tariffs between the Netherlands and the US at the level decided "de facto" by other countries' carriers.

The Netherlands obtained two additional points to serve in the United States.

— *Israel*

The Protocol between the United States and Israel, signed August 16, 1978, was the most liberal agreement at the time.

The agreement freed charter services entirely (lifting the charter ban which Israel had imposed previously) and granted new gateways in the US to Israel (whose access to the country had been restricted to the New York gateway). In that sense, the agreement appeared to be an opportunistic settlement of a particular bilateral situation, rather than a profound modification of the principles on which previous agreements had been based.

In tariff matters, the "double disapproval" clause was introduced for the first time. Governments would only interfere with capacity for technical or operational reasons or on account of circumstances related to the safeguard of the environment. Multidesignation of carriers was permitted.

### — Peru

One Latin-American country which found some basis for agreement in the new policy was Peru. But this success was mitigated, the US having accepted, for the sake of striking a deal in the region, concessions as important as the specification of authorised frequencies in the agreement.

The date is October 1978.

### — Federal Republic of Germany

In the agreement with the FRG, dated November 1, 1978, the "country of origin" rule prevailed both for the tariff regime and for the charterworthiness criteria.

The FRG was reluctant to grant unlimited fifth freedom rights to US carriers, who would enjoy tariff freedom.

Multiple designation was accepted. German carriers could serve six points in the US, with beyond rights.

### — Belgium

A very liberal agreement, but quite in line with the Israeli or Dutch agreements, the Protocol signed with Belgium (December 12, 1978) has two remarkable features :

1) its tariff clause is complete, in terms of the US policy in the matter. It is a double disapproval clause, extending the freedom to establish fares to air transportation effected between the two countries in fifth and sixth freedom and by air carriers of third countries, with sweeping matching possibilities.

2) the full "open sky" concept was applied in the granting of complete freedom to operate *all-cargo services* to Belgian designated carriers.

### e) *IATA challenged*

Since the creation of IATA, its activities had never been challenged by a government, and IATA fares had consistently been, when approved, incorporated into the bilateral agreements. After 33 years of approving IATA tariffs in line with the other governmental agencies, the United States CAB issued its Order 76-6-78 on June 12, 1978, directing IATA to "show cause" why the Board should not rule that IATA tariff agreements were no longer in the public interest and, therefore, should no longer be approved in compliance with Section 512 of the Federal Aviation Act, and immunised from the application of anti-trust law in compliance with Section 414 of the Federal Aviation Act.

As a result of the provisional decision, the practices of Tariff Conferences, as well as the tariff agreements stemming from them would be rendered illegal in the United States to the extent where tariffs to and from the United States, affecting the commerce of the United States according to the "effect doctrine" would be concerned. Such a sweeping exclusion would be paramount to an American unilateral withdrawal from IATA.

The US was apparently determined to terminate the existence of the mechanism of international air fares, established and recognised by the great majority of the countries involved in bilateral air transport agreements : the only multilateral component of the regulatory system.

The CAB appeared insensitive to the international effect of such a decision. The generally negative reaction of the international community came quickly. In its Order 79-5-113, dated 14 May 1979, the CAB could not but acknowledge that the consequences for the system of international air transport would be far-reaching. Meanwhile — and not only because of the pressure exercised by the Order to Show Cause — IATA had felt compelled to re-evaluate its procedures and to proceed with a structural reorganisation.

IATA developed a two-tier membership plan : one tier would allow a member to participate in the trade association activities, while the other would permit carriers to participate in both trade association and tariff coordinating activities. Moreover, in Traffic Conferences, a simple majority vote replaced the sacrosanct unanimity rule which had seemed inseparable from the Conference mechanism. A procedure was created by which special innovative fares might obtain approval, thereby departing from the old "package" agreement concept.

All these changes were timely. In its 1979 Order, the CAB removed part of the previous charges tentatively levied against IATA, and granted interim approval of the new IATA constitution. The trade association activities of IATA were not being challenged, and the CAB continued to grant exemption from the anti-trust law to IATA tariff agreements for an interim period, without prejudice to its final decision at the term of the SCO procedure.

Some commentators wonder, retrospectively, whether the CAB ever had a genuine intention to denounce the US participation in IATA and to trigger off its complete disappearance. Possibly, the CAB essentially sought to impress upon the aviation community the necessity to move earnestly towards the liberalisation of air fares.

At any rate, the CAB's change of attitude also resulted in a reduction of the scope of the 1978 Order to the North Atlantic Traffic Conferences. Even the restricted scope — still involving the densest routes in the world — was later criticised, together with the Show Cause Order itself, in US political circles. Former DOT Secretary Brock Adams expressed scepticism as to the entitlement of the United States to export its anti-trust laws into the international aviation community. Preventing US carriers from meeting with 90 % of the world's airlines through IATA, he felt, would be a tragic mistake.

Such concerns with respect to the interests of the US air transport industry were shared at Congress level. A Sub-committee on Investigations and Oversight of a Committee of the House of Representatives was set up in 1981, with the following objective : „the improvement needed in the implementation of the United States international aviation policy". The policy followed by the Carter Administration in trading with foreign countries, pricing freedom for additional access rights („soft rights" against „hard rights"), was denounced by this Sub-committee, who decided on the following changes of policy :

"We will not trade hard rights for soft rights.

We will not negotiate aviation rights for benefits in other economic sectors.

We will continue to seek flexible air fares within zones of reasonableness.

We will return to active participation in IATA and other international forums" [109].

The "Show Cause Order" of the CAB, scheduled to become effective in September 1981, was again extended and the effective date postponed for one year following the "Levitas Amendment", introduced by Congressman Elliott H. Levitas, Chairman of the Sub-committee referred to above (an Amendment brought to the so-called "Appropriation Bill") [110].

One of the reasons for the new postponement was related to the negotiations undertaken between the US and ECAC which might achieve, in the meaning of the US Administration, a more competitive and there-fore acceptable pricing system on the North Atlantic.

Upon the conclusion and later annual extensions of the Memorandum of Understanding, interim agreements have been reached and extended since July 1982.

On the other hand, most of the Third World States were included in the majority that opposed the US deregulation policy at both Special Air Transport Conferences called by the Organisation in 1977 and 1980.

Clearly, the Order directed against IATA was doomed to fail. It was finally withdrawn and the procedure terminated around the time the CAB itself ceased to exist. But this is more recent history. IATA, under pressure, had brought about some changes in its structures and proce-dures that would facilitate a smooth transition from multilateral pricing to more flexible approaches.

At the level of the international aviation community, the assault against IATA had created an unexpected reaction and had caused a number of governments, who had previously supported it rather reluc-tantly, to rally around the association. In general, the two Special Air Transport Conferences gave rise to a question : *to what extent was it necessary to amend the international regulatory system of air transport?*

## 6. An Australian Development

The IATA tariff coordination activities and resulting tariff agreements were the object of an investigation by the Australian Trade Practices Commission, at the time of a renewal of the authorisation granted to IATA as required by Australian competition laws.

The procedure resulted in the Commission granting authorisation to an application by IATA, dated 31 October 1984, subject to restrictive conditions.

Under Section 90(7) of the Trade Practices Act 1974, the Commission is forbidden to grant an authorisation unless it is satisfied that the arran-gements for whatever authorisation is sought have resulted or are likely to result in *a benefit to the public* and that that benefit outweighs or would outweigh the detriment to the public constituted by any lessening of competition that has resulted, or is likely to result, from giving effect to the provisions of the arrangements.

The Commission, in its 31 October 1984 decision, accepted that there is public benefit in IATA's *trade association activities*. It also accepted that this condition is met as far as preparation and availability of *tariff information* are concerned : agreements arrived at with respect to fares to the Australian market meet the condition by reason of the fare information extracted from them. Such tariffs provide a *point of reference*. However, the Commission *does not accept that these tariffs should be enforced*, which would preclude competitive pricing (or discounting!). IATA later applied for interim authorisation to continue all its activities *other than* compelling members to charge the fares set by carriers within IATA, not advertising tariffs they are charging or requiring agents to charge them or not to advertise them.

In effect, this attempt to outlaw IATA activities misfired, as it did in the US, for most practical purposes; IATA activities were essentially safeguarded.

But there were signals everywhere that caution was needed, and that tariff arrangements between carriers should leave room for innovation, if they were to be continued, in accordance with the various anti-trust laws.

Also, as a result of the Australian episode, there would be reasons to doubt that compliance actions would be permissible under most anti-trust legal systems.

The compulsory character of IATA tariff agreements was threatened, and this would largely contribute, in the long run, to a modification of the tariff activities themselves.

## 7. The Emergence of a Liberalising Policy in the United Kingdom

That the scene was changing was illustrated by the changing course of the United Kingdom : by, if not reversing its traditional policies, at least striving for its own original method of liberalising air transport.

### a) *The regulatory scene*

The main responsibilities for international civil aviation in the United Kingdom lie with the Department of Transport, which has an International Aviation Directorate headed by an Under-Secretary.

The Civil Aviation Act specifies the various duties of the Civil Aviation Authority, which include the regulation of the commercial activities of British airlines. The CAA is obliged to publish a statement of the policies which it will follow in pursuit of its economic licensing duties. Due account must be taken by the CAA of the interest of users as well as of airlines, "with the emphasis perhaps rather more in the users' favour than the airlines", according to one of its leading members, Ray Colegate in 1986 [111].

Parliament has taken an interest in air policies on several occasion and some of the most profound and accurate assessments of the problems of air transport are to be found in reports to the House of Lords. The Foreign and Commonwealth Office is the major Department where drafting and interpreting Air Transport Agreements are concerned, and it provides legal advice on the international law aspects of civil aviation.

b) *A new air policy*

The UK government decided to change its domestic air transport policy in 1980. In May 1981, the CAA made public its intentions regarding commercial aviation at large.

The CAA policy statement dealt with routes and pricing regimes. A more competitive environment was advocated, not because competition was a goal in itself, but because it would serve the interests of the users and foster the development of the national air transport industry. Scheduled air services did not need to be exclusively operated by specialised scheduled carriers : the distinction between scheduled and charter carriers, already blurred by the market evolution, was to disappear. However, the CAA put some safeguards on the indiscriminate lowering of air fares or launching of capacity beyond the predictable needs of the market : there was no intention whatsoever to recommend measures that might eventually endanger the economic activity sector.

According to the same line of reasoning, the allocation of routes to UK carriers should not be prejudiced by rigid pre-arranged areas of influence, as was the case previously. The profitability of the operators and the competitive ability of the carriers should be matters of concern to the licensing authority. A series of cumulative criteria were set out.

This set of balanced principles certainly served as guidelines to the UK government for the deployment of its policy, and may even be referred to as an early indication of what a European-style deregulation of air transport might look like — although, at the time, it certainly did not appear so on the Continent, and the UK itself would at later stages radicalise its position.

But the main feature of the British deregulation lay in the facts of air services : the Laker "Sky Train" operation and, more essentially, the difficult privatisation of British Airways.

In 1979, the novelty of the concept of denationalisation applied to Britain's most prestigious state-owned company made it appear like little more than a slogan reflecting "a forlorn Tory hope".

It took, indeed, eight years to complete the privatisation of British Airways in 1987. BA went through the painstaking process of a "fitness cure", following the criticism expressed in 1981 and 1982, and the various difficulties it experienced, which might have affected the position of the airline on the market of private investors.

At the time, the Conservative government had decided, in 1979, to sell at least half its ownership off to the private sector. One of the most significant developments which affected BA's privatisation, and tested the intentions of the Government was also to have an influence on European and even world-wide deregulation of air transport : the *Laker phenomenon*.

We have referred earlier to the legal vacuum left by ICAO regarding the *nature* of charter flights offered to the public in systematic series. In such cases, it was left to the government authorities to decide whether such flights were treated as scheduled or non-scheduled, in conformity with their domestic rule.

Freddy Laker's "*Sky-train*" operation threatened any clear cut definition. In common with charter flights, it offered a simplified low-cost product, but without the intervention of intermediairies and reservation of seats in the classic sense and without sophisticated in-flight meals. The "no-frills" "first-come-first-served" air service was invented.

However, the "Sky Train" was operated on a regular basis on major routes. In that sense, it required the type of authorisation which scheduled services received and it was to compete on the same markets as those on which scheduled airlines operated. Sir Freddy met some problems in obtaining this authorisation from the UK government, a time-consuming process, but the uphill fight went on for an even longer period in the United States, even though this country had begun advertising its "open sky" policy. The sharp fall of the pound against the US dollar after 1980 damaged the "Sky Train" operation more than bureaucratic obstacles. Laker Airways' debt, contracted to purchase a fleet of DC 10 aircraft, had considerably exceeded its equity by early 1981, when Sir Freddy borrowed another huge amount to purchase three of the new A-300 Airbus planes.

As traffic figures had been discouraging for some time, further banking support was refused to Laker Airways, and desperate lasthour attempts to rescue the airline failed. Sir Freddy was convinced that he had been the victim of a conspiracy and decided to claim compensation from competitors and manufacturers in what was to become the mammoth *"Laker case"*. This lawsuit raised a number of legal issues that were to modify the legal landscape of international air transport. A conflict was created after a judgment on jurisdiction had shown where the "long arm" of the US anti-trust law was now extending in air transport matters. The extra-territorial application of domestic law was becoming a major issue. The amounts of money involved were rocketing sky-high. But the principles at stake were no less important and pitfall had been created, which might cause enduring damage to international air relations. The case was settled.

But judges and magistrates of the highest level in the United Kingdom were made aware of the problem, and bodies like ICAO and the International Chamber of Commerce were alerted.

To review this important development in further detail would take us far beyond this brief outline of British aeronautical policy.

The implementation of the United Kingdom's new liberal policy on the international scene can be found in the *bilateral agreements* concluded by the UK since 1977, essentially with a number of European countries [112].

The direction followed in those bilaterals is the following.

a) *Routes*

The United Kingdom, interestingly, returned to the open route structure. For instance, in the June 1984 arrangement with the Netherlands, each country is authorised to operate over any route between the United Kingdom (including the Channel Islands) and the Netherlands, with one qualification only, relating to toutes on which demand for traffic is low. The aeronautical authorities will consult each other before designating an airline to operate a service on such a route if such action would seem likely to threaten the economic viability of the service provided by an incumbent airline.

An equally general drafting may be found in the UK-Federal Republic of Germany arrangement of December 1984. The limitation here is that airports must have sufficient facilities to accommodate the proposed service.

Furthermore, the above arrangements allowed for the combination of services to any two points in the territory of the other country.

### b) *Traffic rights*

Full traffic rights are exchanged between parties, *except fifth freedom rights* (unless specifically agreed).

These "open" third and fourth freedom rights are related to the new routes described in the arrangement between the two countries, in the strict territorial sense. For all other routes on the existing bilateral agreement, nothing new is introduced.

The granting of traffic rights to all "points in the United Kingdom" facilitates the development of regional services, hence regional airports, whether by aircraft operated by UK or foreign airlines. This objective is an important part of British air policy.

### c) *Multidesignation*

The faculty to designate several carriers on all routes is essential to the philosophy of the UK new style agreements, as it was for the US liberalising agreements.

### d) *Capacity*

The approach of the United Kingdom has always been essentially pragmatic. "Whether the United Kingdom prefers capacity to be regulated by Bermuda 1 principles or predetermined will depend largely on the circumstances; and in some cases it will have no choice if the other Government insists (as they often do) on predetermination. In some cases predetermination may be necessary in order to shield UK airlines against either powerful foreign airlines (such as US airlines) or against foreign competitors who in practice abuse their rights by wholesale discounting of fares, carriage of an undue proportion of 6th freedom traffic (albeit disguised by devices such as double ticketing), or where the foreign Government places UK airlines at a competitive disadvantage, for example by fiscal or administrative measures which distort free access to the market or delay the repatriation of earnings". (Tony Aust, Legal Counsellor, Foreign and Commonwealth Office) [113].

In new liberal arrangements, as with the Netherlands, each designated airline is free to provide the capacity it deems appropriate without the prior agreement of the other country's aeronautical authorities or an agreement with the airline designated by the other country. However, the aeronautical authorities must consult each other if either of them considers that the interests of its own airlines on a particular route are being seriously damaged.

Only in the arrangement with Luxembourg did the UK conclude a deal on the basis of the primary traffic criterion This more classic approach was destined to prevent an excess of traffic with third countries on the low density route between the United Kingdom and Luxembourg — a new example of the pragmatic approach ...

e) *Tariffs*

*Considering their obligations under the Rome Treaty*, the governments of the United Kingdom and the Netherlands have agreed no longer to require their respective airlines to consult other airlines before filing tariff proposals. The UK government had already stated in 1984 that it no longer considered itself bound by this "mandatory consultation" clause of the 1967 Paris Agreement for the Establishment of Tariffs for Scheduled Air Services : this clause was, in its view, incompatible with its obligations under the EEC Treaty.

The UK Administration, of course, favoured the double disapproval clause which was adopted in several of the new arrangements, on the condition of tariffs not being predatory. (Netherlands and Belgium), and additionally (Belgium) that it could not be demonstrated that the fares used had detrimental effects on the normal profitability of the operations.

However indicative of the new policy intentions of the United Kindgom, these "arrangements" (which did not replace previous bilaterals, but superseded them partially and temporarily) were essentially designed to demonstrate the positive effects of this policy and to pressure the other European governments into following the same course to a certain extent : once they had compromised on such bilateral deals, it would become more difficult for those governments to oppose bluntly, in the EEC Council, the very principles they had adhered to bilaterally with the British.

To substantiate their doctrine, the UK negotiators and politicians could demonstrate the positive effects of the domestic deregulation on the traffic between London and regional airports in the UK. While some routes (London-Edinburgh) progressed beyond average, air traffic growth on domestic routes, in the first year of deregulation, averaged some 7 % [114]. Deregulation also resulted in some lowering of fares.

The trend in question would be questioned, later on, when figures showed a stabilisation of both traffic and fare levels.

The UK air policy was vigourously pursued, defended in the European Parliament, and argued with considerable skill in the Council of Ministers of the EEC. Quite distinct from the US "open sky" policy, this mitigated policy finally found echos on the Continent and definitely paved the way for increased competition on European routes. While it was apparent that the UK airlines were more numerous and stronger than those on the Continent, and their national potential and transit possibilities were by comparison unlimited, there was, on the other hand, no alternative policy worth mentioning, and the US push in the same direction could not, in the long term, be resisted by industrialised countries. UK airlines, such as British Caledonian Airlines, engaged in a merciless combat with British Airways, cleverly showed its colleagues that additional aggressiveness on the market was compatible with a cautious course and sound management techniques, and even preserved some forms of airline cooperation, such as tariff coordination through IATA.

Ultimately, the trend towards concentration, that goes along with liberalisation would be illustrated in the United Kingdom by the merger between British Airways and British Caledonian Airways, subsequent to the privatisation of British Airways. (However, the scope for cross-border mergers and equity stakes in foreign airlines remained constrained, as shown by the CAA decision in considering a proposal of SAS in 1987).

All in all, it is important to note the particular influence of the British policy on the de-regulation of air transport.

PART V

# The developing world

# CHAPTER 1

## AN OBSERVATION
## ON THE DEVELOPING WORLD

In theory, the latent revolution in the international regulatory system, not unlike the system itself, was a worldwide phenomenon. If all nations of the world were declared capable and entitled to participate in aviation activities, the weakest among them would logically be most interested in maintaining this system of law because they would be most severely hit by its disappearance : the harsh facts of economic life alone could not secure their rights.

The developing nations, made aware of their number and political influence on the international scene, indeed worked within the system to assure its existence, while strenghtening the equalising principles of the Chicago Convention and inclining the bilateral air transport agreements towards additional protective measures and the sharing of economic benefits.

They certainly made some headway in the Special Air Transport Conferences of ICAO in moderating the influences that threatened to break the structures. For instance, the considerable support obtained by Recommendations in favour of the continuation of multilateral tariff coordination was due to the convincing arguments of speakers from developing countries.

This trend was contrary to the impulse towards a more competitive environment felt in other parts of the world. Developing nations sought for their aviation more international legal protection, more national rights, a less discriminatory access to the market, a more equitable repartition of aviation resources and adequate aid from the international community to compensate for their economic weakness for as long as was necessary to secure their ability to compete on an equal footing with the large airlines of the industrialised world. They advocated modifications of the Chicago system to the extent required by those conditions. The industrialized nations advocated a different modification, towards more flexibility than the system itself allowed for. The latent revolution was a different one for each of the two groups of nations concerned.

Basically, the general economic evolution which we observe is a malaise that necessarily spreads to the whole body : all the components of internal civil aviation are interconnected and interdependent. But the symptoms are different in the North and in the South, in the industrialised countries and in the Third World, because of the overall dissymetry in economic and social developments. The feeling, let alone the obligation of global solidarity has faded away, and possibly disappeared for some time.

In 1978, the final Report of a "think tank" on a Coordinated Policy for international Commercial Aviation, convened by the Graduate Institute of International Studies in Geneva was published. After only a few years, the main concluding remark of this report may appear somewhat naive : „The regulatory system for international civil aviation should be considered as a whole, embracing all types of carriers, all types of services, and all governments ... Any regulatory policy action taken with respect to any region of the world inevitably spreads and affects other regions as well.

The major need not being met today is the need for a common international approach to the regulation of international civil aviation services ... It is important that great care be exercized by governments intending to take unilateral or bilateral action that will force change on the system, even if such action seems to be well-conceived and justified ..." [115].

Yet this advice has never been better timed. It would be a tragedy if the governments of the industrialised world underestimated or lost sight of the fact that developing countries have specific problems and hold different views, and did not realise the deep-reaching effects of their actions on the legal international structure and the global solidarity of interests.

# CHAPTER 2

## SOME COMMON CHARACTERISTICS

In his report to the Club of Rome in 1980 [116], Maurice Guernier described the structural imbalances between the developed countries and the Third World. Specific factors taken into account were the following : the demographic explosion : the generally tropical conditions; the lack of adequately trained professional and managerial elites; social structures inappropriate to the demands of technological development; economic distortions brought about by international aid even when foreseen; and free international trade "which ends up by imposing the law of the most powerful" [117]. Being a technology and a trade, civil aviation is a favourable ground for the convergence of most of these evils.

There exist wide disparities in size and wealth between developing countries. But "they share a common plight which will assume greater proportions in the future, notwithstanding the easing of oil supplies though not so much of oil prices". "They are essentially primary producing countries and the terms of trade have historically shifted against them" [118].

The problem facing airlines in developing countries, against this common background, offer many similarities.

# CHAPTER 3

## SIMILAR PROBLEMS

These problems include "large capital investment requirements, steep fuel cost increases, obsolescent fleets, economic recession, diminishing yields, inadequate airport facilities, the need for adequately trained personnel and for availibility of expert advice, and problems of sparse route networks and narrow market penetration. Worse still, they share the harsh industry climate with the large airlines with vast resources" (Laban Agala) [119].

Some commentators add to the list, specifically : "deregulation in civil air transportation which was prompted by the US at the urging of US consumerism" (Khaled Bitar) [120].

Indeed, the great majority of airlines are state-owned and "their fate, by definition, *cannot be left to the free and occasionally devastating forces of the marketplace*" [121].

All the developing countries together account for, at the most, 40 % of world traffic. They often depend on Western or Eastern industrialised countries for hardware, technology, financial and expert assistance : given the thin air traffic and large distances between their hubs and their meagre resources, they can seldom afford large airlines and their competitive strength is a victim of this vicious circle.

In fact, facing so many similar problems, the airlines of the developing world need to rely more on *cooperation* than on *competition*, if a choice has to be made between the two driving forces underlying the regulatory system of international air transport.

Their countries need, first of all, to cooperate with each other on a regional basis and to seek solutions together to their common problems. The route network and market problems, for instance, have been envisaged for the whole of Africa by regional organisations and would include the exchange of fifth freedom rights to improve the African Grid. The common use of traffic rights by a group of States would strengthen their negotiating hand in bilateral discussions with third countries. Staff exchange programmes, such as cross-postings, "will result in cross-fertilization of ideas which will have a most beneficial effect" [122].

But the question remains as to where the boundaries lie between regional and international cooperation.

Cooperation with industrialised countries, though aimed at more direct remedies, is just as essential.

CHAPTER 4

## DEVELOPING COUNTRIES
## AND THE REGULATORY FRAMEWORK

The observation made at the beginning of this section already reflected the main direction in which the Third World would go, if it were given a chance to express itself : towards a *more equitable access* to the air transport market, within the existing global legal and institutional structure. However, if the present structures do not satisfy its needs, alternatives should be developed (like an African Tariff Conference to substitute for IATA, if needed, or the concept of resorting to UNCTAD to benefit from more equitable conditions of services).

The regulatory policy is developed at national, bilateral and multi-lateral level.

a) *National air policy*

National identification with their airlines is particularily strong in developing countries. These play an essential role in their economic and social development, promote trade and tourism, secure often indispensable supplies of goods, generate employment, bring in foreign exchange and help the national image and prestige of new nations. But financial resources are in many cases scarce : the decision to set up an airline is a costly one, implemented to the detriment of other necessities, and the airline must serve social, as well as commercial goals, thus contributing to its national importance.

The legal status of the national airline is therefore usually protective and weighed down with constraints and obligations for the carrier, who is obliged to operate services or offer fares for social reasons.

Public ownership and control of national airlines is normal in the developing world in view of their quasi-"public utility" role, not to mention extraneous political reasons, like strategy and defence.

Political and economic reasons may exist together to strengthen the importance of national carriers, as in the case of enclosed countries surrounded by politically hostile neighbours and cut off from seaports.

There are a number of different situations which entail the need to maintain, protect and develop national airlines.

b) *Bilateral negotiations*

Within the bilateral framework which remained intact, the Third World countries have developed policies of their own.

Essentially, the "fair and equal opportunity" principle was deliberately stretched to the point where it amounted to equal sharing of national resources, air traffic rights being regarded as resources in limited supply, and the opportunities coinciding with economic returns.

This philosophy is based on the necessity to minimise the negative effect of a weaker position at the outset and to ensure an adequate balance of *benefits*, despite the disparity of means which generally works to the advantage of the other contracting country.

The original concept of the Chicago Convention and the Bermuda Agreement related to the principle *framework* in which capacity could be supplied by the designated carriers. This framework consists of complete equality of chances to gain access to the market and to compete, provided the airlines are willing to supply the capacity and have the means to do so. The extent to which each of them uses this possibility depends on their judgment and on the means available to them; equality of chances is not a requirement that the carriers on both sides of a bilateral transaction should provide the same capacity.

The dilemma lies in the disparity of means which, in the case of developing countries, corrupts the equality of chances and makes it purely nominal. While the interpretation given by developing countries to the Bermudian capacity clause may be deemed consistent with the basic rationale of the rule — to ensure equal access to all aviation markets of all nations of the world — the distortion is ultimately dangerous for all concerned in that it leads to the most rigid form of bilateralism and the final deadlock of a confrontation of national protectionism.

What the situation of developing countries requires is a new and different assessment of their essential interests in commercial aviation, and what benefits they need to derive from international deals in this area, due account being taken of the context of those relations.

Innovative clauses should be introduced to take account of the *nature* of the advantages to be gained in the bilateral trade-off. For instance, if the priority of technology transfer, in the form of personnel training, has been recognised, it would be conceivable to organise an exchange of rights for which the "quid pro quo" would be weighed in such terms of value within a bilateral "ad hoc" arrangement with an industrialized country. Traffic rights traded for training funds and sessions : would the long term aviation interest of the developing country not be better preserved in such an exchange than if commissions or royalties were to be paid by a foreign operating carrier under the umbrella of a questionable legal principle?

In other areas covered by bilateral agreements, the instrument of regulation has served the purpose of balancing interests through a strict adherence to the principles of the Chicago-Bermuda orthodoxy. On such matters as entry, designation and foreign carrier fifth freedom rights, the careful observance of established practice contributes to economic equity and protects the weakest partners. In tariff matters, similarly, "divergent economic approaches were balanced in the context of multi-laterally agreed minimum prices, through the medium of IATA". (Gideon H. Kaunda) [123]. The multilateral coordination of air tariffs is indeed in the interest of the airlines of developing countries, provided it is *effectively* conducive to equality of participation in all tariffs and, in particular, that through-fares are made available on all IATA member airlines by means of interlining. Unfortunately, this has not always been the case, as some European airlines have launched so-called "point-to-point" fares in which African airlines, for instance, could not participate. The bilateral reference to the concertation of fares in IATA was thereby deprived of its anticipated harmonising and equalising effect.

African airlines have opposed such practices as being contrary to the principles of equal access and non-discrimination which are rooted in the international regulatory system. Their objections on those grounds appear to have been legally founded.

Understandably, few of the developing countries adhered to the US deregulation policy and concluded liberal bilateral air transport agreements. "The distributional implications of such a policy to many airlines of developing nations require a different formula. Free capacity and free entry would favour the stronger aviation countries by the sheer size of their market and other resources. In fact, the bilateral process itself is predicated upon prior regulatory arrangements and cannot be construed as a concept by the competitive market model" (Gideon H. Kaunda) [124].

### c) *Multilateral level*

The popular picture that negotiations that count are bilateral is false. The recognition of the specific requirements of emerging countries in aviation was achieved in ICAO. There the political weight of the Third World could be felt.

In particular, the three ICAO Special Air Transport Conferences provided ample opportunity for disclosing the views and wishes of the Third World, and the meetings achieved at least a better understanding of the problems, if not a narrowing of the gap between countries. In some instances, a consensus was reached because of such mutual understanding, based on a common appraisal of common interests, despite recognised differences. For instance, air fares are a dividing issue. Yet the fear of unilateral pricing and a kind of "implosion" of the system was largely shared by the developing countries and the Conference supported the view that multilateral coordination of fares and rates was in the interest of all and should be continued.

In matters relating to capacity, it was argued by the developing countries, and more or less recognised by others, that the "fair and equal opportunity" clause really meant "equality and mutual benefit", in other words that the concept of "opportunities" was to be translated in financial terms, on the basis of the yield derived by the airlines operating services between the territories of the contracting States.

*This, incidentally left no doubt about the desire of third world countries to develop a stricter conception of capacity, for both scheduled and non-scheduled services.*

The 1984 Conference rejected unilateral application of national anti-trust laws on a motion which received massive support from the developing countries.

It was obvious in the 1977 and 1980 Conferences that "the majority of States that resisted US deregulation policy included most of those in the Third World" [125]. Generally speaking, any doctrine or practice that might constitute a threat to their fragile economy gave rise to reactions from the developing countries. These reactions were not necessarily conservative, and some new interesting ideas emerged. But there are limits to what such meetings can achieve, under the circumstances.

d) *Conclusion*

The complementarity of States and airlines is often greater in developing countries than in others, but the nationalistic reaction is finally identical in all.

On the other hand, these countries tend to join forces with their neighbours. Regionalism is at work and this is another aspect to take note of. Regional *cooperation* between developing countries and between their airlines is an important development, consistent with the evolution in other parts of the world (Europe).

But the main question that now needs to be posed is whether the developing countries will be forced to choose a *separate* regulatory solution to their problems, instead of remaining with the rest of the world. The international air transport system benefits from a unique worldwide integration. It is not impossible that dislocation will result from the *unconscious* choices which developed countries, for instance in Europe, will make for themselves. Their choice should be inventive with regard to the forms of cooperation with the Third World in aviation matters, and inspired by the necessity to accommodate different paces of development within a single system.

The President of the Club of Rome, Aurelio Peccei, has warned in the conclusion of his reflections : *"In order to make human affairs manageable, it is essential for the South to be integrated organically into the global system* [126].

# PART VI

# The State of Europe

# CHAPTER 1

## "LEARN FROM AMERICA"

The offensive of the United States in favour of its "open skies" policy met with mitigated success and even encountered massive opposition in ICAO. But the conjectural element of foreign policy could make it succeed in the end, even though it was doomed to fail in appearance. Ideas may fall on fertile grounds and yet take some time to ripen.

Possibly, the US Administration, when launching its campaign, had planned to exercise that sort of influence rather than to re-shape the international landscape overnight. To achieve at least a "greater competition in international aviation" was a reasonable aim to pursue by different methods [127].

The exportation by the US of their domestic policy certainly was one such method, but perhaps too simplistic a method to be the best. Henry A. Kissinger had warned that times were changing and that a "direct" "operational" concept of international order was proving too simple. *"Political multipolarity makes it impossible to impose an American design. Our deepest challenge will be to evoke the creativity of a pluralistic world"*[128].

The consumerist movement proved such a vehicle apt to carry certain questions from one side of the Atlantic to the other. After all, there were some striking similarities between the situation in Europe in 1979-80 and in the United States in 1975-76, as Professor Löwenfeld observed : "controls on market entry, absence of price competition, low load factors, high fares, and inadequate profits".

Of course, there were also substantial differences, essentially legal and political : instead of one country, there were twenty-two sovereign States with different social needs and legal systems which subjected that many air transport markets to the dictates of sovereignty and national interests.

But as the same questions occur to the European consumer, there was little wonder, Löwenfeld concluded, that the Commission of the European Community "asks whether Europe cannot learn from America, even as it borrowed the basic idea of a customs union from sea to shining sea" [129].

Hans Raben, Director General of the Civil Aviation Authority of the Netherlands, concurred with the American expert in air law, Löwenfeld, when he declared : "Today air transport in Europe is a fully grown industrial activity, operating in a well developed market characterised by an extensive and diversified demand. It would be normal under any circumstance to check whether the regulatory system devised for one situation is still adequate for the other" [130].

Others (the BEUC, Bureau Européen des Unions de Consommateurs) put the question even more bluntly : who was to take the blame, if not the airlines? "Europe has a sophisticated air transport market mainly oriented to the interests of airline staffs and ill adapted to the needs of users" [131]. As gross an exaggeration as this statement may have been, airlines were bombarded with reports criticising their modes of operation. Then some politicians in the UK and elsewhere took to the game. Several of them have made "airline bashing" a full time job and "have used the courts as well as the hustings to pursue their cases against the alleged shortcomings of the air transport system" [132].

We have analysed the tendencies reflected in extreme liberal statements issued on many occasions [133].

In the middle of this turmoil, the EC Commission kept its calm. It knew from experience that powerful political obstacles were in the way of liberalisation of air transport. A radical overhaul of the regulatory system was not needed in the short term. Copying the deregulation policy of the United States "just could not work within the Common Market, with its completely different structure of the industry in comparison with the USA", an official of the Commission declared. The Commission stated in its first Memorandum that it was seeking to find *an original solution*, while recognising the need to "learn from America".

An objective was also to increase the efficiency of European carriers following the US model : "Without competition, what will discipline carriers to achieve efficiency?", the last CAB Chairman, Marvin Cohen had asked. The new ideas were definitely floated in Europe. And no alternative philosophy was advanced ...

# CHAPTER 2

## MIXED FEELINGS

The willingness to examine these new ideas, let alone to apply them, was far from universal. The advocates of liberalisation were vocal, but received political support of some significance from only three or four countries of the Communities, at least for some time.

The Netherlands and the United Kingdom were the leaders. But a majority of ECAC Member States, among which were the Southern members of the European Economic Community, resented or opposed any attempt to destabilise the present regulatory system. They would agree, eventually, on the necessity of "achieving a greater degree of controlled competition" and even on "the urgent need for promoting a more innovative, competitive and efficient air transport system in Europe" [134].

But the concept of *controlled competition* implied a general recognition of the need to avoid any disruption of the regulatory framework.

New entrants to the EEC, Portugal and Spain, and likewise Greece, used arguments from the international framework derived from the Chicago Convention, which protects the right of all countries irrespective of their state of development to participate evenly in the air transport market. But they also cited the Rome Treaty :

"One of the theoretical purposes of the Community is the reduction of inequalities between the level of development of Member States", noted Mr. Mota, an official of TAP, the Portugese national airline. "It would be quite illogical that concrete measures would result in elevating inequalities and favoring those who already have the strongest positions" [135].

This impeccable line of reasons marked a potential political fracture among EEC Member States on an issue which was indeed to divide them for a long time and cripple the means of decision of the Council of Ministers as long as the unanimity rule of Article 84, paragraph 2 of the EEC Treaty was applicable to common measures of policy in the air transport field.

However, the quest for an European identity in air transport had been going on for a long time.

# CHAPTER 3

## A LONG QUEST

## 1. First Approach

For a brief moment, after World War Two, Europe was an ideological society. It would become a bureaucratic-mercantile society somewhere in the sixties. (Nothing prevents it from being born again as an ideological-pragmatic society, in the nineties).

The primary concept of a united Europe, as seen by Schumann, Adenauer, de Gasperi and the other statesmen who carried the idea through its first experiments, like Paul-Henry Spaak, included political, as well as full economic solidarity of all the countries of Western Europe. This certainly involved transport as a basic vehicle of freedom of movement in trade and services. It would not have been logical to leave air transport aside, and indeed a common airspace for all the parts of the new entity seemed a fairly obvious concept to formulate and test.

It was, in fact, envisaged that transport integration would precede common policies aiming at economic union at large' of which a coal and steel union under an High Authority was, in the early fifties, a precursory step. The Vice-President of this High Authority for coal and steel, Albert Coppé, noted on this point :

"If the revolution of the sixties in transport had taken place earlier, Schumann and Adenauer would never have limited their goals to coal and steel integration" [136] But did they limit their goals? "No political solution withouth an economic solution, and vice-versa", Paul-Henri Spaak declared. In 1955, transport was an important objective of the preparatory working sessions which were to set up a common market. The Val Duchesse Castle sessions of July 1955 in Brussels, which prepared the ground for the Rome Treaty, dealt with transport (specifically *incluiding air and sea transport*) and public works as one of the four essential areas to be investigated.

"The means of transportation cross borders constantly : that is where Europe could sweep away obstacles and regimes of nationalistic inspiration" [137].

It was a disappointment that transport happened to be the most difficult activity to accommode in the Treaty.

As early as 1950, the *Bonnefous plan* and the *Sforza plan* envisaged a common European airspace and a single airline for the whole of Europe. A variant, the *Van de Kieft proposal* (1951), referred to a consortium or syndicate of airline companies and put forward the idea of calling an international European Conference to examine the constitution of this joint operating agency, to be put in charge of providing intra-European air services. The Parliamentary Assembly of the Council of Europe retained this suggestion, but the Council of Ministers considerably restricted the objective of the conference which it decided to convene, in that it refused to prejudge the issue of a common air transport company. In its 1953 decision, it left the choice of the means to the Conference : the objective was to improve the commercial and technical operations of the airlines engaged in air transportation between participating countries, and the cooperation between them with respect to commercial traffic rights in Europe.

Reference was made to the Sforza plan and to "a European Air Union", as one of the possibilities to explore.

Clearly, *the initial concept of an air transport policy in Europe was based on a political vision of a unified European system and essentially relied on cooperation to realise this vision.*

The modern technology of aviation would soon prove the national structures obsolete. Air transport was a privileged field for European integration, which a unified air transport system would foster by its momentum.

## 2. SAS and AIR UNION : Experiments in Joint Ventures

The closest Europe came to an original formula was the attempt to set up a joint operating airline company. As seen above, the inspiration was political. In a report of the Commission on Economic Questions of the Consultative Assembly of the Council of the Europe, dated 26 November 1951, reference was made to the inadequate dominant political forms and the necessity for the European airlines to achieve together "through a logical distribution of work, the reduction in production costs, the lowering of fares, and the development of air traffic".

### 1. The Scandinavian Airlines System (SAS)

*The example of SAS* gave food for thought to those who dreamed of a common European air transport industry.

Denmark, Norway and Sweden concluded in 1951 an Agreement relating to cooperation in civil aviation matters [138].

The legal basis for the creation and functioning of the SAS is this intergovernmental Agreement, as amended and complemented by subsequent instruments. The three Contracting States ensured coordination of their regulations and air transport policies. The consortium itself was set up, also in 1951, with, as its main objective, the "harmonious expansion of European air transport in the worldwide competition".

The complex system by which the support of the governments involved was ensured made the existence of SAS safe in a number of respects and more dependent on a public law system and inter-Scandinavian politics than any ordinary commercial company in any particular country. But the company itself, curiously devoid of a legal personality of its own and relying on its components, the three original national airlines, is a commercial entity with a flexible form which has proved efficient. Each participating airline remains the owner of its fleet, registered in its own country.

Bilateral agreements have been re-negotiated to include a waiver of the normal clause of designation, in respect of nationality of aircraft and crews.

## 2. *The pre-conditions of AIR UNION*

To extend such concept to other European countries required a political consensus to do away with competition and national individual images. Moreover, an international body should be in control. The Contracting States would have to relinquish part of their sovereignty prerogatives to this institution. The airline would take its decisions on commercial criteria of its own, not necessarily in line with narrowly conceived "national" interests. This system would actually result in the creation of a *common air space*.

Regarding traffic rights, the example of SAS would be followed, "mutatis mutandis". The common airline would, one day, through a gradual process, be designated as the instrument of each bilateral agreement involving Contracting States. At the outset, the negotiating capabilities of all partners would be pooled.

A pre-condition was that the participating airlines would agree within AIR UNION on their respective share of the markets.

### 3. *The structure of AIR UNION*

#### a) *The AIR UNION Convention*

The Contracting States (the Federal Republic of Germany, Belgium, Italy and France) were to sign a Convention approving the constitutive Pact and creating certain obligations for the governments which included entrusting the AIR UNION member airlines with the right to exercise their current and future traffic rights on international scheduled services.

The draft Convention referred to Articles 44, 77 and 79 of the Chicago Convention.

#### b) *The Pact of Association*

The airlines, Air France (acting also on behalf of UTA), Alitalia, Deutsche Lufthansa and Sabena (KLM had withdrawn from the project in 1959), agreed to proceed with the commercial operations in relation to their respective traffic. Certain exclusions were provided for. However, *their middle term objective was full integration*, through gradual coordination of their operational and technical means.

They allocated capacity among themselves according to agreed *quotas*.

### 4. *Failure*

The discussion for the quotas was long and difficult. Despite the delays, due in part to the excessive desire of the would-be partners to finalise the project in detail, the airlines worked steadily towards their objective and all but met their target.

But time passed; the fear of the consequences of the introduction of jet aircraft diminished and the pressure within the airlines for a reduction of competition was reduced accordingly. The high performance aircraft were less of a threat than had been anticipated.

Politically, the concept weakened rapidly. France became reluctant to give away parcels of its sovereignty. Considerations of defence were involved : in the end, De Gaulle vetoed the project. In 1966, it was evident that the governments concerned would not consent to the Convention and the AIR UNION project, to which much effort had been devoted, was given up.

## 3. The European Economic Community

#### a) *The conclusion of the EEC Treaty (1957)*

The EEC was established in March 1957 under the Rome Treaty [139]. Six countries (France, the Federal Republic of Germany, Italy, Belgium the Netherlands and Luxembourg) decided to create a *"common market"*, which included certain *freedoms* enumerated in the Treaty. Transport activities were indispensable to the implementation of those freedoms.

However, transport was difficult to include in an organisational scheme, particularly air and sea transport, due to their wide international context. A section of the Treaty dealt with the subject in a general manner, providing summary guidelines for a sectorial policy, but even those guidelines were not applicable to air and sea transport, which might be subjected to further measures to be decided unanimously by the Council of Ministers at a later stage.

*Note :* Twelve countries are currently Members of the EEC [140].

b) *Treaty provisions*

Consistent with these developments, the Treaty contains the following relevant provisions :

*Article 3*

"For the purposes set out in Article 2, the activities of the Community shall include, as provided in this Treaty and in accordance with the timetable set out therein" :

"c) the abolition, as between Member States, of obstacles to freedom of movement for persons, services and capital;

d) ...

e) the adoption of a common policy in the sphere of transport;

f) the institution of a system ensuring that competition in the common market is not distorted;"

*Article 74*

"The objectives of this Treaty shall, in matters governed by this title, be pursued by Member States within the framework of a common transport policy".

*Article 84*

"1. The provisions of this title shall apply to transport by rail, road and inland waterways.

2. The Council may, acting unanimously, decide whether, to what extent and by what procedure appropriate provisions may be laid down for sea and air transport".

c) *Immobilisation until 1974*

Legally, the thesis was sustained for several years that air and sea sectors were virtually outside the Treaty in its entirety, subject only to any Council decisions, adopted on the basis of Article 84 by unanimity.

The opinion of air law experts, such as Louis Cartou, was firmly in favour of this thesis [141]. Community law experts were hesitant. The point was argued that Article 84 even precluded the Commission from making proposals in the fields of air and sea transport. At any rate, when Regulation 1017 was adopted in order to implement the competition rules of the Treaty in the sector of transport, air and sea transport were explicitly excluded from its scope.

The legal discussion did not prevent the Commission from putting forward a proposal in 1970. The European Parliament discussed this proposal on the basis of a report of the Italian Senator Luigi Noe. The proposal intended to "rationalise" the intra-European air services network and emphasised the necessity to reinforce cooperation between European airlines : their equipment should be integrated and commercial traffic rights beween European countries would be automatically exchanged.

The report was followed by a draft Council's Decision [142] which was approved by the Council (19 October 1972) and again submitted to the Assembly and to the Economic and Social Committee. These bodies expressed opinions, in respectively, a second "Noe Report" and a "De Grave Report", *both concluding in favour of a strong integration of EEC airlines and a "common air space" upon which the Commission would exercise regulatory jurisdiction.*

However, the political winds were already changing and the adoption of the Council's Regulation in application of Article 84, para. 2 of the Treaty seemed more remote than ever. The Commission felt that no real progress could be accomplished in a direction where national interests inevitably interfered. Moreover, its powers of initiative were considerably impaired by the legal deadlock.

d) *The "French Seamen's case".*

Developments of a legal nature have been important in the difficult history of the EEC common air transport policy.

The first of such developments was the judgment of the European Court of Justice in Case 167/73 (Commission v. France) known as the "French Seamen's case" [143].

This decision, dated 4 April 1974, is a landmark. Not only did the Court declare the principle of the applicability of the general rules of the Treaty to sea (hence to air) transport, it also created the basis for a common policy in these fields, legally speaking, and opened a process of successive legal clarification of the Treaty's intentions.

The case had to do with a provision of a French law (the Code du Travail Maritime) which required that a certain percentage of personnel of French nationality be employed on board French merchant vessels. The Commission won its case in a proceeding founded on Article 169 of the Treaty. The French Republic had contended that the maritime sector did not fall within the scope of the Treaty, by virtue of Article 84, while the Commission found the discrimination by nationality to constitute an infringement of the provisions of the Treaty and of other relevant Community law (Council's Regulation 1612/68). The Court resolved the controversy born from Title IV of the Treaty (on Transports), inserted in the general structure of the Treaty, and from the rather obscure language of Article 84, par. 2. The Court came back to the basic principle of the Common Market, which should, according to Article 2, embrace all economic activities within the Community. Therefore, the Court considered that the fundamental rules of the Treaty contained in Part II could not be waived unless by explicit stipulation of the Treaty. Article 84 does not bring about such an exclusion. The only exclusion entailed by Article 84, par. 2, the Court said, is from the provisions of Title IV, as long as the Council has not otherwise decided, as set forth in this article. Consequently, air and sea transport *remain, like other modes of transport, "subject to the general rules of the Treaty"* (Whereas n° 32).

This decision clarified the issue but it created, quite unnecessarily, a new ambiguity by referring to the "general rules" of the Treaty, a terminology unknown in the Treaty itself. Was the Title on Transport, Title IV, included among the "general rules" which, according to a certain doctrine, could only mean the first and second Parts of the Treaty? The third Part, which includes the rules on competition, would not be covered.

This new doubt was only to be lifted by the Court itself in 1986, in the so-called "Nouvelles Frontières" decision.

All in all, this 1974 judgement was a step forward, and an encouragement for the Commission to proceed.

### e) The Commission's proposals

The Commission did not take advantage of the Court's 1974 decision to act completely on its own and in fact came closer to governments of the Member States and their national carriers and manufacturers. The "Spinelli Report" (1975) and the "Scarascia-Mugnozza Communication" (1976) were sweeping attempts to reconcile a number of factors, including the interests of the European aircraft manufacturing industry. Air transport being a complex activity in itself, the ambitiousness of the Spinelli project more or less blurred the issues.

The Commission's activities gained momentum *in 1978*, when the Council adopted an informal working programme listing priority items for consideration, and the Commission followed its own line of thinking in a *first Memorandum* on the subject.

But this "Community approach" contained few concrete proposals and there were notable omissions : air fares, application of the competition rules. In 1981, the Commission complemented this approach by introducing a proposal for a directive containing procedures and criteria for the fixing of scheduled *air tariffs* for carriage between Member States.

During that period, the underlying concept became *increased competition* rather than *improved cooperation* : the political pendulum swung in the direction in which common views could form, at some stage ...

In 1984, *Memorandum nr. 2 of the Commission* [144] brought forward, at last, a coherent set of concrete proposals for the establishment of a common air transport policy.

This document, modestly described as : "Process towards the development of a Community air transport policy" was introduced in March 1984. It contained an accurate analysis of the situation of air transport in the world and in Europe and came up with the conclusion that a gradual liberalisation, rather than US style deregulation, "evolution rather than revolution", would serve the interests of all parties concerned. The proposals dealt with :

1) bilateral agreements between Community States to be harmonised with respect to *tariff* and *capacity*, and

2) the application of the *competition rules* of the Treaty.

Those three main issues would focus the discussion, yet a fourth important subject was dealt with in a subdued tone : *market access*. This subject would soon prove to be inseparable from the others. Furthermore, the Commission indicated the broadlines of its policy on *State aid*.

Regarding *capacity*, the Commission proposed a zone for free capacity introduction : States would intervene only to protect their national carriers if their part fell to 25 % of the market.

In *tariff* matters, the proposal introduced the concept of *zones* of non-intervention or approval by one State only, as an optional means of introducing more flexibility and permitting the introduction of innovative fares.

As to the *competition rules* of the Treaty, they would apply *between Community airports only for an initial period of seven years*.

The proposal contained exemptions from the prohibition set forth in Article 85 and specified exceptions in favour of certain cooperative activities of the airlines, such as tariff coordination and commercial agreements, under certain conditions and provided the entire package of the Commission's proposals were adopted by the Council of Ministers of the Community.

The problem of *market access* was cautiously approached by the Commission — too cautiously perhaps, as governments themselves found it necessary, at a later stage, to deal with the subject somewhat more explicitly.

In fact, the Commission proposed, and the Council adopted in 1983, a *Directive on inter-regional services* [145]. The scope and actual importance of this Directive had been considerably reduced in comparison with the proposal made by the Commission. Nevertheless, as far as principles were concerned, and the regulatory mechanism set to work, Madame Simone Veil, then President of the European Parliament, was right in seeing this initiative as *"the prefiguration of an integrated European network of air services"*.

The principle is very simple : between airports of certain categories, and provided aircraft with a limited capacity are used, the Member States waive their ability to refuse permission to open scheduled services within the Community. Under the general conditions of distance, airport categories and specified capacity, the procedure is almost one of automatic approval : if the home State of the applicant air carrier agrees to the application, it forwards it to the other State affected, which is *bound to authorise* the service.

The implications of this kind of regulatory system on the *international public law regime* by which *air traffic rights* are exchanged in the world were not perceived at first, due to the limited scope of this primary legislation, but should be fairly obvious now and deserve to be reflected upon.

In *September 1986*, the Commission made a proposal to enlarge the scope of the inter-regional air services Directive. In its Communication of 1986, the Commission re-asserted its 1984 proposals, with some nuances. Meanwhile, discussions had been continuing on the Commission's proposals and on related political and legal issues in the European Parliament and the Economic and Social Committee; a certain evolution could be felt in the airlines' way of thinking and that of the government officials involved. ECAC was working out its own positions. Within the scope of this book, we can only refer to the most significant developments of this evolution. Significantly, as indicated, legal developments have been particularly important, as they related to obligations already contracted by EEC Member States and followed a logic which could be translated in judicial terms.

## f) *Essential legal developments*

### *A certain amount of confusion ...*

The legal situation had been at a standstill for a long time, following the 1974 European Court's decision in the "French Seamen's case", referred to earlier. Regulation 17, generally implementing the competition rules of the Treaty, was still not applicable to air transport (by virtue of Regulation 141 of November 26, 1962).

A Regulation of 1968 (1017) provided rules of procedure and of substantive law exclusively for rail, road and inland surface transportation. Air and sea transport remained out of reach. Even the applicability of the rules *in principle* was still being questioned or even denied by some governments. It was understandable that governments did not see clearly whether they were under any particular obligation to apply and rules, notably the competition rules of the Treaty, to air transport.

### *Lord Bethell and "Freedom of the Skies"*

With the political pressure, based on consumer interests building up, and some very high air fares on intra-European routes, a Euro-MP from the United Kingdom, Lord Bethell took some initiative to have the situation redressed in the Courts. He was at the head of a user's association "Freedom of the Skies", which backed his efforts to a certain point. He first attempted in 1981 to have the EG Commission investigate air fares, but the Commission found at the time that tariff fixing was a process placed, in most cases, under the responsibility of governments, and that it therefore could not constitute an infringement of Article 85 of the Treaty.

The Commission also answered that it was examining the question in relation to Article 86, which deals with abuse of dominant position and the obligations of Member States, and would put forward legislative proposals. Lord Bethell requested the European Court of Justice to void this answer and declare the Commission in fault for failure to act. The Court of Justice rejected the claim as inadmissible, Lord Bethell lacking a proper cause of action [146].

Lord Bethell continued his campaign against the allegedly abusive conduct of established airlines and filed a complaint against Sabena for charging too high fares on the Brussels-London route, a procedure that dragged along for some time in the English courts.

### The "Sterling Airways" case

These efforts remained inconclusive, as did a complaint lodged against the Scandinavian airline, SAS, by a Danish independent carrier, Sterling Airways. The Commission was asked to find that excessive air fares were charged on the Copenhagen-London route, because of the monopolitic concession enjoyed by SAS, which thereby allegedly abused its dominant position on this market, even though the said air fares had been duly approved by the Danish government. Another relevant feature of the situation — Sterling Airways argued — was the blockage of any access to the market of international scheduled services and certain charter flights, which were all exclusively conceded to SAS. The complaint raised important issues of international public law in air transport, and a decision could have far-reaching effects. Being deprived of its usual investigative powers by the lack of applicable regulation, the Commission resorted to the assistance of the Danish government, as provided for under Article 89 of the EEC Treaty. At the outcome of a slow-moving procedure, the Commission found that an abusive situation had existed during a certain period, but that it had now ceased to exist due to the lowering of fares, and therefore no formal decision was needed.

As regards the right of access to international air services, the Commission recognised (rightly, in our judgment) that it did not hold the power to interfere with the decision of a Member State's government to concede air services to a particular carrier of its choice, and not to others. The reasons were derived from the sovereign power of States, according to international conventions, to control the airspace above their territories — from which the right derived to designate the airlines to operate air services between their respective territories. A provision of the Treaty dealing with situations of that nature is Article 90, which protects certain activities from being caught by Articles 85 and 86. The situation could only be remedied if application was made of Article 61, par. 1 and Article 84, par. 2 of the Treaty, in other words, if the Council took the responsibility for a policy relating to these issues. However, the Commission declared that there could be no doubt that the competition rules (Articles 85 and 86) were applicable to air transport companies [147].

It remained to be seen how they could ever be applied ... Despite the comments to the contrary, the "French Seamen's" decision of 1974 had been ambiguous. It was high time that all these legal difficulties were resolved, and the Commission was looking for an opportunity to obtain a clarification of its power and of the obligations imposed by the Treaty on Member States and undertakings by the Court of Justice of the European Communities.

### The "Nouvelles Frontières" case

The Court of Justice had refrained from including air transport among the sectors of transport where it had found, in an action filed by the European Parliament, that the Council had failed to act in fulfilment of its Treaty obligations.

Strictly legally speaking, the situation was indeed different for the various modes of transport (Politically, the pressure was on anyway).

The opportunity was offered to deal with air transport, as such, by a question asked the Court of Justice by a Paris Police Court, pursuant to Article 177 of the EEC Treaty. The Court's judgment was delivered on April 30, 1986 (Cases 209 to 213/84, Lucas Asjes and others).

Certain airlines and travel agencies were accused of applying tariffs other than those approved by the civil aviation authorities in infringement of certain provisions of the French Civil Aviation Code.

The Paris Court requested an interpretation of the Treaty so as to enable it to verify the compatibility of the provisions of the Treaty "with those provisions of the compulsory procedure of approval, foreseen by French law, for air tariffs" (Decision, par. 1).

The reference was "for a preliminary ruling as to whether Articles L 330-3, R 330-0 and R 330-15 of the French Civil Aviation Code are in conformity with Community law".

The observations presented by several governments, the Commission, two airlines (Air France and KLM) and the company called "Nouvelles Frontières" — the tour operator and travel agent initially incriminated — were conflicting on the fundamental issue of the applicability of the competition rules to air transport, in view of Article 84 of the Treaty.

The Court ruled that *"like other means of transport, air transport remains subject to the general rules of the Treaty including those concerning competition".*

This was really the basic clarification that the Commission had been seeking to enable it to progress with authority derived from the Treaty. Others, like "Nouvelles Frontières", had also hoped for a clarification of this nature, but one which would open a course of action for them before the national courts. However, they were disappointed. The Court indeed balanced its judgment by the finding that the applicability remained theoretical in the case of air transport as long as no action was taken either by a Member State (under Article 88) or the Commission (under Article 89), or that no implementing Regulation was adopted by the Council. The direct applicability of the rules can only result from one of the three situations described.

*Legal and political consequences of the "Nouvelles Frontières" judgment*

The "Nouvelles Frontières" judgment was a landmark of its own, essentially of a transitional nature and based on the necessity to hasten a Council's decision while maintaining the legal security which the airlines' Councel had avocated in the absence of clear obligations incumbent on Member States. All parties concerned could find reasons of satisfaction in this judgment.

We should note, however, that the Court did not prejudice the issue of the compatibility of certain cooperative practices of the airlines with the Rome Treaty. The language used by the Court was only slightly ambiguous in this respect : logically, any such finding was left to the competent national authorities. If the Council takes responsibility, it must do so in the context of the application of Article 84, par. 2, i.e. by adopting a comprehensive air transport policy. There is no obligation, but clearly a possibility, for the Council to issue group exemptions under such a policy, by using the legal powers conferred under Article 87.

Another observation is that the Commission was the only party in a position to take advantage of the judgment by pressing its proposals to the Council and, if needed, by proceeding against the airlines and the Member States under the authority derived from the Treaty.

Indeed, the Commission instituted proceedings against the major scheduled airlines of the Community countries for infringement of the competition rules, pursuant to Article 89 of the Treaty. These proceedings served to add to the pressure put on the Council to make a decision and helped the Commission to develop, through dialogues with the airlines, norms of its own in respect of the application of the Treaty rules to airlines' cooperative agreements.

The proceedings were dropped when the Council adopted a legislative package, on December 14, 1987.

g) *The rules adopted by the Council : a first step towards the integration of the market*

Prior to December 14, 1987, the Council had not adopted any legislation of major political significance. An exception might be the Directive on interregional air services of July 25, 1983.

However, the implications of this Directive were not obvious at the time, and its scope was limited.

The Council's decision of December 28, 1979, establishing a procedure of consultation between Member States in their relations with third countries and international organisations (80/50 EEC) is noteworthy.

But the commitment of Member States had been reduced to an exchange of information.

The few other norms adopted by the Council in connection with air transport were essentially technical, on subjects such as noise abatement at airports and consultation in case of air accidents.

After years of discussions, the Council adopted in July 1987, and formally decided in December, on a package based on the Commissions's proposals. The Council, in the process, inserted its own views. A high level working group had worked towards the difficult compromise.

*The "EEC package on air transport"*

The "package" adopted on December 14, 1987 was published in the Official Journal of the European Communities dated 31 December 1987.

It includes :

— Council Regulation (EEC) N° 3975/87 of 14 December 1987 laying down the procedure for the application of the rules on competition to undertakings in the air transport sector;

— Council Regulation (EEC) N° 3976/87 of 14 December 1987 on the application of Article 85(3) of the Treaty to certain categories of agreements and concerted practices in the air transport sector;

— Council Directive of 14 December 1987 on fares for scheduled air services between Member States;

— Council Decision of 14 December 1987 on the sharing of passenger capacity between air carriers on scheduled air services between Member States and on access for air carriers to scheduled air-service routes between Member States.

Briefly summarised, the measures enacted here are the following :

— *On competition rules :*

The Community regulation is applicable to intra-Community operations only. The scope is restricted to air services operated between Community airports. Defined group exemptions are provided for some types of agreements between airlines. However, these exemptions are granted for a limited period, (until 31 January 1991) "during which air carriers can adapt to a more competitive environment". (Whereas clause, Council Regulation 3976/87).

This implies a proviso that the burden will shift to the airlines to demonstrate the need for continuation of such exemptions beyond 1991.

The regulation spells out the conditions for exemption of, for instance, pooling arrangements and tariff agreements. (While joint operations agreements are not included, they might qualify for individual exemptions).

The Commission is called upon to issue its own Regulation in accordance with the Council's policy (cfr. E.C.O.J., August 31, 1988).

The procedure is being set forth by the Commission. Whatever the modalities, the competition rules of the Treaty apply to the air transport sector from January 1, 1988.

The conditions for exemption of tariff consultations (whether multilateral-IATA- or bilateral) are worth mentioning :

a) such consultations must be voluntary;

b) air carriers may not be bound by the results;

c) the Commission as well as Member States will be given the opportunity to participate as observers in any such consultations.

### On air fares

While the double approval regime is recognised, some criteria are set for the approval of fares by governments, including the needs of the consumers, a satisfactory return on capital and the competitive market situation.

But the main innovation lies in the recognition of *zones of flexibility*, meaning pricing zones within which air fares qualify for *automatic approval* when they meet certain conditions.

Within the zones of flexibility, the States concerned shall allow *third and fourth freedom* air carriers to charge discounts and deep discount air fares of their own choice.

N.B. The *discount zone* extend from 90 % to more than 65 % of the reference fare, which is the normal economy fare.

The *deep discount zone* extends from 65 % to 45 % of the reference fare. A zone of additional flexibility is created, which extends from 10 % below the bilaterally approved level of a fare to the ceiling of the deep-discount zone, provided the conditions are met.

### On capacity and market access in bilateral relationships

*The Member States may no longer avail themselves of an entitlement to an equal capacity sharing on their bilateral intra-Community air services.*

"In the period between 1 January 1988 and 30 September 1989, a Member State shall allow any third- and fourth-freedom air carrier(s) authorized by the States concerned under the arrangements in force between them to operate routes between their territories to adjust capacity provided that the resulting capacity shares are not outside the range 55 % : 45 %" (Article 3, 1).

"... the range within which a Member State shall allow the air carrier(s) of another Member State to increase its (their) capacity share shall be extended to 60 % : 40 % from 1 October 1989" (Article 3, 2).

Remark : As a matter of fact, this system might lead to a considerable increase of capacity through the matching possibilities it provides. The innovation lies, as in the conept developed by ECAC, in the principle of zones of automatic approval in the field of capacity.

*As far as market access is concerned*

*"Multiple designation" by a Member State on a country-pair basis has to be accepted by the other Member State concerned.*

*On a city-pair basis, multiple designation has to be accepted under certain conditions.*

*Subject to the capacity-sharing provisions, Community air carriers are permitted to introduce third or fourth-freedom scheduled air services between category 1 airports in the territory of one Member State and regional airports (categories 2 and 3) in the territory of another Member State.*

However, some exceptions were introduced, on a temporary basis, by Member States.

Under certain conditions, a Community air carrier is permitted to operate a *fifth freedom* scheduled service; the combination of points on air services between Member States is widely permitted.

### Perspective

These new rules adopted by the Council have to be considered as a first stage towards the completion of a single European market, which the legislation refers to as "the internal market in air transport".

### h) *The Single European Act*

*The main political decision regarding air transport in the EEC was taken by the Heads of State and Government, at their meeting in June 1986.*

The so-called "Summit" of the Community is not, institutionally, a Community body, as it is not referred to by the Rome Treaty and has no formal power. Nevertheless, the now traditional meetings of the Heads of State and Government determine the main political orientations of the Community.

Following suggestions made by the Commission, the Summit decided that the transport sector, including air and sea transport, must be part of the Single European Market.

The concept is defined and the target date is set in the Single European Act, which entered into force on July 1, 1987. The Single European Act provides for the progressive establishment, over a period expiring on 31 December 1992, of *"an area without internal frontiers in which the free movement of goods, persons, services and capital is ensured in accordance with the provisions of this Treaty".*

The Single Market, which is drawing considerable attention from all parties concerned in Europe, is nothing more than a full and modernised application of the objectives and principles of the Rome Treaty; however, considering the internal competitive situation and nationalistic interests as well as economic and social discrepancies in the Community, it is a formidable challenge.

In the air transport sector, where bilateralism and nationalism prevail, the introduction of the Treaty freedoms would sooner or later, even if the target date is not met, dismantle the regulatory system within the Community and have far-reaching implications in the air relations of EEC Member countries with third countries.

The legal nature of the freedoms of the air, cabotage and other economic rights exchanged bilaterally will have to be reviewed; bilateralism itself will lose its significance between Member States; the national identity of air carriers will be dissolved; out of necessity, agreements with third countries will need re-negotiating; national identities of air carriers will be blurred, multinational airlines may emerge and be designated to operate formerly "national" routes; the designation clauses will be reviewed, both in terms of national control and ownership and in terms of multi-designation; new ideas and practices will spread in the wider aviation world.

A situation of "quasi-cabotage" in Europe and the creation of a common air space will or would result very quickly in traffic rights negotiations conducted by the Community on behalf of its members, with some other countries and parts of the world.

Although it is far from clear at the time of this writing how the Single Market concept is going to be applied to air transport, and at any rate serious doubts exist regarding the date of December 31, 1992, nevertheless a process of thought has begun and both the financial and commercial market places reflect the tendencies of airlines and associated concerns to adjust in time to a new competitive situation.

In a changing world, few developments may be of such significance as the progress towards the completion of the Internal EEC Market, in 1992 or somewhat later.

## 4. The Council of Europe and ECAC

The intensive activity of the EEC in air transport matters gave a new impulse to the search for a common attitude on essential regulatory questions at the larger level of the Council of Europe and of the European Civil Aviation Commission.

## The ECAC policy statement of 1985

At its Twelfth Assembly in 1985, ECAC adopted a new policy statement on intra-European air transport [148]. The statement recognised the need for more flexibility in the system, while rejecting total deregulation. A gradual change should permit differences in competitive ability to be taken into account.

More flexibility in capacity sharing and a review of the 1967 Agreement in Tariffs were advocated. The conditions of competition should be harmonised, giving particular consideration to state aid and social conditions where fair competition could be affected. Non-scheduled flights should be regulated by harmonised liberal conditions. ECAC also recommended cost-effective standards for airports and airways, with consultation procedures for airline users.

This 1985 document has been called "an important statement of intent on a Europe-wide basis" [149].

As a policy statement, it reflected perhaps more than mere intentions, and provided moderate, balanced and often precise guidelines, of which the EEC (composed of 12 out of the 21 ECAC Member States) would necessarily have to take account when establishing its own Community policy. Seen from other parts of the world, the overlap may well appear somewhat confusing. From the mere *legal* angle, there is a clear difference in status between such a policy statement by a consultative body and any measures adopted by the Council of Ministers of the EEC in application of the EEC Treaty. But a certain progress had been made, politically.

## Multilateral Agreements on Tariffs and Capacity

The next step laid the foundation for a legally binding situation.

At the meeting of the Directors General of ECAC on 17 to 19 December 1986, two draft Multilateral Agreements on tariffs and capacity-sharing were adopted, and a majority of the Directors General agreed to conclude Memoranda of Understanding committing their aeronautical authorities to apply the principles and procedures contained in the draft Agreements as from January 1, 1987.

Three Directors General made reservations.

a) *Agreement on Tariffs*

The International Agreement on the Procedure for the Establishment of Tariffs for Intra-European Scheduled Air Services — as adopted in draft form in December 1986 — replaces the Paris 1967 Agreement. It has the same scope and the same objective : to establish tariff provisions applicable to intra-European scheduled services, the term "intra-European" applying exclusively to the territories within Europe of Member States of the European Civil Aviation Conference. (Articles 1, (1), a and 2, a).

The main differences are the following :

1) *Consultations among airlines are no longer mandatory*

"The importance of inter-airline multilateral tariff consultations and the role of the International Air Transport Association in these consultations are recognised by Parties to this Agreement. Nevertheless, inter-airline consultations, whether multilateral or bilateral, shall not be made a mandatory requirement for the filing and establishment of tariffs. The filing of tariffs by an airline shall be permitted on an individual basis or, at the option of that airline, following consultation with any other airline(s)" (Article 3, 2).

2) *Zones of flexibility are defined*

Any tariff "which meets the requirements of the zonal scheme as specified in the Annex shall be automatically approved" (Article 5, 2).

It may be observed here that both conditions meet the essential requirements for the compatibility of any tariff coordination and approval system with the provisions of the Rome Treaty, according to the EEC Commission. Technically speaking, the system of the "zones of flexibility", in which government approval is automatic, had been developed by ECAC and United States delegations when concluding the Memorandum on North Atlantic tariffs and was further studied in the ECAC's so-called "COMPAS Report" for application to intra-European services.

b) *Agreement on Capacity*

The International Agreement on the Sharing of Capacity on Intra-European Scheduled Air Services contains the principles and procedures for the sharing of capacity between Member States of ECAC and replaces and supersedes any other bilateral arrangement which would be more restrictive than this Agreement. (More flexible arrangements are permitted on a bilateral basis or amongst a group of States) (Article 1, 2).

The original feature of this Agreement is the *concept of zones of flexibility applied to capacity.*

The zonal scheme described in the Annex is valid for a trial period of three years. Within a zone of 45/55 %, the designated airlines are free to offer, without possibility of regulatory intervention, the capacity they consider necessary to meet market demands. Under certain conditions, Tier 2 of the scheme provides for an automatic increase of one percentage point in capacity share.

(Annex).

This Agreement was concluded "for the purpose of achieving a greater degree of controlled competition in the intra-European market, and as a first practical step in the field of capacity sharing" (Memorandum, Article 1).

### Council of Europe

It must be mentioned here that the Council of Europe has consistently shown great interest in the progression of an European air transport policy. The 1985 Twelfth Assembly called for the harmonisation of ECAC and EC approaches in an effort to liberalise air transport all over Europe. This resolution strongly supported the efforts of ECAC to achieve a comprehensive scheme, including the zone type arrangements contained in the COMPAS report, new charter concepts and expanded regional services. The report of Mr. Anders Bjork, which brought about this resolution, reflects the Council of Europe's great interest in civil aviation.

## 5. Regulation of Non-scheduled Services

One of the characteristics of the European situation is the importance of charter services and of charter-priced journeys in the total volume of passenger traffic. *About half the passengers travelling in Europe use charter flights or pay low "promotional" fares.* On several major routes, the competition of charters has either chased away scheduled services or considerably reduced their profitability through "seat-only" sales and the spread of special fares.

A number of large and medium-sized, non-scheduled airlines compete with scheduled airlines and among each other, many of them equipped with the jet aircraft types suitable for European scheduled services.

The liberalisation of charter rules has developed gradually in Europe and the "inclusive tour" charter operation has been allowed to develop, notably by the United Kingdom, into the simple offer of seat-only sales on a regular series of flights to holiday destinations. This in turn has encouraged new entrants to compete on the air tourism market. Some enterprising tour-operators have strongly pushed politicians and civil servants in the direction of more flexible conditions and free pricing. The deregulation policy in Europe contributed to this effort, and the 1986 "Nouvelles Frontières" decision was — this is only an example — used as an argument to obtain from the Belgian Minister of Transport, in 1987, the suppression of the existing regulation on minimum selling prices in Belgium.

The pressure exercised by independent carriers to gain freer market access and to compete fairly with established airlines is likely to become an important, if not decisive factor in the process of liberalisation of air transport in Europe.

# CHAPTER 4

## POSSIBLE INTERNATIONAL EFFECTS
## OF AN EEC COMMON POLICY

The objectives of the Chicago Convention and of the Rome Treaty are not incompatible in themselves. However, some problems of conciliation exist. International practice has created forms and principles which have become the norm and have acquired a status of their own. For instance, bilaterals set out rules on the coordination of air fares, norms of designation of carriers, etc. The general recourse to bilateralism has itself established a practice of international law by which countries recognise each other and deal with each other's sovereignty as Contracting States. The application of the principles of the Chicago Convention resulting from the bilateral practice cannot easily be dissociated from these principles themselves. Equality of chances, fairness and non-discrimination of treatment are principles embodied in the rules of law by virtue of customs and international comity. Nonetheless, a multilateral approach can be worked out.

A status-quo is out of the question. The Rome Treaty, in its Article 234, obliges the EEC Member States to adapt their previous arrangements with third countries, whenever such arrangements are incompatible with the Treaty.

No indication has been given so far by the European Court of Justice as to the application of this provision to air transport relations : much will depend on the rules of policy and law which the Community will decide to follow and the external policy it will determine for itself.

The Chicago Convention is obviously the earliest Treaty. The question of amendments may be on the table at some time. Bilateral agreements will have to be re-negotiated. Another question of interest is the extra-territorial application of EEC law. As far as the competition rules of the Treaty are concerned, the scope of which cannot be limited by an implementing regulation, their extra-territoriality will occur procedurally in a manner different from US anti-trust law, but it will occur in some areas.

Other points requiring attention are : designation of airlines, (European) cabotage rights, fifth freedom rights exchanged in Europe, capacity shares, etc [150].

The effects of a common European policy will be felt in neighbouring and other parts of the world; such effects are too important to be taken lightly by the authorities concerned.

# CHAPTER 5

## CONCLUSIONS

We believe in a certain "denationalisation" of airlines.

The Single European Act, when in force, may open a new era where such a process will take place. But we also believe in the necessity for airlines to be allowed to pool their resources, in order to ensure true equality of chances, as well as an intelligent use of the available means. The basic legal and administrative conditions for the interchange of aircraft have been studied for many years and we have taken part in these studies [151]. ECAC has been involved in this type of research practically since its creation.

States may have to accept that their national interests are not necessarily identical with those of national airlines, as such. New types of enterprises will emerge, in various formats, with different roles to play. New patterns of traffic rights exchanges will be developed, as a *multinational airspace* is formed.

"As international air transport develops, new regulatory structures are needed. Europe with its sizeable air transport market and advanced structure of international cooperation, will play a key role in developing these new structures" [152].

The author's own views on the prospects are, broadly, the following :

1) The airlines of the European Community would establish a precedent if they were no longer run on narrow nationalistic principles and were no longer treated like State property. They should be open to financial participation by other airlines, be encouraged to cooperate and enter into joint ventures and operations, and to merge, provided no undue distortion of competition results to the benefit of the largest airlines.

2) Airlines should be able to compete on a fair and equal basis throughout the Community. This will require a comprehensive policy which should take into account differences in size and primary market volume. Such a policy should not only deal with possible state aids, but should seek to control air fares and market practices in order to prevent predatory pricing, dumping and misleading advertising. Distri-

bution systems should be regulated by Community legislation to prevent abuses of operation of computer reservations systems. A number of questions of a similar nature will have to be legally resolved.

3) It is important that Community law be developed and that disruptive actions by national courts and piecemeal approaches to political and operational problems be avoided. Legislative coordination and harmonisation are required from EEC Member States.

4) There is simply no alternative to a common attitude towards air traffic rights. The single market, even though it falls short of realising a European unity, implies a unity of decision on fundamental economic questions which involve *freedoms*. The exchange of freedoms of the air between Community Member States belongs to the public order in formation, but has to be accompanied at the outset by a certain awareness of what the policy towards non-EEC countries is going to be. In some areas of Europe, there is vocal support for *"the creation of a Community cabotage zone in view of negotiating with third countries"*.

In that case, a common negotiating authrity will have to be established — normally the European Commission. Such a stage cannot presumably be reached without transition. The credibility of the policy should be strengthened gradually by taking appropriate steps. Bilateral agreements with third countries will be construed and applied according to a common policy and renegotiated following commonly agreed positions of Community Member States.

It will be an interesting juncture when the Community is recognised as competent to negotiate on behalf of Member States and actually begins to move in that capacity. Strictly speaking, nothing in the Chicago Convention prevents States to negotiate together, in the framework of regional cooperation. Such process might even simplify matters to some extent, if only by reducing the number of bilaterals. But such new style arrangements will be rather complicated to work out, both because they require an understanding among EEC Member States on various accounts and because third countries may be in a position to raise difficulties on their own. Yet this may stimulate the creation of other regional coalitions of forces and contribute to the overall de-nationalisation of the rules of the game.

If Europe establishes the precedent, we believe in the possibility of interregional negotiations and agreements to substitute in the future for the nationalistic approaches of the current bilateral air transport agreements.

# PART VII

# Perspectives

# INNOVATIVE THINKING REQUIRED :

## A NEW BALANCE

The writer has had some experience in air negotiations and international conferences : enough to fill him with a certain amount of caution and make him recommend avoidance of simplistic views when approaching a new era.

For this is a new era for international air transport, and it will require a careful consideration of the facts and a great deal of innovative thinking.

Different parts of the world are in different stages of development. It is therefore unlikely that any blueprint will fit. It may prove attractive to consider applying a solution like the GATT agreements to services like air transport, but past efforts to fight national protectionism within that framework are not encouraging. On the other hand, the Chicago-Bermuda plan has brought about a distressing fragmentation of the world of civil aviation. To maintain this framework at all costs would be unwise, unless serious adaptations are made to the system. The complexities of the problem should be examined from a number of vantage points, in order to achieve as balanced an overall view as possible.

At any rate, we should have little confidence in any disorganisation which professes to cure the evils in any sort of activity, let alone one like air transport, which constantly puts human life at stake, affects the environment and concerns vitally important social interests.

Factors likely to influence the future can be discerned in the present. Perspectives can only be traced from clearly defined starting points.

One of these starting points is the state of international cooperation among governments and airlines.

# CHAPTER 1

## COOPERATION : CAN WE DO WITHOUT?

A very big question indeed is now being asked : do we still need institutionalised cooperation? Do we need ICAO and IATA, in their present forms, the references to inter-airline cooperative arrangements in inter-governmental agreements, and the instricate, costly network of interline dealings, which the existing structure have encouraged and that, in the opinion of some, the public pays for?

Perhaps a good way to approach this question is to consider the reasons for cooperation in the first place.

The Chicago Convention established a principle of fair and equal access of all nations to civil aviation activities. It also based the entire system on the absolute sovereinty of States over their airspace. Allowing for the diversity of means and needs, the only way to reconcile the aim of equality with the sovereign powers of States was to ensure the highest possible degree of international cooperation. This cooperation would be multifold at the level of civil aviation authorities as well as of airlines. A large consensus would be achieved on the main issues, and in areas of common concern government prerogatives would be relinquished in the interest of the worldwide aviation community. Multilateralism and standardisation would be the tools of this policy, centred on ICAO. In the field of air traffic rights, the chosen pattern of bilateralism certainly enabled States to assert their authority over their national airspace and to control competition, while strictly governing market entry, but the Bermuda Agreement contained a number of principles aiming at multilateralism and the pattern itself standardised the practice. That these principles should govern such key elements as rights and rates was accordingly a major objective of the negotiators at Bermuda. They succeeded. A pattern was provided for the exercise (as distinct from the granting) of traffic rights, agreement was reached on the overall coordination of rate-making, and principles were laid down for "orderly development of international air transport through cooperation and understanding" [153].

If a new set of rights of the air were to be defined, who would dare contend that "cooperation and understanding" were no longer required to compensate for inequalities and permit an orderly development of air transport throughout the globe?

The gap between the rich and the poor has never been wider.

A review of some forms of cooperation shows the variety of these forms and the strength of the impulse to which they respond *despite the shortcomings of public law* in the matter.

"The *need to cooperate* must be vital in air transport, as it is seen to remedy the deficiencies of public law in the matter, and to prevail in spite of the worldwide bartering systems which continue to govern the exchange of air traffic rights ..." [154].

The difficulties of developing air transport in some harmony are numerous. As stated by a South American commentator : "The most positive solution found in the practice of air policy by governments and airlines, to counter these negative factors, is to adopt methods of collaboration and integration at their respective level; they have sought, through the coordination of efforts, means and policies, the best way to achieve a prosperous future for air transport" [155].

It is hardly surprising that Professor Chauveau spoke of air transport as of "the ground of election of cooperation".

a) *At government level*

ICAO itself is the best example of cooperation between governments within the wide scope of its activities, ranging from the exchange of in-depth statistical and economic information to full integration of the air navigation systems.

The other intergovernmental organisations described above also fulfil cooperative objectives to various extents.

One could expect that such cooperation, in the wide sense of the world, would have become common place in international jargon, and that it would not be questioned. But it is being questioned, at least as far as the *worldwide specific* methods of cooperating among States are concerned, — in other words, the issue of a proper forum for civil aviation.

A forum like UNCTAD would, according to certain countries, be more adequate than ICAO to deal with international air transport as a commodity, while others would favour the GATT Agreement to provide the

answer in a new era of free competition. However, none of these frame-
works, not even regional organisations, can supply the kind of cooperation that ICAO has made possible.

That, in itself, should be a sufficient reason to keep ICAO alive and
to develop its activities, because international air navigation and air
transport cannot possibly dispense with precisely that kind of cooperation.

The two other reasons are :

1) the kind of cooperation needed is essentially technical, and any
other forum would, in fact, give a much more *political* connotation to
the international debate on aviation;

2) regional coordination of interests may be a very positive element,
*provided it finds ways of expression and therefore self-assertion in a wider
forum where compromise is made possible.*

In other words, regionalism has to be balanced by the existence of an
international organisation, open to all.

Cooperation is only as good as the men who cooperate. It is humanly
very rewarding that people engaged in the same activities and confronting
the same types of problems, called upon to meet again in bilateral
confrontations, should know each other personally and share their
experiences in a neutral environment where the differences that appeared
gigantic when each of them was sitting at home, blur and look ridiculous
in retrospect. Civil servants may accede to a truly political view of the
problems when seeking solutions together. This will not prevent political
differences from getting in the way, but beneath the options of that
nature, men will know with whom they are dealing and somehow assess
the true dimension of the problems.

They will not entrench themselves in their positions, but they will
at least cooperate in that sense, that a telephone call may often prevent
a diplomatic incident from occurring.

It is true that the underlying thesis of the recommendation to place
international air transport under, for instance, the auspices of GATT
is that getting away from *bilateralism* would improve, not diminish international cooperation and make it considerably more efficient. The
problem of bilateralism is a different one. We will discuss it briefly, a
little later in these pages. Institutions such as OEEC (Organisation for
European Economic Cooperation) and GATT, on which rested, to a

later extent, the task of freeing trade through multilateralism, have evolved their particular *methods* of international cooperation. Yet methodology is no absolute key to success, particularly when recession hits. In that sense, multilateralism is no more a guarantee of liberalism than proclaimed devotion to liberalism — a barrier against protectionism.

Moreover, cooperation in the strict sense of the term as it is now widely used, i.e. between developed and developing nations, is an absolute necessity in air transport and is far from having reached a stage of significant development. There is no particular sign that, for that matter, institutions such as OEEC and GATT have met the economic necessities of the developing nations in international trade.

Some concrete examples of the development of international cooperation are : the Yaounde Convention of AIR AFRIQUE and the EUROCONTROL convention.

1) *AIR AFRIQUE and the problem of common operating agencies under the Chicago Convention*

The Treaty relating to air transport in Africa was signed in Yaounde on March 28, 1961, between several West African States.

The Treaty instituted an airline, jointly owned and operated by the Contracting States : the "AIR AFRIQUE" company, which each Party undertook to designate as its chosen instrument to operate its international traffic rights. (Title 1, Ch. 1, Art. 2) [156].

Regardless of detailed differences with other forms of cooperation of this type (for example, SAS or East African Airways, a common airline that did not survive the dissolution of the East African Community), the AIR AFRIQUE agreement had distinctive legal and political features.

The Ministers of Transport (Civil and Commercial Aviation) of all the Member States set up a Committee in which they discuss "their common policy, perspectives of development of air transport and programmes as well as, generally speaking, all questions relating to Civil and Commercial Aviation" (Article 8).

The Contracting States are committed to coordinate their positions for the negotiation of air traffic rights within the framework of intergovernmental agreements, taking into consideration the exploitation and the interests of the common Society AIR AFRIQUE (cf. Article 10).

Such a close and political cooperation, formally based on the existence of an common enterprise, nevertheless falls short of being an integrated political structure : a common air space, regulated by a common authority. The Committee of Ministers is only consultative.

Seen globally, a distinctive achievement of the AIR AFRIQUE cooperation has been its legal repercussion in an Amendment brought to the Chicago Convention, giving birth to the present Article 77.

It is a significant sign of the importance of cooperation in the Third World that developing countries have brought about the only substantive Amendment to the Chicago Convention, which goes in the direction of more cooperation and less nationalisation of air transport.

Technically, this Amendment is only an addition to the last paragraph of Article 77. It provides that the Council will determine the manner by which the provisions of the Convention concerning the nationality of aircraft will be applied to aircraft operated by international operating agencies. Pursuant to Article 6, all aircraft must have a nationality, which is established by their inscription in the register of the State where they were registered. The Resolution of the Council of ICAO dated 14 December 1967 has defined the criteria applicable to any common or international registration of aircraft.

A common registration implies that States which have formed an international operating agency establish a *register other than a national one* in order to realise a joint registration of aircraft operated by the said agency.

An international registration system means that aircraft operated by an international operating agency are registered, not on a national basis but by an international organisation, with a legal personality, whether or not of the States which have formed the said agency.

*In the case of common registration.*

*A.* The States which have formed the international operating agency accept jointly the responsibility imposed upon Member States by the Chicago Convention;

*B.* These States identify among themselves, for each aircraft, one which will act towards third States parties to the Chicago Convention;

*C.* The operation of those aircraft shall not discriminate against other Contracting States in relation to the provisions of the Chicago Convention. (The geographical area of the multinational grouping may not, for instance, constitute a cabotage zone).

*Note :* This non-discrimination clause has to be noted in context with the intentions of other regions, like the EEC, to assess the need and the method of conciliating international conventions with the Chicago Convention as a prior treaty.

*D.* The laws and regulations of the States involved with respect to aircraft and crews must conform with the obligations imposed by the Chicago Convention and its Annexes; this conformity must be ensured in a uniform manner.

### In the case of international registration.

The same criteria are applicable, and the Council may adopt additional conditions, to ensure that the other ICAO Member States are given sufficient guarantees that the provisions of the Chicago Convention have been observed.

### 2) The EUROCONTROL Convention

Another example is the International Convention of Cooperation for the Safety of Air Navigation, which was signed in Brussels on the 13th of December, 1960, and entered into force on the 1st of March, 1963.

The signatories were Belgium, the Netherlands, Luxembourg, France and the Federal Republic of Germany.

The Treaty set up an international organisation which aimed, as its main objective, at intensifying cooperation in the field of civil aviation and, in particular, of organising the control of air navigation in the upper air space (above 7.600 m.).

This cooperation was theoretically a model of design and efficiency within a regional concept of air navigation control; however, it did not work smoothly and Member States forced the institution to deviate somewhat from its original aims.

A Protocol amending the Convention reflects its new orientation (cf. sub. Note 61).

### b) At airline level

Inter-airline cooperation is under discussion much more at present than inter-governmental cooperation, the forms of which are more classical in a number of areas.

The focus placed upon competition has prejudiced indiscriminately the intricate network of arrangements which prevail among airlines and, admittedly, may be confusing for the outsider. How is one to distinguish normal and generally *useful* agreements from those unduly restrictive of competition?

The cartel connotation attached to the IATA fare-setting activities has particulary damaged the reputation of the entire set of IATA designed or patronised cooperative activities of the established airline industry.

## 1. *IATA*

Inter-airline multilateral cooperation is the essence of IATA. We have enumerated some of IATA's activities and will not revert to them. In general, the integration of all networks is largely the work of IATA, and a major role in this integration is played by the *interlining* system.

The IATA Multilateral Interline Traffic Agreement provides for a uniform system of handling, transfer, re-routing and relating procedures for all passengers, baggage and cargo between participating carriers.

By enabling through-transportation on a single document, the Agreements play a vital role in speeding up the movement of the vast amount of interline traffic carried through the world today.

When Knut Hammarskjöld, the Director General of IATA, outlined to the US CAB the arguments showing the importance of the interlining system for the traveller, even the most determined adversaries of IATA were convinced. On the other hand, experiments in simplified low cost transportation, like Laker's and People Express, often left the passenger distressingly in need of interlining facilities. Carriers of the USSR, Eastern Europe and China participate in the interlining programme of IATA, thus exemplifying its importance.

Another set of circumstances in which IATA can play, and has started to play an important role is in the cooperation between airlines of developed and developing countries, particularly in the field of personnel training.

Of course, other areas are more exposed to criticism and likely to disappear wherever pro-competitive forces are exercised and use available legal means : cooperation among airlines relating to agency programmes, for instance, is probably in jeopardy.

### 2) *Other examples of inter-airline cooperation*

But inter-airline cooperation is so much *in the nature of things*, despite commercial competition, that it is far from being the privilege of IATA

or IATA airlines. *Charter* carriers cooperate, *regional* carriers cooperate.
Airlines cooperate efficiently and quietly in *telecommunications* through
SITA (Société Internationale de Télécommunications Aéronautiques).
They have achieved remarkable cooperation in the *technical* field : among
Arab airlines, for instance, or among European airlines in the two
groups known as ATLAS (Air France, Deutsche Lufthansa, Alitalia,
Sabena) and KSSU (KLM, SAS, Swissair and UTA). Under such
cooperative arrangements, the work of maintenance and overhaul of
aircraft is shared and distributed among the technical departments of
the partners. The specialisation agreement is completed by other arrangements, like interchange of aircraft during the planned major overhaul
of the respective fleet components.

Much depends on regional circumstances. Strong inter-airline cooperation is needed in continents like Africa, to permit equal access to
*technical and training facilities*, pool resources in *equipment*, etc. However, the usefulness of cooperation is far from restricted to developing
countries. In Europe, due to the short flying distances and the high
density of traffic on certain routes, it is indispensable that airlines
*coordinate their schedules*, in their own interests, but essentially in the
interests of the public, which would otherwise suffer from a concentration
of services during the most profitable times of the day and from a spread
of services insufficient to meet the public demand. Pooling agreements
in Europe have become pragmatic and almost operational arrangements,
on account of the specificities of intra-European operations. Capacity
sharing clauses — which look highly suspicious in the light of precedents
in anti-cartel law — in fact are only dusty survivals of old times in the
vast majority of cases. By contrast, *joint operations* are tailored to meet
challenging situations and respond to particular requirements : for
instance, in cases where the creation of a service would not be justified
by the initial volume of traffic produced on the route considered, if such
were to support a two-carrier operation at the outset.

Predictably, some European airlines are looking for even closer cooperation, reaching the stage of *integration*, in order to meet the challenge
of increased international competition, including that of the US mega-
carriers to which deregulation has given birth on the other side of the
Atlantic. The US authorities have not opposed, for instance cooperation
between Sabena and British Caledonian Airlines on the Brussels-London-
Atlanta route. SAS and Sabena have looked into close cooperation, an
example which made other European carriers think, not all of them part
of the establishment of designated scheduled airlines. The European

Regional Airlines Organisation (ERA), at its 1986 annual meeting, seriously considered the suggestion that they should discard their individual identities in favour of merging into "potentially the largest regional carrier in the world outside the US".

Aside from code-sharing agreements, the US scene shows examples of cooperative arrangements involving airlines of all sizes. The pooling of resources of commuter airlines and ultimately their merger has demonstrated the strength of the need to regroup in a deregulated environment. The first example was Allegheny Commuter, created in 1967 by an airline of the same name and very well known since under the name of USAir.

In Europe, *legally speaking*, the EEC rules allow airlines belonging to nationals of different Member States, and prohibit exclusivity based on nationality. Provided the market is open to competition and such agreements are entered into on a voluntary basis, there would be few reasons to oppose most types of close cooperative agreements tending to the formation of independent multinational economic entities of exploitation of air transport. Such operating agencies would act in conformity with Article 77 of the Chicago Convention, which would contribute to the conciliation of the Chicago Convention and the Rome Treaty. Clearly, the days of inter-airline cooperation are not over.

But new days are coming as well.

# CHAPTER 2

## COMPETITION : WAYS AND MEANS OF PROGRESS

For some time, aviation appeared to be a romantic occupation : an activity pursued by sportsmen in a country club. If an intruder of questionable reputation disturbed the atmosphere, the gentlemen of the club requested the police to double the guard at the gate. This view of the history of civil aviation, although not without some foundation, is far from the real story.

The air transport scene was once peaceful, but not for long. Various forms of competition from the inner circle of national carriers developed fiercely in the fifties, and were exacerbated by the number of competitors in the sixties.

Around that time and later, a wild competition from charter and other independent carriers developed in a practically deregulated environment, as we have seen earlier in this book. The conquest of international markets, if not the control of its own national market demanded a spirit of adventure from an airline in the sixties and earlier seventies.

The author has known or met some of the men of that generation of entrepreneurs, who built up "their" airlines in the US or in Europe (Velani, Hagrup, Combart, Dieu, many others) : their methods were not smooth, their environment was not gentle. Middle-sized airlines with small national markets could only survive economically by means of a shrewd and aggressive commercial policy and by developing products of quality. By the second part of the seventies and during the eighties, harassed by lower-cost operators who abided by other rules, and confronting the economic crisis, many established airlines that had meanwhile softened and expanded like government departments entrenched themselves in their positions and fell back on various forms of State invention; they also took the easy way out commercially, allowing their own revenues to deteriorate under the pressure of the market-place.

The international structures reflected the diminution of the international spirit. Bilateral agreements served more and more as shields for national airlines and ambushes were set to narrow the fields of competition. Protectionism resulted in unilateral initiatives by which domestic laws were applied to foreign airlines to protect the interests of national carriers. While in some geographical areas the industry was mature and could take care of itself, restrictions to free competition multiplied, due to States' policies often inspired by lazy national airlines, incapable of facing competition on proper grounds. It was high time to relax the intervention of governments, at least whenever the economic strength of a nation allowed for the admission of international competition as the basic rule for the production of international services.

Competition was nothing new in air transport; but the time had come in some regions to retrieve at least the original flexibility of the regulatory system, and to create additional exposure for airlines by removing some of the artificial protection provided by governments for the national carriers of their choice.

A mature industry has to be *independent*. Pricing should be a voluntary process, market entry should permit competition and the provision of capacity should essentially respond to the needs of the market. In a sound economic doctrine, of liberal tendency, the public should benefit from a wider choice of products, in quality as well as in prises, and more efficient enterprises will benefit from their own efforts and become more profitable economic entities.

It is time that we regard, in the light of current development in Europe, for instance, *revenue pooling* and *capacity sharing* inter-airline agreements as having outlived their utility, as they unnecessarily reduce competition.

The economic regulation of international air transport has become a popular topic for politicians and international conferences. The controversy invariably turns to the most popular anthem on this popular subject : competition, leading to lower air fares. Competition has only one drawback, which is due to the simplicity of its formulation and the faith of those who see in it an end instead of a means to achieve progress for communities and mankind at large.

In perspective, the trend towards increased competition is sound and will contribute to the modernisation of the regulatory instrument. Properly channelled, it may mean the return to genuine internationalism in regulation. The absence of international norms of competition, however, would result in confrontation of unilateral competition policies and laws and to conflicts without any possible arbitration. The ways and means of progress are numerous, and will never, in this complex world, be reduced to a slogan. Competition as a fact is nothing more than the rule of nature which ensures the survival of the fittest. As a regulatory tool, it has to be governed by law.

# CHAPTER 3

## PROSPECTS FOR A LEGAL ORDER

### a) *Coming of age at a time of erosion of principles*

To reconcile the large and the small, the "have"'s and the "have not"'s, protectionism and liberalism has always been a challenge for internationalists.

The efficiency of any legal system depends on its application more than on its merits. The Chicago-Bermuda system was essentially *applicable;* that was its principal merit. It was not conceptually perfect and the authority it bestowed on international institutions was limited. However, the concepts existed, the guidelines were provided, the rules were established. It was left to the States to apply the law in the spirit in which it had been conceived : for a safe and orderly development of civil aviation, taking into consideration the equal right of all nations to participate.

The erosion of legal principles and the bending of the rules in favour of narrowly conceived national interests have exemplified the weakness, not so much of the regulatory system itself but of its legal support. It was just too easy for each State to pull the blanket to its side and still look like a law-abiding member of the community. Everybody was right and wrong. Arbitration was practically non-existent, if at all theoretically possible. The bilateral procedure encouraged pragmatic compromises concluded in short-term business terms at the expense of clear definitions of principles. Even States which stood for some principles were willing to betray or at least to silence them for the sake of immediate success.

Through these kinds of deals, the customary law of air transport evolved like an unheatlhy public law arrangement, exceedingly tainted by business interests and borrowing from public law only the language of sovereignty that gave strength to protectionism. The law of contract is normally more explicit than customary law, as its terms are not left open to inference, but are spelled out and put into words. In air transport agreements, the ambiguity was maintained as a new rule of reason, up to the time it became evident that national law, clear-cut and usable by lawyers, would somehow regain precedence.

Indeed, no *superior*, truly international norm governed the parties to a bilateral air transport agreement at least, not in as far as norms of economic law were concerned.

Ostensibly, *unilateral measures* began affecting the economic and technical modalities of international air transport : currency transfers, noise constraints, marketing and selling activities of foreign airlines, and, last but not least, national competition laws.

So competition entered through the legal back door of protectionism, prior to becoming the motto of liberal regulation. The difference in actual inspiration and effect is, to our eyes, negligeable.

As Wassenbergh has put it : "The propensity of States to make exclusive arrangements to assert their preferences and predilections internationally in political, legal, economic, financial and social affairs, or to extend their jurisdiction to this effect, gradually replaces "open" bilateralism and "open" multilateralism by "unilateralism", including "closed" bilateralism and "closed" regionalism". (The author uses the terms "open" and "closed" to indicate, respectively, non-discriminatory arrangements, open also to other States on condition of reciprocity, and arrangements exchanging privileges reserved to the parties and not available to or negotiable by other States.)

Wassenbergh gives the example of the waiver imposed by the US CAB, in its time, upon designated foreign air carriers with respect to the possibility to invoke sovereign immunity in US courts if claims based on the operations authorised under the bilateral agreement at stake were concerned. That certainly is a case in point. It amounts, Wassenbergh says, to "a condition which unilaterally imposes US law on foreign airlines and finds no basis in the standard air agreement itself nor in international law" [157].

In 1979, the International Chamber of Commerce adopted a statement on air transport which addresses this problem.

"In a system based on competition, governments may wish to impose their regulations relating to restrictive business practices/antitrust, subsidies and other similar measures. But to avoid situations in which industry is faced with unilateral action and in which disputes arise between governments concerning the extraterritorial application of such regulations, the ICC proposes that an international conference on such application be convened" [158].

The third Special Air Transport Conference of ICAO (October/ November 1985) issued a Recommandation directing the Council to develop guidance material for avoidance of conflicts resulting from the unilateral application of domestic competition laws to international air transport, in particular where bilateral air services provisions were affected. Contracting States should, under this Recommendation, ensure that their national competition laws are not applied in such a way that a conflict arises with their obligations under their air services agreements and/or under the Chicago Convention, and in such a way that they have no extra-territorial application which has not been agreed upon between the States concerned. The Recommendation also requests the Contracting States to endeavour to agree bilaterally about methods to ensure harmonious air transport relations between those of them whose competition policies are at significant variance with each other [159].

The economic regulation of international air transport is in the process of being fundamentally reviewed in the light of the awareness that air services are commercial activities which require freedom and diversification of products. The legal order, under the circumstances, can only be re-established through a new assessment of the principles and norms that govern the relations between States on the subject of air transport, and of States and airlines. Particular difficulties are to be expected on account of the continuing involvement with international relations at large. But the main problem lies in the differences in the state of economic and social development between different parts of the world, and between countries within geographical regions. Moreover, there also is the basic reason that common legal norms are, more than ever, required.

b) *Plan of action in the legal field*

1) *Subjects to be dealt with*

It is necessary that international lawyers address, at last and at least, the following major areas of problems :

a) the legal norms required by the evolution of the economic regulation of international air transport : rights and obligations of States and international authorities, market access, capacity distribution, tariff approval, multinational operating instruments, fifth freedom rules, prevention of new forms of discrimination and distortions of competition, etc.;

b) the new forms which international relations will take in a changing environment : evolution of bilateralism, the prevention and sanctions of unilateral actions, arbitration, etc.

c) the integration of scheduled and non-scheduled services in a single legal and regulatory regime;

d) the responsibility of air traffic controllers and airport authorities;

e) the development of additional instruments for the prevention and sanction of acts contrary to the security of international civil aviation : (in complement to the Tokyo, Hague and Montreal Conventions on military interception fo aircraft);

f) the harmonisation of the legal regimes of liability of air carriers, and related matters (evolution of the system of the Warsaw Convention);

g) the harmonisation of the rules of air and space law, which the development of techniques and technologies will require. Spacecraft will effectuate air transport operations (carriage of traffic, with or without lucrative purpose, from one point of the earth to the other via the atmospheric space). The law of the air and the law of space are based on a different set of principles.

Several of these tasks are undertaken or in process under the auspices of ICAO or in academic institutions, like McGill University's Institute and Center of Air and Space Law; all should be pursued with renewed energy.

2) *The structures of international public law* which concern civil aviation should be adapted to a changing world, in which regional institutions will evolve as independent intergovernmental organisations with political drives and a legal apparatus; a central organisation, ICAO, should have reinforced powers and be assigned newly defined tasks. The various aspects and implications of the contingency plans for inclusion of air transport among the services subject to the rules of the GATT Agreement should be carefully scrutinised. Opinions should be developed on those subjects from the legal as well as the practical angle and conclusions suggested to the international community.

3) *The shaping of international relations*, although more dependent on political evolution than on theoretical thinking, should be considered carefully and worked out with a constantly global view of the problem. The controversy surrounding bilateralism is more or less dissolving in the more general turmoil surrounding the gradual deregulation of air transport. Legally speaking, means should be devised to encourage multilateral provisions which will govern bilateral relations and supersede any diverging provisions of bilateral agreements. In order to become directly applicable, the provisions of bilateral air transport agreements should be incorporated in domestic laws [160].

# PART VIII

# Conclusions

The political challenge is such that major issues of competitive implications continue to emerge and to make the realities of tomorrow more difficult to grasp. For instance, new technologies, not only in air transportation, but in related fields may transform the commercial configuration of the markets, making the survival of some competitors problematic and posing constant questions to governments and airlines. Matters such as computerised reservation systems become key issues of market control and competitive ability : an adequate regulatory framework has to be provided, if not improvised. Such developments occur very quickly. The time in which governments and enterprises have to react becomes shorter and shorter.

The perplexity of the observer is therefore understandable.

And we will avoid the arrogance of pretending to conclude.

## CHAPTER 1

## A REMINDER OF SOME FACTS

Let us simply recall a few facts :

1. *Air transport is an activity that puts human life and the human environment at some risk*

The basic concern of regulators of air navigation and related techniques, as well as of air transport as an economic activity has to be the *security and safety* of the flights. In addition, the nuisances created by this activity have to be controlled and kept to a minimum.

No relaxation of government control over air transport to whatever degree could ever entail, nor be justified to entail a diminution of operational safety of the aircraft, whether in flight or on the ground, due to equipment standards, crew qualification, navigational aid failures or congestion at airports.

While this may sound self-evident, words of caution are being spoken in various quarters, such as international pilots' associations, European institutions, and so on, because of signs that deregulation in the United

States has resulted in "corner-cuttings" in aircraft maintenance costs by some operators under competitive pressure. The other major challenge posed by intensive competition and open market access is the increase of the number of aircraft movements at airports. The infrastructure of such developments has to be planned ahead to maintain proper security standards.

On the other hand, the conservation of the natural environment and the quality of life have become major concerns of humanity, in its struggle to survive its own technological performance. Recently, hundreds of young people "occupied" a forest which was to be cut down to permit the construction of a new runway at Frankfurt airport. Numerous litigations have taken place against noise at airports, resulting in increasingly restrictive rules on noise abatement conditions and procedures. The pollution caused by airplanes, notably in the upper atmosphere, has also to be taken into account in the long term.

## 2) *Air transport is an expensive and energy-consuming activity*

No matter how successful efforts have been to increase the access of passengers to air transport, this activity remains expensive. The development of aircraft technology, security devices and infrastructures requires huge investments; the price of new generation aircraft shows no sign of diminishing — on the contrary, and despite progress made in saving fuel, the operational expenses in this field are still substantial and globally on the increase. Moreover, these expenses are linked to the world prices of petrol. The 1974 crisis, which resulted in a major shake-down of the air transport industry for several years, showed its vulnerability to the price fluctuations of the fuel market.

Air traffic control and airport charges are constantly being raised, and an important proportion of operational costs are beyond the control of airlines. The privatisation of airlines and their economic deregulation should be accompanied by measures to counter operational costs, which should escape the ceaseless avarice of governments and be strictly cost-related. Otherwise a policy of low fares may result in bankruptcies and loss of employment — unless state subsidies are reinstated, which would defeat the whole purpose.

The objectives set out in Article 44 of the Chicago Convention should be borne in mind, in particular those of responding to the needs of the peoples of the world for a safe, regular, efficient and *economic* air transport system, and *of preventing the economic waste resulting from unreasonable competition.* The waste of economic resources, which are limited worldwide, should be prevented. International cooperation can play a supplementary role in this respect, but the thrust of the effort must be made by governments taking a global view of this essential problem of the preservation of resources, through policies in which air transport must be integrated.

The developing countries, whose resources and financial ability to purchase equipment and fuel are particulary scarce, are therefore also particularly interested in keeping this activity under control.

*But there is not one country in the world that can afford chaos nowadays.*

### 3) *Air transport is an indispensable activity*

We will not emphasise the various functions of air transport which, like maritime navigation for centuries, has fulfilled the essential mission of bringing peoples together. Nothing replaces such human contact. Even telecommunications are no substitute.

The fact is that air transport has become a key factor in the chances of economic and social, if not political survival and development in many countries of the Third World.

In the industrialised countries, it is a commodity whose disappearance is simply inconceivable.

The main point here is that air transport is indispensable *for different reasons and to different degrees in different parts of the world.* To maintain equal chances of participation for all countries, the inequalities must be compensated by a system of international law and cooperation that somehow has to be globally conceived and practically integrated.

### 4) *Air transport is a commercial activity*

In itself, air transport is merely a commercial activity, and should be governed by the rules of trade in services, whenever and wherever the extraneous constraints due to high cost technology and social and economic circumstances are being taken care of.

Products offered on the market-place should be diversified and respond to the demands of the public. The competition in services should not be distorted internationally, which means that national laws on competition should neither interfere, nor conflict with each other, but should respond to an international competition law governing the overall commercial aspects of international air transport.

## 5) *Regionalism is a normal trend in civil aviation reformation*

The re-appraisal of the economic regulation of air transport is, logically, being undertaken and pursued at regional level, because the variety of situations mentioned above encourages neighbouring countries to seek common interests and attitudes based on common features specific to their region.

However, there is a further tendency for regions to talk to each other. It could be envisaged that a *new bilateralism based on inter-regional dialogues* might be developed at some further stage. It would be progress compared with the present reductive forms of bilateralism used in air transport relations.

The sense of solidarity between nations certainly deserves to be encouraged without excessive fears that worldwide structures would thereby be shaken down and dissolved. The parallel tendency should be, on the contrary, to reinforce the structures capable of international legislation and arbitration.

The only danger in regionalism is the indifference of one region to the requirements of the others, and the predominance of political ideologies over the factual needs of an integrated worldwide air transport network.

## 6) *This is a small world*

*"Air transportation, along with modern communications, has transformed this vast globe, almost in a single generation, into a small world"*. ("Project Horizon" (1961) US Government policy statement on international aviation.)

The stable and productive period in which air traffic could develop in an orderly manner under the single Chicago-Bermuda regime has been a thing of the past for a long time now. In a sense, the fragmentation was predictable. The non-innovative concept of state sovereignty over airspace "meant sowing a seed of fragmentation at the basic legal level" [159].

This fragmentation is now multifold and multiple. Nevertheless, the wide-ranging, worldwide implications of any change in air transport policies by States or groups of States can be felt instantly and cannot be overlooked.

There is a cultural revolution in progress due to the abolition of distances, both physical and informative, worldwide. It would be paradoxical if air transport, which has been instrumental in bringing about this revolution, were itself to lose its global regulatory framework and its legal integrity. There is no basic, valid reason for such a dramatic development. On the contrary, the only hope for the peaceful development of humanity at large in the next century lies in a reinforced structure of international cooperation based on the solidarity of poor and rich nations.

No interest would be properly served by selfish reactions at whatever level. What the Chairman of the Chicago Convention Adolf Berle said in his opening statement, in 1944, remains true :

"All agree that an effective form of world organization for air purposes is necessary. This does not exclude regional organizations from having a primary interest in the problems of their particular areas; but no regional organization or group of regional organizations can effectively deal with the new problems resulting from interoceanic and intercontinental flying".

A new pattern and a new style of international air transport relations has to be invented. The dogma of absolute state sovereignty in its customary applications has to be revised. Multilateral agreements must gradually supersede bilateral provisions. *This is a world of common ground.*

### 7) *Politics will not save the day*

The excessive politisation of air transport problems is a direct consequence of the exclusive rights the national States have exercised over their air transport industry as owners of the air resources. Air traffic is no more a national entitlement than air is a negotiable national resource. A sounder legal philosophy would have prevented the abusive trade-off among nations of commodities which should be treated as international by nature.

No wonder that general politics and ideologies have corrupted the commerce of the air.

But even the a-political theory introduces politics by the back door. Economic liberalism makes the market a political aim, and regards the consumer as a potential voter. Air transport is so commercial in essence and so tainted by public interest that it is a specific animal, pushed ahead by its almost unpredictable technology.

We would be reluctant to admit that the current political language, with its *repetitiveness*, its *immobility*, its *self-serving* assertions, its generality and servility to pre-conceptions, could ever reflect the versatility of particular sectors like this one. A simple recipe will not save the day where complex services like transport or communications are concerned, and technology or social problems will make nonsense tomorrow of today's truth.

## 8) *Market growth is a key factor*

The early post-war market was small and inelastic; air traffic has expanded dramatically in the sixties and the market is now highly differentiated, and will double in size by the end of the century. Clearly, the regulatory perspective can never be the same as at the time when collective action was all that was required. "The individual approach has thus been confirmed and appears to be a solidly entrenched concept in regulatory thinking. "We are in a phase of compromise. "International air transport", as the current Director General of IATA, Dr. Eser has concluded, "in its present phase is experimenting with this system in an attempt to preserve the advantages of both approaches."

# CHAPTER 2

## AN ATTEMPT TO CONCLUDE

By putting all these elements together, in a rapidly changing environment, we can begin to perceive a future which will reconcile the various social and economic requirements.

The pattern is still vague, and it is doubtful whether it will ever bring about perfect legal security; but who could dream of perfect legal security in economic law nowadays? The international order, in particular, is in serious danger for multiple reasons and there is no reason why international air transport should escape the common lot, being closely related to the evolution of international relations.

The general regulation of air transport must rest on some of the essential principles of the Chicago Convention of 1944.

A *safe* air transport system and an *orderly development* of air services are such principles. In this context, the value of human life and of the human environment for the future must remain essential preoccupations, and take precedence over merely economic considerations. Air navigation must remain safe, air transport must be economical.

As far as economics are concerned, views may of course differ, but facts must be taken into account in the light, on the one hand, of the orderly development criterion and, on the other, of the requirement to ensure the *equality of chances* of all nations. In our view, the essential guideline inspired by these principles is to respect the legitimate interests of all and bear in mind the solidarity of all nations in confronting the future. Any valid policy should take account primarily of the needs of the countries for which air transportation forms the backbone of economic development and social progress. This does not mean that a uniform economic regulation should necessarily apply worldwide; on the contrary, it is time to accommodate the system to the stage of development of the industry and of the society in particular areas of the world. But these regimes must be reconciled in a wider framework.

One of the emerging concepts seems to be the distance gradually introduced between the interests of nations and the identities and nationalities of airlines. This distance is likely to lay the foundation for a common re-appraisal of the respective roles of governments and airlines. As enterprises, the airlines will develop their commercial activities according to their judgment and compete on an equal basis with each other, within a commercial-legal environment. To a large extent, the competition law principles will have to receive international recognition, in order to avoid disruptive unilateral action by governments. If left to national courts, the legal order will run great risks of quick disruption and jurisdictional conflicts will multiply. Someone has paraphrased Clemenceau's words and stated that air law is too important to be left to the lawyers ...

As nations, the States that signed the Chicago Convention and engaged in so many bilateral arrangements will have to reconsider some of their options and re-define their true responsibilities. Primarily, those responsibilities bear on the interests of the groups concerned, but they imply regulatory interventions in the functioning of the air transport industry. Such interventions are, of course, required in security and safety matters, as well as in the area of adapting the infrastructure to the demands of traffic. But, economic regulation is far from outruled or outdated; on the contrary, it will be more necessary than ever to prevent and punish dumping practices and anti-competitive behaviour at large. It is clear from experience that deregulation calls for re-regulation. In economic terms, it would be abhorrent to allow overcapacity to develop to the extent staf tariffs would be entirely de-regulated. Even those services which are indispensable to the communities in some or even all countries may be in jeopardy and the belated intervention of the richest country in favour of its ailing industry, in a sudden protectionist reaction, would not only defeat the purpose of deregulation and work against public interest, but would further aggravate the imbalance of forces in the world. It should not be forgotten that air transport is extremely sensitive to conjuncture, to oil prices and currency variations. Governments who did not provide certain safeguards would not be meeting their responsibilities. The eminent economist of air transport, Stephen Wheatcroft, has identified consumerism and deregulation as "twin forces" to be considered "in explaining the severity of the world airline crisis" during the 1980-1983 recession. This formidable crisis has cost the airline industry almost six billion US dollars over those few years. How many airlines, and countries, could afford a shake-down of a similar magnitude again?

. In some ways, the system must accommodate markets by dramatic expansion and thinly spread networks, nevertheless necessary for the communities concerned. It must reconcile competition and cooperation, balance collective and individual inputs in different blends, whether at government or airline level. Yet an integrated documentary format of operation is necessary, as in the past, for the convenience of the users and the promotion of air transport. Service to the passengers cannot be degraded but, on the contrary, should be improved. The pattern of inter-governmental agreements will have to be revised : diversified altogether on specific points and standardised on others. Governments will have to regulate competition, take account of the diversity of services, clear possible financial difficulties which would affect the fairness of the deal and include, as the case may be, transfer of technologies to developing countries, and so on. It is important that, for an increasing number of items, they abide by a multilaterally agreed set of principles, rules and procedures; in this case, "multilateral" may boil down to "regional".

We have noted the objection that inter-regional disputes can substitute for international power struggles. They would be just as difficult to arbitrate, maybe more. This is indeed a danger. The international community should provide guidelines — a "code of conduct" — to prevent such a problem from arising. That will be the role of the larger international institution, ICAO, which alone can provide the type of framework required to put thoughts and facts together and arbitrate if necessary. We have to face the fact that complete multilateralism will fail to materialise for a long time. Any form of international solidarity is better than outright nationalism. It is a step forward in the right direction, provided there is one.

The new society, anyway, does not need to resemble the battlefield of today. New thoughts will be injected into the system. Consumerism (as well as environmentalism) provokes such thoughts. Consumerism is a new phenomenon, not yet fully explored legally, but of great social importance, provided it is not focused on the primacy of the market. It must be centred on the human being who is entitled to a life of quality. The discriminate user of air transport will be a different sort of person from the bewildered passenger in crowded airports. Or else consumerism will fail in turn to achieve its purpose.

No existing ideology will by itself do justice to the requirements of the people : the man in the street, passengers on business or leisure trips, shippers, airline employees. They want an ad hoc, unobtrusive system, one with which they can live and travel safely, send goods, for the right transparent price, with a choice of adapted products. They do not want to notice the system, but to be able to call on it if anything goes wrong.

The employees of this large industry, beginning with the crews, are highly qualified. They have to be. The reliability of the service depends on them. Their training has often been a substantial investment. They should expect, especially in countries with few or no equivalent job opportunities, a certain stability of working conditions under which airlines operate. This is not a question that can be solved in theory, but by taking into account the specificities of the air transport industry.

Bearing in mind the quality of life — rather than the number of automobiles on the road or of aircraft in the air — requires a certain approach to the production of goods and services. Past theories are hardly appropriate to present situations. This is not new in itself. At the time of the industrial revolution, the new technology of factory production generated problems that neither Locke nor Smith had faced. We are coming up to a time of new technologies, new labour problems, a new style of life with more leisure time. It is predictable that diversified products will respond to these demands. Anyway, a shrinking world will need more than ever fast, reliable and massive transportation means as an essential factor of social cohesion.

Let business be business, but over and above the business life of aircraft manufacturers, airlines of all kinds and intermediaries, the regulators of air transport economics should bear in mind that the interdependence of all countries is a key factor in this line of activity. The Chicago Convention of 1944 is not a monument to be preserved at all costs. But it has established a worldwide framework that can be improved and completed to respond better to the progress of mankind — an ideal of our fathers not to be forgotten by our sons.

# APPENDIX 1

## (Notes)

## INTRODUCTORY REMARKS

The following Notes are meant to provide quick references. They are based selectively on pertinent material immediately available to the author at the time of writing. (The author has relied on other material as well and largely on his own professional experience.) The references are therefore far from comprehensive. Other sources and excellent studies, including a number by some of the writers we cite, can be found. In fact, an abundant literature exists on the economics and economic law of international air transport. It is, however, largely disseminated in specialised reviews and monographs published over a period of some forty years. Effective research can be sometimes difficult under those circumstances. On the other hand, the textbooks on air law cover the whole area in general terms, but do not usually reserve an extensive place for the consideration of issues which are frequently difficult to grasp, require professional attention to market developments and depend heavily on politics while requiring legal thinking at the same time. The legal writers, more academically inclined and documented, will naturally indulge more in developments of private law or criminal law issues raised by international air transportation.

"Ad generalia", we refer the reader to ICAO, IATA, AEA and ATA documents, and to material gathered in the libraries of such institutions as the Institute and Centre of Air and Space Law of McGill University in Montreal, the Institut du Transport Aérien in Paris or the International Institute for Air and Space Law of the State University of Leiden. On European, in particular EEC developments, we recommend the publications of the Institut d'Etudes Européennes of the Free University of Brussels. Last but not least, we refer the reader to the *International Bibliography of Air Law*, by Wybo P. Heere, which is updated on a regular basis (Kluwer Law and Taxation Publishers). A selected bibliography is attached in Appendix 3.

J.N.

[1] Cfr. Bury vs Pope (1586), 7-8 English Reports 375; Baten's case, 77 English Reports 810. Also : John COOPER, "Roman Law and the Maxim : 'cujus est solum' in International Air Law", *The McGill Law Journal*, 23 (1952)185.

[2] Cfr. A. McNAIR, *The Law of the Air*, Butterworths, London, 1932, p. 15.

[3] Cfr. Nicolas MATEESCO MATTE, *Traité de Droit Aérien-Aéronautique*, Pedone, Paris, 1980, pp. 56-57.

[4] Hoffman vs. Armstrong, cfr. A. McNAIR, *op. cit.*, p. 33.

[5] *72 U.S. Stat. 740*, Tit. I, par. 104 (1958), *49 U.S. C.A.C. 20*, par. 1304 (1958).

[6] Cfr. International Law Association, 28th Report, Madrid, 1913.

[7] Convention Relating to the Regulation of Aerial Navigation, Paris, October 13, 1919; ratified by 32 countries.

[8] M. MILDE, "The Chicago Convention — After Forty Years", *Annals of Air and Space Law*, 121 (1984).

⁹ On the Conference, cfr. *Proceedings of the International Civil Aviation Conference*, Chicago, Illinois, Nov. 1-Dec. 7, 1944, The Department of State, p. 13.

On proposals made at the Conference by delegates, cfr. W. J. WAGNER, *International Air Transportation as Affected by State Sovereignty*, Bruylant, Brussels, 1970, pp. 95 sq.; DIEDERIKS-VERSCHOOR, *An Introduction to Air Law*, Kluwer, Deventer, 1983, p. 9.

¹⁰ M. MILDE, *op. cit.*, id.

¹¹ On the achievements of the Chicago Conference, notably in air transport related politics, cfr.; Bin CHENG, *The Law of International Air Transport*, Stevens, London, 1962, pp. 18-28; W. J. WAGNER, *op. cit.*, pp. 95 sq.

¹² Cfr. Bin CHENG, *op. cit.*, p. 120.

¹³ Cfr. Bin CHENG, *op. cit.*, p. 21.

¹⁴ Cfr. Michel FOLLIOT, *Les Relations Aériennes Internationales*, Pedone, Paris, 1985, p. 287.

¹⁵ Cfr. H. A. WASSENBERGH, "Parallels and Differences in the Development of Air, Sea and Space Law in the Light of Grotius' Heritage", *Annals of Air and Space Law*, 171 (1984) : "Article 6 of the Chicago Convention has become the starting point for the present restrictive bilateralism in the exchange of operational and traffic rights for international scheduled air services".

¹⁶ Cfr. *I.C.A.O.* D.O.C. 7070, vol. I (Resolution A2-18, Definition of the "scheduled international air services") also D.O.C. I.C.A.O. A1-EC/2 (Resolution A1-39, same title).

¹⁷ Cfr. ICAO DOC 7278 C/814, (10-5-1952).

¹⁸ Cfr. U.N.T.S. 389 (1944).

¹⁹ A. GARNAULT, "Les Conventions et Résolutions de Chicago", *R.F.D.A.*, 29 (1946-47).

²⁰ A. KOTAITE, "The Chicago Convention, an Act of Faith in Civil Aviation", *39 ICAO Bulletin*, Nov. 1984, p. 14.

²¹ Y. LAMBERT, "The Chicago Convention has met the need in 40 years' use", *30 ICAO Bulletin*, Nov. 1984, p. 15.

²² Cfr. a.o. E. D. GAGGERO, "En el 40ᵉ aniversario de la Convención de Chicago — Homenaje a la OACI", *CIDA*, Montevideo, 1984, pp. 79-80; H. A. PERUCCHI and A. L. SANES, "Las enmiendas a la Convención de Chicago-Homenaje a la OACI", *CIDA*, Montevideo, 1984, pp. 19-65.

²³ Air Services Agreement between the Government of the United States of America and the Government of the United Kingdom of Great Britain and Northern Ireland, Fefruary 11, 1946; "Annexes and Final Act of the Civil Aviation Conference held at Bermuda", January 15-February 11, 1946, TIAS 1507.

²⁴ Albert W. STOFFEL, "American Bilateral Air Transport Agreements on the Threshold of the Jet Transport Age", *J.A.L.C.*, 122 (1959) "Such an agreement was necessary between the two leading civil aviation powers of the world because of the difference in their approaches to the problem of the exchange of commercial air rights which had become evident in Chicago. The agreement constituted a compromise between the liberal American and the restrictive British concepts."

²⁵ Cfr. J. COOPER, "The Bermuda Plan : World Pattern for Air Transport", in *Explorations in Aerospace Law, Selected Essays*, Mc Gill University Press, Montréal, 381 (1968); BAKER, "The Bermuda Plan as the Basis for a Multilateral Agreement, in VLASIC and BRADLEY, *The Public International Law of Air Transport*, Vol. 1, Mc Gill University Press, Montréal, 1948; N. M. MATTE, *op. cit.* (ed. 1980), p. 230, "Ad generalia", cfr. ICAO DOC, SATC 1977, nr. 3, pp. 5-6-7 and App. 3, p. 39; LISSITZYN, "Bilateral Agreements on Air Transport", *J.A.L.C.*, 248 (1964).

²⁶ P. VAN DER TUUK Adriani, "The Bermuda Capacity Clauses", *J.A.L.C.*, 411, (1955).

[27] Albert W. STOFFEL, *op. cit.*, p. 129.

[28] J. Z. GERTLER, "Law of Bilateral Air Transport Agreements : ICAO Air Transport Regulation Panel and the Regulation of Capacity in International Air Services", *Annals of Air and Space Law*, 52, (1984).

[29] Consult, a.o. : J. C. McCARROLL, "The Bermuda Capacity Clauses in the Jet Age", *J.A.L.C.*, 120 (1963); J. CRIBBETT, "Some International Aspects of Air Transport", *J.R.A.S.*, 678 (1950); BIN CHENG, *op. cit.*, p. 429; SHAWCROSS and BEAUMONT, *Air Law*, 4th ed., vol. II, pp. 362, 366, *et al.*; N. MATEESCO MATTE, *op. cit.*, pp. 230 sq.; LOWENFELD, "The Future determines the Past : Bermuda I in the light of Bermuda II", *Air Law*, 5 (1978); A. MERCKX, *Post-Bermuda II Trends in the International Economic Law of Air Transport*, unpubl. L.L.M. thesis, Inst. of Air and Space Law, McGill Univ., Montreal, 1981, pp. 107 sq.; DIAMOND, "The Bermuda Agreement Revisted", *J.A.L.C.*, 419 (1975); J. Z. GERTLER, "Bilateral Air Transport Agreements : Non-Bermuda Reflections", *J.A.L.C.*, 818 (1976).

[30] On the subject of ratemaking in general, cfr. essentially P. P. C. HAANAPPEL, *Ratemaking in International Air Transport : A Legal Analysis of International Air Fares and Rates*, Kluwer, Deventer, 1978; on the approval of the IATA Traffic Conferences machinery by the U.S. under the anti-trust laws, cfr. also, f.e. A. MERCKX, "New Trends in International Bilateral Regulation of Air Transport", *E.T.L.*, 1984, pp. 131 sq.; P. P. C. HAANAPPEL, *id.*, p. 30, note 32.

To be noted that the intention to approve the machinery for one year had been expressed by the U.S. in the Bermuda Agreement, itself : cfr. Annex II, par. b.

[31] "Although in certain circumstances a lesser amount is required", following opinion of Prof. DIEDERIKS-VERSCHOOR, *op. cit.*, p. 11; cfr. also H. A. WASSENBERGH, *Post-War International Civil Aviation Policy and the Law of the Air*, Nijhoff, The Hague, 1962, p. 117.

[32] A. W. STOFFEL, *op. cit.*, p. 128.

[33] A. W. STOFFEL, *op. cit.*, p. 127.

[34] P. CHAUVEAU, *Droit aérien*, Libraries Techniques, 1951, p. 65.

[35] ICAO Resolution A1-3L; *ICAO Lexicon 1952*. (Italics added).

[36] M. LE GOFF, *Manuel de Droit Aérien*, Dalloz, Paris, 1964, p. 246.

[37] Cfr. ICAO Circ. 135 (1977), *Tariff Enforcement;* ICAO Circ. 144 (1977), *Regional Differences in Fares, Rates and Costs for International Air Transport;* ICAO Circ. 150 (1980), *Surveys of International Air Transport Fares and Rates* (1978-1979).

[38] Cfr. ICAO DOC 9228-C/1036 (1978).

[39] Cfr. ICAO DOC 9199 and 9297.

[40] P. P. C. HAANAPPEL, *op. cit.;* G. O. ESER, "Airline Pricing in a Liberalised Regulatory Environment", *Annals of Air and Space Law*, 3 (1985); J. W. BRANCKER, "IATA and what it does", Sijthoff, Leiden, 1977.

[41] Report of the D.G. to the 1949 General Assembly; cfr. IATA Documentation.

[42] M. LE GOFF, *op. cit.*, p. 123.

[43] Current membership of ECAC includes : Austria, Belgium, Cyprus, Denmark, Finland, France, the Federal Republic of Germany, Greece, Iceland, Ireland, Italy, Luxembourg, Malta, the Netherlands, Norway, Portugal, Spain, Sweeden, Switzerland, Turkey, the United Kingdom and Yugoslavia.

[44] Resolution formally constituting ECAC : ECAC/1-Res. 1, 1955, 3). Texts of documents relating to the constitution of ECAC in ROSENFIELD, *The Regulation of International Commercial Aviation*, Oceana, 24-2, booklet 14.

[45] Constitution of the ECAC, Sec. B(4) (a); Rules of Procedure, Sec. B(4) (b).

[46] Constitution of the ECAC, id., art. 5.

240APPENDIX 1

**⁴⁷** Id. art. 6.

**⁴⁸** Id. art. 7.

**⁴⁹** Id., art. 15.

**⁵⁰** Prof. I. H. Ph. DIEDERIKS-VERSCHOOR, *op. cit.*, p. 37.

**⁵¹** On specific problems of air transport in Europe, consult, a.o., BONNEFOUS, "Le Problème des Transports Aériens en Europe", *Revue Générale de l'Air*, 307 (1951); S. WHEATCROFT, "The Economics of European Air Transport", *Harvard University Review*, 1956; D. GOEDHUIS, "The Role of Air Transport in European Integration", *J.A.L.C.*, 273 (1957); DE VILLENEUVE, "Les Transports Aériens Régu- liers de l'Europe Occidentale", *Revue Générale de l'Air*, 4 (1961); S. VEIL, "L'Europe et l'Aviation Civile", *Bull. ITA*, 1159 (1980); J. NAVEAU, *L'Europe et le Transport Aérien*, Bruylant, Brussels, 1983; S. WHEATCROFT and G. LIPMAN, "Air Transport in a Competitive European Market", The Economist Intelligence Unit, Sp. Report 1060, 1986.

Also cfr. EC documents, a.o. : European Community. Civil Aviation Memoran- dum Nr. 2 — Progress towards the Development of a Community Air Transport Policy, 1984; European Community. Opinion on Memorandum Nr. 2, Economic and Social Committee, 1985; European Community. Report on Memorandum Nr. 2, European Parliament Transport Community, 1985.

**⁵²** L. WEBER, "Les éléments de la coopération dans le cadre de la Commission Européenne de l'Aviation Civile (CEAC)", *R.F.D.A.*, Nr. 394, (1977).

**⁵³** Cfr. ECAC Doc.; cfr., a.o. P. P. C. HAANAPPEL, *Pricing and Capacity Determi- nation in International Air Transport*, Kluwer Law and Taxation Publishers, Deventer/ Boston, 1984, pp. 164-167, notably footnote 34.

**⁵⁴** The consensus to create the AFCAC as a specialized agency of the OAU was formulated in the Agreement between the Organization of African Unity (OAU) and the African Civil Aviation Commission (ACAC) establishing AFCAC as a specialized agency of OAU, signed at Addis Abeba, May 11, 1978; text in : ROSEN- FIELD, *op. cit.*, 84-2, booklet 15; on organization see *ITA Bull.* nr. 18, 9 July 1971; *ITA Bull.* nr. 30, 28 may 1973; sp. *ITA Bull.* nr. 30, 12 September 1977.

**⁵⁵** Current membership of the AFCAC includes : Algeria, Angola, Benin, Burundi, Cameroon, Central African Republic, Chad, Congo, Egypt, Ethiopia, Gabon, Gambia, Ghana, Guinea, Ivory Coast, Kenya, Lesotho, Liberia, Libya, Madagascar, Malawi, Mali, Mauritania, Morocco, Niger, Nigeria, Rwanda, Senegal, Sierra Leone, Somalia, Sudan, Swaziland, Tanzania, Togo, Tunisia, Uganda, Upper Volga, Zaire, Zambia.

**⁵⁶** Cfr. Declaration of General Policy in the Field of Civil Aviation, 1980, A, 1.

**⁵⁷** Cfr. Declaration of General Policy in the Field of Civil Aviation, II, 7 AFCAC has associated itself to the Lomé four-years Plan (1978-1981).

**⁵⁸** Convention on the Establishment of the African Air Tariff Conference. (Text in : ROSENFIELD, *op. cit.*, 67).

**⁵⁹** Cfr. Preamble of the Convention : "Considering the urgent need to improve the existing worldwide tariff coordination machinery to respond more adequately to the specific needs of air transportation in Africa ...".

**⁶⁰** Current membership of the LACAC includes : Argentina, Bolivia, Brasil, Chile, Colombia, Costa Rica, Cuba, Dominican Republic, Ecuador, El Salvador, Guatemala, Honduras, Mexico, Nicaragua, Panama, Paraguay, Peru, Uruguay, Venezuela; cfr. SHAWCROSS and BEAUMONT, *op. cit.*, Vol. 1, pp. 117-119; J. C. BOGO- LASKY, "Air transport in Latin America : the Expanding Role of LACAC", *L.A.L.C.*, 1978, pp. 75-107.

A. LAMAISON, Consideractiones preliminares sobre la Comisión Latino-Americana de Aviación Civil, Montevideo, 1975, 17, note 1.7.

[61] International Convention Relating to Cooperation for the Safety of Air Navigation, Brussels, 13 December 1960; Protocol (Amending the International Convention ...), Brussels, 12 February 1981; Revised 1981 Multilateral Agreement Relating to Route Charges; on changes, cfr. Mousse, "Eurocontrol, The Changes Effected in the International Organisation by the Instruments signed on 12 February 1981" *Air Law*, Vol. VII, 1982, nr. 1, p. 22. Cfr. Texts of multilateral and bilateral agreements relating to Eurocontrol in ROSENFIELD, *op. cit.*, 84-2, booklet 18.

[62] Multilateral Agreement on commercial rights in Non-Scheduled International Air services within Europe, Paris, 30 April 1950, ICAO DOC 7695; cfr. L. CARTOU‘ *Droit Aérien*, P.U.F., Paris, 1963; M. LITVINE, *Droit Aérien*, Bruylant, Brussels, 1970, 32.

[63] Cfr. DIEDERIKS-VERSCHOOR, *op. cit.*, p. 13; J. J. GOUDSMIT, *Het internationale ongeregelde luchtvervoer en artikel 5 van het Verdrag van Chicago* (thesis Utrecht, 1953, p. 5 English summary; J. W. F. SUNDBERG, *Air Charter, A Study in Legal Development*, 1961; E. DU PONTAVICE, *Le statut juridique des affrètements aériens dits "charters"*, RGAE 241-257 (1970); J. P. HARI, *Les transports aériens commerciaux non-réguliers en Europe*, thesis Lausanne, 1969; J. KAMP, *Air Charter Regulations, a Legal, Economic Consumer Study*, 1975; O. J. LISSITZYN, "Freedom of the Air, Scheduled and Non-Scheduled Air Services", in MCWHINNEY and BRADLEY, *Freedom of the Air*, 1968, pp. 89-105; S. D. BROWNE, "The international angle", *Aeronautical Journal* 29 (1973); A. A. WASSENBERGH, *Aspects of Air Law and Civil Air Policy*, Martinus Nijhoff, The Hague, pp. 79-103; J. THOMKA-GAZDIK, "The Distinction between Scheduled and Charter Transportation", *Air Law*, 66 (1976).

[64] H. A. WASSENBERGH, *Public International Air Transportation Law in a new Era'* Kluwer, Deventer, 1976, p. 44.

[65] Tony AUST, "Air Services Agreements : current United Kingdom procedures and policies", *Air Law*, 189 (1985).

[66] M. FOLLIOT, *op. cit.*

[67] Cfr. O. J. LISSITZYN, "The Legal Status of Executive Agreements on Air Transportation", *J.A.L.C.*, 436, (1970), p. 436; also nr. 18, 1951, p. 12; Bin CHENG, *op. cit.*, p. 46; "*ad generalia*", U.N., Laws and Practices Concerning the Conclusion of Treaties, 1952. Subject discussed in various works of H. A. WASSENBERGH.

[68] *Proceedings*, p. 451.

[69] Cfr. Bin CHENG, *op. cit.*, pp. 373-374; Clause to be found, for instance, in bilateral agreements of the U.K. with Uruguay, Peru, Italy, Sri Lanka, Spain, Thailand, Israel, Egypt, Iraq, Dominican Republic, Panama, Burma, Libya.

[70] P. VAN DER TUUK ADRIANI, *op. cit.*

[71] Amir ALI MAJID, "Impact of Current U.S. Policy on International Civil Aviation", *Zeitschrift für Luft- und Weltraumrecht*, 295 (1983).

[72] A. STOFFEL, *op. cit.*

[73] Cfr. A. BALTENSWEILER, "The Flight from the Freedom of Choice", *ITA Doc.*, Not. 11.735.

[74] H. A. WASSENBERGH, *op. cit.* sub (64), p. 44.

[75] ICAO DOC. 8681.

[76] T. AUST, *op. cit.*

[77] Cfr. A. F. LOWENFELD, *Aviation Law, Cases and Materials*, Matthew Bender, N.Y., 1972; E. WESSBERGE, "Arbitrage et Accords Internationaux", *R.G.A.*, 3 (1951); J. NAVEAU, "Away from Bermuda? An Arbitration Verdict on Capacity Clauses in the Belgian-Ireland Air Transport Agreement", *Air Law*, 50 (1983).

[78] H. A. WASSENBERGH, "Regulatory Reform — a Challenge to intergovernmental Civil Aviation Conferences", *Air Law*, 44 (1986).

[79] Cfr., a.o., Bin CHENG, *op. cit.*, p. 3; Bin CHENG, *The Right to Fly, Grotius Society Transactions*, 1956, pt 99, pp. 105 sq.

[80] Bin CHENG, *op. cit.*, Preface.

[81] M. LE GOFF, *op. cit.*, p. 9.

[82] M. G. FOLLIOT, "Nouvelles Orientations des Organismes Intergouvernementaux d'Aviation Civile", *R.F.D.A.*, 314 (1976).

[83] R. STAINTON, *Civil Aviation, The Economic Future : A Worldwide Perspective*, Lloyds of London Press Conference, New-York, 25 May 1979.

[84] Harriet Oswalt HILL, "Bermuda II, The British Revolution of 1976", *J.A.L.C.*, 113, note 15 (1978).

[85] Albert W. STOFFEL, *op. cit.*, p. 127.

[86] H. A. WASSENBERGH, *op. cit.* sub (64), p. 54.

[87] H. A. WASSENBERGH, *op. cit.*, sub (64), p. 74.

[88] Morton S. BERGER, *Aviation Daily*, 31 Aug. 1973.

[89] K. HAMMARSKJÖLD, Director General IATA, Symposium of the U.S. Department of State, Kingston, Jamaica, 31 January 1979.

[90] R. STAINTON, *op. cit.*

[91] R. STAINTON, *op. cit.*

[92] H. A. WASSENBERGH, *op. cit* sub (15).

[93] M. G. FOLLIOT, *op. cit.*, sub (82), p. 319.

[94] Air Transport Services Agreement between the United States of America and the United Kingdom of Great-Britain and Northern Ireland, July 23, 1977; TIAS 8641n, 811, 28 (UST, Department of State, Washington D.C.).

[95] Air Transport Services Agreement between the United States of America and the Kingdom of Great-Britain and Northern Ireland, Amending the Agreement of July 23, 1977, as Modified. Effected by Exchange of Notes signed at Washington, April 25 1978; TIAS 8965.

[96] F. VIDELA ESCALADA, "Air Transport in International Law", in *International Air Transport in the Eighties*, ed. by H. A. Wassenbergh and H. P. van Fenema, Kluwer, Deventer, p. 173.

[97] D. D. SANDELL, "Deregulation — Has it finally arrived? The Airline Deregulation Act of 1978", *J.A.L.C.*, 799, (1979).

[98] Cfr. 49 U.S.C., 1321 (1976).

[99] "Rep. Norman Y. Mineta", quoted in M. COHEN, *Regulatory Report*, (CAB's new Chairman charts an independent course, Nat'l J., 1975, pp. 1559-1566).

[100] Raymond A. YOUNG, Deputy Asst. Secretary DOT, Symposium of May 1978 at Georgetown University.

[101] B. R. DIAMOND, *op. cit.*, sub (29), p. 462.

[102] R. Thornton, in MCWHINNEY and BRADLEY, *op. cit.*, pp. 179-189; cfr. note 10, at 25 quoting Sackrey, "Overcapacity in the U.S. International Air Transport Industry", *J.A.L.C.*, 30 (1966).

[103] Cfr. BARLOW, *The Extraterritorial Application of U.S. Antitrust Laws and International Air Transportation : A Legal or Political Question?* LLM Thesis, McGill University, Montreal, 1983.

[104] P. P. C. HAANAPPEL, "Deregulation of Air Transport in North America and Western Europe", in *Air Worthy, Liber Amicorum Dr. I. H. Ph. Diederiks-Verschoor*, Kluwer, 1985, p. 98.

[105] Fulda, International Aspects of Aviation *J.A.L.C.*, 63, (1967).

[106] R. Thornton, *op. cit.*, p. 89.

[107] K. Hammarskjöld; cfr. Rinck, "The international factors in German Air Transport", *J.A.L.C.*, 102 (1967).

[108] For the list, cfr. Driscoll, "Deregulation, the US Experience", *Int'l Business Lawyer*, 1981, p. 158; A list which perhaps has not been updated includes : the Netherlands, Israel, Federal Republic of Germany, Belgium, Korea, Papua New-Guinea, Jamaica, Costa Rica, Singapore, Fiji, Taiwan, Thailand, Netherlands Antilles, Finland, Jordan, Barbados, El Salvador, Partial liberal agreements were concluded by the US with : Australia, Brazil, Philippines, New Zealand.

For a good analysis of main common features, cfr. A. L. Merckx, "New trends in the international bilateral regulation of air transport", *European Transport Law*, 107, (1982).

[109] Cfr. Report of the Subcommittee on Investigation and Oversight of the Committee on Public Works and Transportation, U.S. House of Representatives on the Improvement needed in the implementation of the United States International Aviation Policy, August 1983, 98th Congress First Session, USGPO 23-934.

[110] FY 82 DOT Appropriation Bill.

[111] R. Colegate, "The U.K. Regulatory Scene", *ITA Magazine*, (Deregulation II), nr. 36, June/July 1986.

[112] Cfr. Gardiner, "United Kingdom Air Services Agreements 1970-1980", *Air Law*, 5, (1982).

[113] T. Aust, *op. cit.*

[114] Cfr. *ITA Magazine, Dereglementation II*, June-July 1986, p. 13.

[115] Final Report of the Think Tank on a Coordinated Policy for International Commercial Aviation, published by Graduate Institute of International Studies, Geneva, 1978, Doc. Series nr. 1.

[116] M. Guernier, *Tiers Monde, Trois quarts du Monde*, Dunod, Paris, 1980.

[117] Khaled Bitar, "Airlines in Developing Countries", in *Commercial Aviation in Developing Countries*, publ. IATA, Montreal, 1985; cfr. on this general subject A. Peccei, (Pres. Club of Rome), One Hunderd Pages for the Future, McDonald, London-Sydney, p. 117.

[118] Laban Agala, *Airlines in Developing Countries*, ref. under 117, p. 1.

[119] Khaled Bitar, *op. cit.*, p. 24.

[120] Khaled Bitar, *op. cit.*, p. 25.

[121] Khaled Bitar, *op. cit.*, p. 29.

[122] G. H. Kaunda, "Regulation — A Government Perspective", in *Future Challenges in African Air Transport*, publ. IATA, Montreal, 1985, p. 44.

[123] G. H. Kaunda, *op. cit.*, p. 45.

[124] G. O. Eser, "Airline Pricing in a Liberalised Regulatory Environment", *Annals of Air and Space Law*, 19 (1985).

[125] A. Peccei, *op. cit.*, p. 160.

[126] M. R. Straszheim, *The Promise and Prospects of Greater Competition in International Aviation*, Symposium on international aviation policy, Kingstown, Jamaica, 30 Jan.-2 Feb. 1979.

[127] H. A. Kissinger, *American Foreign Policy*, Norton and Cy, Inc. New-York, 1974, pp. 57-58.

[128] A. F. LOWENFELD, "Deregulation, — Is it contagious?", in *International Air Transport in the Eighties*, Kluwer, 1981, pp. 30-31.

[129] H. RABEN, in *op. cit.*, sub (128).

[130] BEUC, Bureau Européen des Unions de Consommateurs, Report on Air Fares, 1985.

[131] S. WHEATCROFT and G. LIPMAN, "Air Transport in a Competitive European Market", *op. cit.* under (51), p. 1.

[132] J. NAVEAU, *L'Europe et le Transport Aérien*, *op. cit.* under (51), Chapter X.

[133] In : Memorandum of Understanding on the Procedure for the Establishment of Tariffs for Intra-European Scheduled Air Services, 19 December 1986, Art. 1, first Considering.

[134] MOTTA, Presentation to Seminar of Air Transport, Lisbon, 4 June 1986.

[135] A. COPPÉ, "Souvenirs marquants", *Studia Diplomatica, I.R.R.I.*, Brussels, 1981, nrs. 1-4, p. 258.

[136] J. VAN TICHELEN, "Souvenirs de la négociation du Traité de Rome", *Studia Diplomatica, I.R.R.I.*, Brussels, 1981, p. 327.

[137] ICAO DOC 278.

[138] Treaty establishing the European Economic Community, signed in Rome on 25 March 1957, together with the Treaty instituting EURATOM ("Rome Treaties") : Treaties establishing the European Communities. Treaties amending these Treaties, Office for Official Publications of the European Communities, Luxembourg, Cat. : FX-23-77-963-EN-11.

[139] Current membership of the E.E.C. includes : France, the FRG, Italy, Belgium, The Netherlands, Luxembourg, the U.K., Denmark, Ireland, Greece, Spain, Portugal.

[140] Cfr. L. CARTOU, "La structure juridique du transport aérien à la veille du Marché Commun", *R.F.D.A.*, 101, (1958); M. LEMOINE, "Marché Commun Européen et Transport Aérien", *Interavia*, 1058 (1958).

[141] COM Doc. (72) 134 Final and (72) 695 Final, 18 October 1972. Noé Report in : *EP Doc. 30.248.*

[142] *E.C.J.*, 357, (1974).

[143] Memorandum of the Commission, Progress towards the development of a Community air transport policy, March 1984, COM Doc. (84) 72 final.

[144] Council Directive (83/416/EEC) of 25 July 1983 concerning the authorisation of scheduled inter-regional air services for the transport of passengers, mail and cargo between Member States (O.J. L 237, 26 August 1983, p. 19).

[145] E.C.J. Decision of 10 June 1982, Lord Bethell vs. Commission, cfr. *Cahiers de Droit Europeén*, I.E.E., Brussels, 1982, p. 548, with note Joliet.

[146] Sterling Airways case, in *Bulletin* (1980), 12, n. 2.1.33; *Tenth Report on Competition*, nrs. 131 to 139, *11th Report on Competition* (of the Commission), nr. 5; on related issue (regulation of application of articles 85 and 86 EEC Treaty to air transport undertakings) cfr. Draft Council Regulation, *J.O.C.*, 291, 12 November 1981, p. 4.

[147] European Civil Aviation Conference, Policy Statement on Intra-European Air Transport, June 1985.

[148] S. WHEATCROFT and G. LIPMAN, *op. cit.*, p. 47.

[149] J. NAVEAU, "Interconnexion between the European Development and the Regulatory System of International Air Transport", Seminar on Aviation Law, Groningen University, Rotterdam, October 1986, Aerovision Consultancy Publ.

[150] J. NAVEAU, "La Banalisation des Aéronefs", *Rev. de Dr. International et de Dr. comparé*, 25 (1965) and *Revue Générale de l'Air*, 1 (1968); "Aspects juridiques de la Coopération en Transport Aérien", *E.T.L.*, 1 (1978); "Bilateralism revisited in Europe", *Air Law*, 85 (1985).

[151] K. VEENSTRA, Report to the 1987 Assembly of Presidents of the Association of European Airlines, AEA Doc.

[152] K. HAMMARSKJÖLD, "One World or Fragmentation : the Toll of Evolution in International Air Transport", *Annals of Air and Space Law*, 81 (1984).

[153] J. NAVEAU, "Aspects juridiques de la Coopération en Transport Aérien", *op. cit.*, sub (150).

[154] Alvaro BAUZA ARAUJO, "Nuevos Desarrollos en la Política de la Aviación Internacional", *Editorial M.B.A.*, Montevideo, 1975, p. 8.

[155] ICAO Circ. 98-AT/19. The signature States were : Cameroon, Central African Republic, Congo, Ivory Coast, Gabon, Dahomey, Haute-Volta, Mauritania, Niger, Senegal, Chad.

[156] H. A. WASSENBERGH, "Regulatory reform. National jurisdiction (domestic law) versus international jurisdiction", *Air Law*, 115 (1986).

[157] *ICC Doc.*, Nº 310-297-Rev. 3, statement of Council, Para. 6.

[158] AT-Conf/3-WP/65, 7 Nov. 1985.

[159] The agreements "are binding on the contracting parties under international law" : quoted from J. Z. GERTLER, "Custom in International Air Relations", *Annals of Air and Space Law*, 75 (1985). See also on the subject : H. A. WASSENBERGH, "Decision of 19 July 1984 in the Laker case (House of Lords)", *Air Law*, 44 (1985); Kean, "British Operating Permits : the Philippine Cases", *Air Law*, 49 (1985).

On the evolution of bilateralism, cfr. J. NAVEAU, "Bilateralism revisited in Europe", *op. cit.*, sub (150); "L'évolution du bilatéralisme en droit public international de l'Air", *R.F.D.A.*, 54 (1986).

# APPENDIX 2

## LIST OF CERTAIN
## RELEVANT INTERNATIONAL CONVENTIONS,
## IN PUBLIC INTERNATIONAL AIR LAW

*I. General and Economic Regulation of Air Services.*

1. Chicago Acts : Convention on International Civil Aviation, Chicago, 7 December 1944. 15 U.N.T.S. 295, as amended though the Protocol on the authentic trilingual text of the Convention with Annex, Buenos Aires, 24 September 1968, 740, U.N.T.S. 21.

   International Air Services Transit Agreement (States Parties to the Chicago Acts : cf. ICAO, Public Information Office), 84 U.N.T.S. 389.

2. Agreement on the Joint Financing of Certain Air Navigation Services in Greenland and the Faroe Islands, Geneva, 25 September 1956, as amended through the Protocol for the amendement (of same) Montreal, 3 November 1982, 334 U.N.T.S. 89.

3. Multilateral Agreement on Commercial Rights of Non-Scheduled Air Services in Europe, Paris, 30 April 1956, 310 U.N.T.S. 229.

4. Multilateral Agreement Relating to Certificates of Airworthiness for imported Aircraft, Paris, 22 April 1960, 418 U.N.T.S. 211.

5. International Agreement on the Procedure for the Establishment of tariffs for Scheduled Services, Paris 10 July 1967, 696 U.N.T.S. 31.

6. Memorandum of Understanding (between the Aeronautical Authorities of several ECAC States and the United States of America), Washington, 2 May 1982. As amended and reserved.

7. Agreement between the Organization of African Unity (OAU) and the African Civil Aviation Commission (AFCAC) establishing AFCAC as a specialised Agency of OAU, Addis Ababa, 11 May 1978.

8. Convention on the establishment of the Multinational Civil Aviation Training Centre of Addis Ababa (Socialist Ethiopia), Addis Ababa, 12 December 1980.

9. The International Convention Relating to Cooperation for the Safety of Air Navigation Eurocontrol Brussels, 13 December 1960, 523 U.N.T.S. 117.

10. Cooperative Agreements between Eurocontrol and (several countries) (Spain, Austria, Canada, Portugal, Greece, United States, and the European communities).

11. Protocol amending the Eurocontrol International Convention Relating to Co-operation for the Safety of Air Navigation of 13 Dec. 1960, Brussels, 12 February 1981.

*II. Offences against penal law and other acts which may jeopardize the safety of international civil aviation.*

12. Convention on Offences and Certain Other Acts Committed on Board Aircraft, Tokyo, 14 September 1963, 704 U.N.T.S. 219.

13. Convention for the Suppression of Unlawful Seizure of Aircraft, The Hague, 16 December 1970, 859 U.N.T.S. 105.

14. Convention for the Suppression of Unlawful Acts Against the Safety of Civil Aviation, Montreal, 23 September 1971, 974 U.N.T.S. 177.

# APPENDIX 3

## SELECTED BIBLIOGRAPHY

1. *General works, Books, Governmental publications.*

BAUZA ARAUJO A., *Nuevos Desarrollos en la Politica de la Aviación Internacional*, Ed. M.B.A., Montevideo, 1975.

BRANCKER, *IATA and what it does*, Sijthoff, Leyden, 1972.

*British Air Transport in the Seventies (The Edwards Report)*, Her Majesty's Stationery Office, London, 1969.

BÜRGENTHAL T. H., *Law-Making in the International Civil Aviation Organization*, Syracüse University Press, Syracuse, N.Y., 1969.

CARTOU L., *Droit Aérien*, P.U.F., Paris, 1963.

CHAUVEAU P., *Droit Aérien*, Librairies Techniques, Paris, 1951.

CHENG B., *The Law of International Air Transport*, Stevens and Sons Ltd, London, 1962.

CHUANG R. Y., *The International Air Transport Association*, Sijthoff, Leiden, 1972.

*Competition and the Airlines, An evaluation of deregulation*, CAB staff Report, December 1982.

COOPER J. C., *Aviation, Cabotage and Territory*, Montreal 1952.

*Exploration in Aerospace Law*, Selected Essays by John Cobb COOPER, Ed. by Ivan A. Vlasic, McGill Univ. Press, Montreal, 1968.

DE JUGLART M., *Traité élémentaire de Droit Aérien*, Pichon et Durand, Auzias, Paris, 1952.

DIEDERIKS-VERSCHOOR I. H. Ph., *An Introduction to Air Law*, Kluwer, Deventer 1983.

ESTIENNE-HENROTTE E., *L'application des règles générales du Traité de Rome au transport aérien*, Ed. Université de Bruxelles, coll. IEE, Brussels, 1988.

FOLLIOT M. G., *Le Transport Aérien International, Evolution et Perspectives*, Pedone, Paris, 1977.
— *Les Relations Aériennes Internationales*, Pedone, Paris, 1985.

GIDWITZ B., *The Politics of International Air Transport*, Lexington Books, Lexington/Toronto, 1980.

HAMMARSKJÖLD, K. N., *International Air Transport, Tariffs and Trade*, Royal Institute of International Affairs, London, 1978.

HAANAPPEL P. P. C., *Pricing and Capacity Determination in International Air Transport*, A Legal Analysis, Kluwer, Deventer, 1983.

*House of Lords, European Air Transport Policy, the Report Select Committee on the European Communities*, 26 March 1985, HL 115.

JOHNSON D. H. N., *Rights in Air Space*, Manchester, 1965.

KEAN A., *Essays in Air Law*, Nijhoff, The Hague/Boston/London, 1982.

LE GOFF M., *Manuel de Droit Aérien*, Droit Public, Dalloz, Paris, 1964.

LEMOINE M., *Traité de Droit Aérien*, Sirey, Paris, 1974.

LISSITZYN O., "International Air Transport and National Policy", in *Studies in American Foreign Relations*, New-York, 1942;
— "Freedom of the Air; Scheduled and Non-Scheduled Air Services", in *The Freedom of the Air*, Montreal, McWhinney/Bradley, 1968.

LITVINE M., *Droit Aérien*, Bruylant, Brussels, 1970.

LOWENFELD A. F., *Aviation Law*, Matthew Bender, New York, 1972.

MATEESCO-MATTE N., *Treatise on Air-Aeronautical Law*, ICASL, McGill University, Montreal/The Carswell Co Ltd, Toronto, 1981.

MCNAIR A. D., *The Law of the Air*, Librairies Techniques, Paris, 1951.

NAVEAU J., *Droit du Transport Aérien International*, Bruylant, Brussels, 1980; *L'Europe et le Transport Aérien*, Bruylant, Brussels, 1985.

*Report on Competition in Intra-European Air Services*, ECAC Doc n° 25 (1982).

ROSENFIELD St. B., *The Regulation of International Commercial Aviation, The International Regulatory Structure*, Oceana Publications, Inc., Dobbs Ferry, New York, 1984.

SHAWCROSS and BEAUMONT, *Air Law*, 4th edition, Butterworths, London, 1977.

TANEJA N. K., *US International Aviation Policy*, Lexington Books, Lexington/Toronto, 1980.

THORNTON R. L., *International Airlines and Politics : A Study in Adaptation to Change*, Michigan University Publ., 1970.

VAN BOGAERT E., *Eléments de Droit Aérien*, Story-Scientia, Brussels, 1987.

VIDELA ESCALADA F., *Derecho Aeronautico*, Zavalia, Buenos Aires, 1970.

WASSENBERGH H. A., *Aspects of Air Law and Civil Air Policy in the Seventies*, Martinus Nijhoff, The Hague, 1970.
— *Public International Air Transportation Law in a new Era*, Kluwer, Deventer, 1976.

WASSENBERGH H. A. and VAN FENEMA H. P., *International Air Transport in the Eighties*, Kluwer, Deventer, 1981.

WEBER L., *Die Zivilluftfahrt im Europäischen Gemeinschaftsrecht*, Springer Verlag, Berlin/Heidelberg/New York, 1981.

WHEATCROFT S., *Air Transport Policy*, Michel Joseph, London, 1964.

WHEATCROFT S. and LIPMAN G., *Air Transport in a Competitive European Market*, The Economist Intelligence Unit, London, 1986.

2. *Articles*

ATWOOD J., "Regional Aviation Agreements : a desirable alternative to bilateralism", *ITA Bull.*, 533 (1979).

BRETON J.-M., "Piraterie Aérienne et Droit International Public", *R.G.D.I.P.*, 2 (1971).
— "Organisations économiques régionales et coopération aéronautique : les problèmes posés par l'article 84 (2) du Traité de Rome", *RFDA*, 279 (1970).

BULIN R., "EUROCONTROL : A European Organization", *JRAS*, 160, 1965.

CLOSE G., "Article 84 EEC : the development of a transport policy in the sea and air sectors", *ELR* 188 (1980).

COHEN, M. S., "New air service and deregulation : a study in transition", *JALC 696* (1979).

COOPER J., "The proposed Multilateral Agreement on Commercial Rights in International Civil Air Transport", *JALC 125* (1947).

DAGTOGLOU P. D., "Air Transport and the European Community", *ELR 335* (1981).

DU PONTAVICE E., "Le statut juridique des affrètements aériens, dits 'charters'", *RGAE 3* (1970).

DRISCOLL E. J., "The Role of Charter Transport in International Aviation", *Air Law 74* (1976).

ERDMENGER, J. V., "A new dimension to civil aviation through European economic integration", in *International Air Transport in the Eighties* (o.c. sub 1, cfr. Wassenbergh and Van Fenema).

GAZDIK (Thomka-Gazdik) J., "Anti-trust Laws and International Airline Cooperation", The Hague International Academy, *Recueil des cours* (1972), I, 479.
— "The Distinction between Scheduled and Charter Transportation", *Air Law 66* (1976).

GULDIMANN, W., "Air Transports in International Law — Possibilities and limits in international unification", in *International Air Transport in the Eighties*, o.c., p. 149 sv.

GERTLER Z. J., "Nationality of Airlines : A Hidden Force in the International Air Regulation Equation", *JALC 1* (1982).

GUILLAUME G., "L'arrêt de la Cour de Justice des Communautés Européennes du 30 avril 1986 sur les transports aériens et ses suites", *RFDA*, 161 (1987).

HAANAPPEL P. P. C., "Deregulation of the US system of government regulation of domestic civil aviation seen in the light of the overall structure of international civil aviation", *Akron Law Rev.* (1976).

HAMMARSKJÖLD Kn., "One world or fragmentation : the toll of evolution in international air transport", *Ann. A.S.L.*, 79 (1984).

HELLER P. P., "Flying over the exclusive economic zone", *Z.L.W.*, 15 (1978).

HEYMSFELD D., "An introduction to regulatory reform for air transportation", *JALC 665* (1975).
— "Deregulation of air transportation under the Aviation Act of 1975", *Akron Law Rev.*, 643 (1976).

LANDRY J., "Some plain talk about airlines and deregulation", *Akron Law Rev.*, 635 (1976).

LEVINE M., "Alternatives to regulation : competition in air transportation and the Aviation Act of 1975", *JALC 703* (1975).

LOWENFELD A. F., "A new take-off for international air transport", *54 Foreign Affairs*, 36 (1975).

MAGDALENAT J. L., "The story of the life and death of the CAB Show Cause Order", *Air Law 83* (1980).

MAJID, A. A., "Impact of current US policy on international civil aviation", *Zeitschrift für Luft- und Weltraumrecht*, 295 (1983).

McCARROLL J. C., "The Bermuda capacity clauses in the jet age", *JALC 115* (1963).

MERCKX A., "New trends in the international bilateral regulation of air transport", *ETL 107* (1982).

NAVEAU J., "Away from Bermuda?", *Air Law*, 44 (1985).
— "Bilateralism revisited in Europe", *Air Law*, 85 (1985).
— "L'effet du droit européen sur le transport aérien", *Annals A.S.L.*, 131 (1986).

Nys R., "Etude sur la nationalité des aéronefs", *RFDA*, 159 (1964).

Reiner G., "The jurisdiction of US Courts relating to international disputes", *Zeitschrift für Luft- und Weltraumrecht*, 130 (1985).

Richard G., "KAL 007 : the legal fallout", *Annals A.S.L.*, 147 (1984).

Robinson G. S., "Changing concepts of cabotage", *JALC*, 553 (1968).

Stoffel A. W., "American bilateral air transport agreements on the threshold of the jet transport age", *JALC*, 119 (1959).

Thornton R. L., "Governments and airlines", *International Organization*, 541 (1971).

Tompkins, "The North Atlantic — Competition or Confrontation. The potential impact of United States antitrust law on international air transportation", *Air Law*, 48 (1982).

Tourtellot, "Competitive policy in airline deregulation", *The American University Law Rev.*, 537 (1979).

Tyrell, "Evolution or Revolution", A review of progress on the abolition of restrictions on competition in the air transport sector, *European Competition Law Review*, 91 (1981).

van der Tuuk Adriani P., "The Bermuda capacity clauses", *JALC*, 406 (1955).

Warner J., "How can a multilateral agreement in international air transport be attained?" in *Studia in Onore di Antonio Ambrosini*, Milan (1957), 587.

Wassenbergh H. A., "Innovation in International Air Transportation Regulation", *Air Law*, 138 (1978).

— "Towards a new model bilateral Air Transport Services Agreement", *Air Law*, 197 (1978).

— "New aspects of national aviation policies and the future of international air transport regulation", *Air Law*, 18 (1988).

— "Regulatory Reform : a challenge to inter-governmental Civil Aviation Conferences", *Air Law*, 31 (1986).

— "The application of international trade principles to air transport", *Air Law*, 84 (1987).

Weber L., "The application of European Community Law to Air Transport, Comments on a Decision of the Court of the European Communities of April 4, 1974, French Seamen", *Annals of A.S.L.*, 233 (1977).

— "The Eurocontrol Route Charges Litigation before the Court of Justice of the European Communities", *Annals of A.S.L.*, 355 (1978).

Wessberge E., "Prospects for international air transport under open competition", *ITA Bull.*, 43 (1980), p. 1081 sq.

IMPRIMÉ EN BELGIQUE

ETABLISSEMENTS EMILE BRUYLANT, société anonyme, Bruxelles
Admin.-Dir. gén. : JEAN VANDEVELD, av. W. Churchill, 221, 1180 Bruxelles